D1429456

A story of survival

ALICK DOWLING

RINGPRESS

Dedication

For Janek and Mary's children, Nela, Kati, Mark, Clare, Gabrielle and Joe to whom much of this story is new, and for their children.

Published by Ringpress Books 1989.

An imprint of Ringpress Limited, Spirella House, Bridge Road, Letchworth, Herts SG6 4ET

Typeset by Area Graphics Ltd, Letchworth, Herts. Production Consultants Landmark Ltd of London Printed and bound in Great Britain by The Bath Press

ISBN 0-948955-45-7

Acknowledgements

My first must be to my friend John Farrell, a tower of strength throughout this project. As a librarian he has known what books and references would be needed, anticipating my requirements by providing them. His experience as an indexer, his knowledge of book production, correcting proofs, his general advice and continual encouragement have been an invaluable stimulant when inspiration flagged.

For professional advice on technique my son Gregory has been very helpful to an inexperienced writer. Other members of my family and friends, too many to name, have been generous with advice and suggestions, only some of which I have been able to accept; many conflicted. For their forbearance when I have disappeared at times into mental abstraction I am grateful.

It has been my good fortune to have in Julia Barnes an editor/publisher whose enthusiasm has been matched by efficiency. Her perceptive editing has added zest to a prosaic account of the historical background.

Last, but obviously not least, I pay tribute to Janek Leja who has provided the material without which nothing could have been written. With the same modesty that prevented him from applying for a commission nearly fifty years ago, he has declined to allow his name to appear as part author; he emphasized the unimportance of the personal element except insofar as it typified the history of his fellow countrymen and encouraged me to write the story in my own way. As a scientist he disapproved of the fashionable obsession for seeking psychological motives to explain his experiences; such speculation finds no place here; we agreed that the forgotten virtue of reticence is preferable. He has been a patient teacher in correcting my ignorance of Polish spelling, accents, and history, and an indispensable source of advice and help with translations of Polish or Russian material. It is a signal honour to have been entrusted with the telling of this hitherto unrecorded story.

Photography

Thanks to Dorothy Smith for first class picture research and to the Hulton Picture Company, the Imperial War Museum and the Polish Institute and Sikorski Museum for their help and co-operation.

Contents

Appendices

Introduction

MY qualification for being associated with Jan Leja in preparing this book is that he and I have been linked for the last forty years by having married two sisters. During this time we have co-operated in a gentle conspiracy of pretended submission to their wishes. Unbiased observers may have a more objective perception that this might be our delusion, but perhaps only a jury of our twelve children—six each—could give a true verdict.

Despite marital encouragement, Janek was reluctant to write this story himself; being too busy was one of his reasons for procrastinating. This excuse was seriously undermined when he retired in 1983 from his position as Professor of Mineral Processing at the University of British Columbia. He finally agreed to the suggestion that as I had a word-processor, I should act as scribe. This meant overcoming his major objection to having his story recorded, for he has always stressed that his experiences during the war were by no means exceptional, and that many of his contemporaries had even more harrowing tales to recount.

Nevertheless his story deserves to be told, not only for the edification of his heirs, but because his triumphant survival over incredible odds is an exceptional story in its own right. It recalls the extraordinary combination of gallantry, humour, ingenuity, and determination that was typical of the Poles' response when their country was invaded by Germany and Russia in 1939.

After Janek received an outline draft of his story, prepared from notes and tape recordings, his memory was further stimulated when he looked again at his old diaries and maps. He was then able to produce such a personal account of his time as a prisoner of the Russians that it seemed appropriate that this private portion of the story, and where he describes his visit to Poland in 1973, should be told in the first person. Parts I and III appear more conventionally in the third person.

Janek Leja, left, his wife Mary and author Alick Dowling.

The decision to form a Polish Army in Russia under General Wladyslaw Anders in 1941 from survivors of the 200,000 Polish prisoners-of-war and two million deportees was a direct result of Hitler's invasion of Russia in June of that year. Deported from their homes in Poland, these Poles had been treated so brutally in Russia, that it is estimated that a third to a half were dead by the time of the Nazi invasion in June 1941. The epic story of how these survivors, still a great multitude, including many women and children, found their way to the collecting centres at Buzuluk on the Volga and later at Yangi-Yul in Uzbekistan has never been fully told.

This present account cannot pretend to do this, but perhaps the story of how one individual fared during these events, the central core of Janek's text, can portray one thread in this large tapestry. Poles came from slave labour camps, Arctic prison camps and the many centres of exile scattered throughout Asiatic Russia. While Janek was journeying from the Vorkuta Arctic region, his elder brother Staszek and his wife Basia were making their way from deportation in Siberia. They were not to meet until October 1942 in Persia.

Janek describes the conditions in slave labour camps and how those who lost faith or abandoned hope of survival were the first to die. This primitive and cruel form of unnatural selection operated to eliminate the psychologically unfit and, coupled with a good measure of luck, produced survivors who were few in number but of unusually high calibre, despite their pitiful physical weakness from near starvation. These disparate individuals, each distinct yet with the typically Polish characteristics, were fused into military units after retraining as parachutists, engineers, commandos and infantry. It was like compiling suits out of surviving cards from broken, dispersed, ill-treated, shuffled packs. Most, like Janek's brother Staszek went on to take part in the liberation of Italy.

The quality of the army formed from these survivors was apparent to Harold Macmillan, then British Minister in Northern Africa, who commented on their "high standard of drill, discipline, appearance and tenue". He also described a more subtle impression of "romance—not gaiety, exactly, but chivalry, poetry, adventure". "It was," said Macmillan, "more than a military formation. It was a crusade."

Others who managed to escape to the West earlier through the Balkans, joined the Allied forces in France. Yet others either played a significant part as aircrew in the Battle of Britain or formed the Carpathian Brigade in Syria under French command. The Carpathian Brigade refused the French order to surrender in June 1940, marched to Palestine and under British command played a distinguished part in the North African desert campaign. Later it became part of Anders' Polish Second Corps joining his army from Russia in Persia and was then involved in the epic battle for Monte Cassino and the liberation of Bologna. Janek's story can be regarded as one individual card and is equivalent to a snapshot or random cross section of the multitude of different but simultaneous events that were happening at that time.

It is intimately connected with historical events, so to help place it in perspective, there is an appendix of parallel charts which chronologically link events that were occurring in Poland, events elsewhere where Polish interests were involved, and what was happening at the same time to Janek and his family. The historical background in Part I sets the scene for Janek's early years. Part III looks at the later months of the war after Janek's escape from Russia, from a Polish perspective.

Between September 1939 and June 1941 Poland was cruelly treated by both partners in its Fourth Partition, Nazi Germany and Soviet Russia. In contrast to the well documented horrors of the Nazi occupation which continued until 1945, the methods used by the

Soviet occupying power to obliterate the Polish nation have received less attention. The systematic destruction of the educated classes by mass deportation in four huge railway convoys to the furthest parts of the Soviet empire, resulted in enormous suffering and many deaths. Numerous examples of this determination to reduce Poland to the state of a slave nation incapable of self rule, which persisted even after the pact which allowed the formation of Anders' army, are touched upon in the course of Janek's story.

There were many factors which affected Janek's decision to remain in exile after peace was declared. Obviously, anyone who suffered under Soviet rule would be reluctant to accept Poland as a satellite state. But his reasons were not all personal. It was the Soviet record of deception and double dealing during the course of the war which made any return to Poland a moral impossibility for him.

This was highlighted by Katyń. In 1940 15,000 Polish officers from Russian prisoner of war camps disappeared. The Soviets denied any knowledge of their fate but in 1943 bodies of Polish officers were discovered at Katyń. The Soviets used the Polish Government's plea to have Katyń investigated by the Red Cross as an excuse to break off diplomatic relations and then insisted on retaining the eastern part of Poland after the war. Coupled to this was the imprisonment of the underground fighting units when the Russians re-entered Poland in 1944 and the betrayal of the Warsaw Rising later that year. The Commander of the Home Army and fifteen leaders of the Underground Government were abducted after an offer of safe conduct in the spring of 1945 and a show trial was conducted in July, that same year. This was at the very moment when a provisional government for Poland was being cobbled together in Moscow.

Janek's decision to remain in exile was shared by the majority of the Polish soldiers and airmen who fought with the Western Allies. It is therefore understandable why Janek and so many of his colleagues were unable, unwilling and indeed not welcome to return to a post-war Poland subservient to the USSR and dominated by communists, where mention of the names Sikorski, Anders, Katyń, or the Home Army was forbidden. The perspective of the later part of this account in Part III does not accord with the conventional perception of Western European observers. Those who remember the war years and others who have accepted the stereotyped portrayal of these episodes in books and films may find this perspective unfamiliar, even disturbing.

The full story of mass deportations, arrests, persecutions and exterminations carried out jointly by the NKVD[1] the Soviet security services and the Security Services (Bezpieka) of the Communist

Government in Poland, during the ten years after World War II has never been disclosed or adequately reported in the West. Not until 1987 was a full account[2] published on the fate of Poles forcibly deported from the parts of Poland ceded to the USSR at Yalta, and those hunted in Poland itself by the Bezpieka under the direction of the NKVD.

The USSR and Polish communist governments have claimed that all prisoners and deportees held in Russia had returned after the various amnesties, but the truth is that only a small proportion were released. Millions were forced to stay behind. Though deportations have occurred over several centuries, the ones perpetrated by the Soviets have been different in both scale and motive from anything that had happened previously. There has been duplicity about the motive for deportation and even denial that such has occurred—neither was the case under the Tsars. The central core of Janek's story is the duplicity of those responsible for Poland's present position.

Alick Dowling
January 1989

[1]NKVD: Norodovy Komisariat Vnutrich Dyel—the Soviet People's Commissariat for Internal Affairs.

[2]Julian Siedlecki — *Losy Polaków w ZSSR w latack 1939 – 1986* (Fate of Poles in the USSR in 1939 – 1986) (in Polish) — Gryf Publications Ltd, London 1987.

PART I

CHAPTER ONE

The Conquest of Poland

"ONCE upon a time," the story would be told to Polish children, "Poland was a strong free country—but that was long ago!"

In the years just before Janek Leja was born, in May of 1918, Poland had virtually ceased to exist. It was a country of the past, a country of the mind, like Utopia or the lost country of Atlantis. It was not shown on any map of Europe for it had been elbowed out of existence by the neighbouring mighty empires of Russia, Austria and Germany, ruled over by the ancient dynasties of the Romanovs, the Hapsburgs and the Hohenzollerns. There was no vestige of independent government in any of the territory that had once been Polish, no Polish control of education and the Polish language was forbidden for official purposes—even in Warsaw, the heart of Poland. Before war broke out, in the summer of 1914, no country seemed more helpless, no nation more hopeless, than the once great Kingdom of Poland.

In 1938 Prime Minister Neville Chamberlain declared his amazement that Britain might be going to war "for a faraway country of which we know nothing." He meant Czechoslovakia, but little more was known of Poland. Even today most Western Europeans know little of Poland's past, other than its tragic history and heroic tradition of fighting for its independence. Yet even more than most countries, Poland today and the people of Poland, have been shaped by their past. To follow the story of one individual Pole—only one of thousands, as Janek himself insists, whose life underwent a similar transformation it is essential to understand something of that past and that tradition.

It is difficult, particularly for those with the secure unchanging frontiers of an island state, to realize how changing boundaries can shatter lives or to appreciate the instability and uncertainty that partition causes and the disruption and chaos that follow it. When

Janek was born, it was five generations since Poland had been free. Every member of his family had been born and had lived under the domination of a foreign power. Even his grandparents could not remember a time when Poland was unoccupied. No one would have dared to hope that any of them, even his sister eight-year-old Maria and his six-year-old brother Staszek, would ever live to see an independent fatherland. It was expected they would all die as they had lived, subjects of an alien power. Yet Janek born in 1918, came at a time of promise, a joyful moment in the history of a country that had seen little enough joy in the last one hundred and fifty years. At last Poland was given her independence, she seemed to be regaining her strength while her masterful neighbours, the three great monarchies of Europe, perished.

The strongest life-line in Polish history was created in 966, when the King of Poland and his subjects embraced the Christian religion and were received into the Catholic Church. Four centuries later the young queen of Poland married Jagiello, the Grand Duke of neighbouring Lithuania, and this union led to the creation of a strong kingdom, more powerful than any neighbouring countries. The marriage was celebrated by the establishment of the Jagiellonian University of Kraków, an ancient centre of learning without parallel in Eastern Europe, comparable with Oxford, Cambridge or the Sorbonne. So a strong Poland, part of the Catholic Church and with an honoured place in Western learning, had come into being. But at almost the same time as Poland became part of the Catholic West, Russia entered the Eastern Orthodox Church and later, Prussia, the neighbour to the West, accepted the doctrines of the Protestant reformation, so Poland was partly cut off from this heritage.

There were other problems, and the greatest of these lay in the land itself. Flat endless plains stretch away from Warsaw to the frontiers broken only by irregular tracts of forest. In Polish polen means plain, so Poland is the Land of Plains. It has no rivers or mountains to form barriers to hinder foreign armies from sweeping across the country and little sea-coast to be defended. History is geography and Poland was vulnerable, a prey to foreign invasion as envious neighbours cast their eyes upon its fertile corn-growing plains. The centuries brought invasions by Mongol hordes from the east, by Teutonic Knights from the north, by Cossacks from the Ukraine, by armies from Sweden. These assaults were all, after a fashion, met and overcome. But the pattern of a country continuously under threat and continuously saved by heroic courage and the prayers of the Church perhaps led to a failure to realize that the ever-present danger might not always be overcome.

The year 1683 was the year of Poland's greatest triumph, as the strength of the huge Turkish Empire was thrust into the heart of Europe. It was the last campaign in a war between Christendom and Islam that had lasted for a thousand years—since long before the Crusades. As well as dominating western Asia and North Africa, the Turks ruled land in Europe where Greece and the Balkans were under their sway. Now the Empire, already past its greatest glories, was making a last supreme effort. A quarter of a million men advanced under the command of the Grand Vizier Kara Mustafa, who declared his ambition of stabling his horses in St Peter's in Rome. The armies reached the walls of Vienna, the capital of the Hapsburgs, where the two-headed eagle looked East and West along the Danube. Once Vienna fell, the road to Western Europe lay open. Vienna appealed for help—and Poland answered the appeal.

Jan Sobieski, King of Poland, had fought the Turks on behalf of his own country for ten years. Now he led the combined Polish and Austrian armies against the Turkish armies besieging Vienna. He forced them to turn and face him on the heights of Kahlenberg in the Vienna woods, and there he won a spectacular and resounding victory. The Turks were forced to give way and retreat. It was the end of the last Crusade. Christian Europe was safe—never again would the armies of Islam menace Christendom. Jan Sobieski became a legend and a hero. He could not have acted differently, but he could not envisage the dangerous consequences his victory would have for Poland. For, by destroying the threat of Turkish aggression, Russia and Austria were freed to pursue their own territorial ambitions and Prussia was not far behind. Now that Poland was no longer threatened by the Turks, the country lay in the path of those three European powers—and they were much closer.

Far from safeguarding against this new threat from her uncomfortable neighbours, Poland seemed intent on digging her own grave. The landowners of the Commonwealth determined to limit the powers of the Crown, had formed a joint assembly, which was called the SEJM, in which every member of the landowning nobility was entitled to sit. They called it a "noble democracy", considering themselves as the Nation, while the other orders of society, the clergy, the merchants in the cities, the common people and the peasants, were merely subjects. When the ancient Jagiello dynasty came to an end, the SEJM claimed that in future the monarchy would no longer be hereditary. The Kings of Poland would be elected by the nobility in the SEJM. This did not make for strong government. In the year 1696 there were eighteen hopeful candidates for the throne—but worse was to follow.

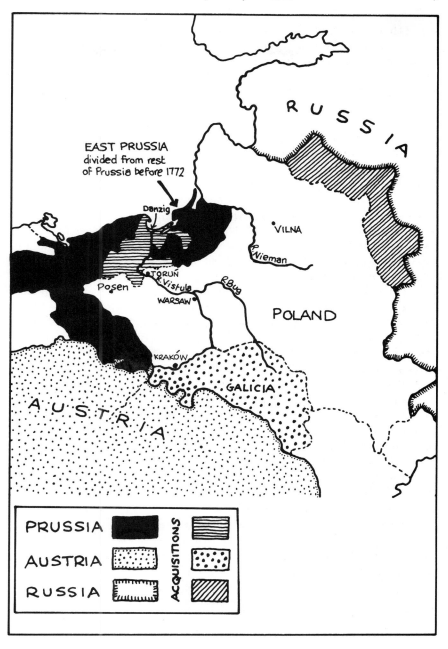

First Partition of Poland: 1772.

To make the noble democracy more democratic, the assembly introduced a veto, so that any single member of the assembly could stand up and say: "I do not permit it", about any decision that lay before it. Democratic possibly, but it meant that remarkably little business was ever carried to a successful conclusion and a single corrupt member could be persuaded or bribed to prevent any projected reform from going forward. The Kings of Poland tried to press forward with reforms, but hampered by the nobility within and pressure from the mighty neighbours without, they could achieve little. The end of Polish independence and the reign of the last King of Poland, was in sight.

In 1764 intrigue by Catherine the Great of Russia secured the election of Stanislaw Poniatowski as king. He had been one of her lovers and she thought if he owed his kingdom to her, she could do as she wished with a puppet king. Yet Catherine under-estimated the Polishness of her puppet ruler and he tried to strengthen the monarchy against foreign pressure. It was no use and his attempts at reform only led to years of bitter struggle.

This was the cue for Frederick the Great, King of Prussia. He was forging Prussia into a formidable military power and it was desirable to strengthen his eastern borders against Russia, and he too looked enviously at the cornlands of Poland. He proposed a partition of Poland—a division of the spoils. Catherine the Great agreed eagerly and Joseph II, the young Hapsburg Emperor, also agreed that it was their duty to step in and end the "chaotic disorder" in Poland. The European powers which had declared themselves saved by the Polish troops under Jan Sobieski less than a century before, showed themselves largely indifferent to the fate of Poland now. It was a pattern that was to be repeated many times.

So in 1772 the First Partition of Poland took place: Russia, Prussia and Austria each awarded themselves a slice of Poland. No Polish approval was sought; no other European power was called in to arbitrate. It was a piece of shameless political connivance such as the twentieth century would find hard to beat and by it Poland lost a third of her territory and a third of her inhabitants. She had not lost all hope. Stanislaw, still king in name, rallied the Polish remnant behind him and too late found support for creating a stronger government and a powerful army, while the occupying powers looked on in disapproval. Meanwhile, the French Revolution exploded upon Europe and occupied the attention of the western powers. Austria was soon at war with the new government of the French Republic. Joseph II was the brother of the beleaguered Marie Antoinette, but it was not sentiment that made him act, it was to prevent the dangerous poison

The Cake of Kings. A satirical engraving of the First Partition of Poland by M. Lemie.
Hulton Picture Company

of republicanism infecting the monarchies of Europe. For Russia and Prussia the chance was too good to be missed. In 1793 they effected the Second Partition, this time without Austria. Russia annexed most of Lithuania and Prussia seized the ancient port of Gdansk—Danzig.

The fires of the French Revolution had sparked off a wave of patriotism throughout Europe—including Poland. Tadeusz Kościuszko appeared as a heaven-sent leader, swearing he would give Poland back her liberty and also give freedom to all the serfs bound to the estates of the landowners. But patriotism and courage were not enough. The occupying powers were deeply alarmed by Poland's new

Second Partition of Poland: 1793

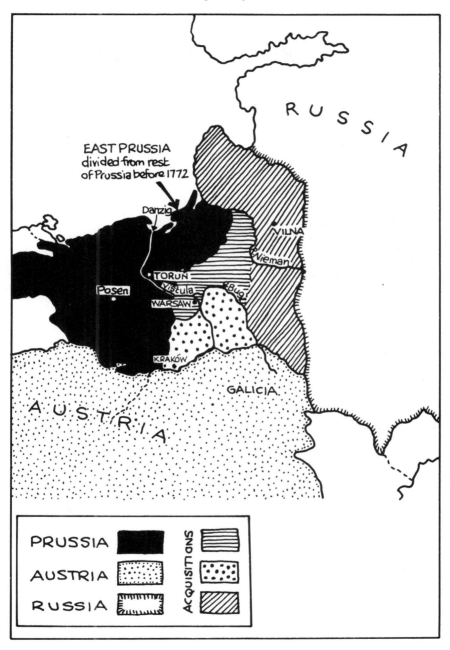

Third Partition of Poland: 1795

ambitions and despite the desperate bravery Kościuszko inspired, the Poles could not stand up to the weight of the Russian and Prussian armies. Kościuszko was made prisoner, Stanislaw was forced to abdicate and Warsaw was occupied. Now the three powers sat down again to the banquet, determined this time to leave no crumbs behind. In 1795 the Third Partition took place, with Austria once more an eager partner. All the remaining Polish territories and Polish nationals were shared out amongst the three powers. In a secret clause they undertook that "the name and designation of the Kingdom of Poland shall remain suppressed as of now and for ever."

Even now, the Poles did not entirely despair. It soon became clear that the policies of Europe were no longer presided over by its ancient rulers, but by the new Emperor of the French—Napoleon Bonaparte. "The future of Europe," Napoleon declared, "depends on the ultimate destiny of Poland." This sounded well and the diagnosis was arguably correct, but it was far from being a policy statement for the new Napoleonic Empire. Romantic history claims that Napoleon created a free Grand Duchy of Warsaw following appeals from his Polish mistress Marie Walewska. But Napoleon was rarely swayed by such considerations. His conduct towards Poland was governed by his own cynical, self seeking purposes. The new state was largely formed out of lands annexed by Prussia and Austria, countries which he had recently defeated, while much of Russia's land was undisturbed.

Yet many Poles believed that, after Napoleon's war with Alexander of Russia, he would remedy this and enlarge the new state. So they flocked to join Napoleon's eagles, foreshadowing the future, when so many Poles joined Polish legions, fighting for an alien power but all the time believing their own country would benefit. These men were not seeking personal rewards, they were fighting for the freedom of their country. It was this spirit that drove young Janek Leja, with so many thousands more, to leave Poland in 1939 and 1940 in order to continue fighting for their motherland.

The Poles who joined Napoleon took part in his thrust into Russia in the campaign of 1812. They were caught up in his defeat and in the appalling retreat from Moscow, ravaged by winter storms, racked by hunger, menaced, attacked and destroyed by Russian troops as ruthless in the defence of their homeland as Poles had ever been. When the twenty-five years war against Revolutionary France and against Napoleon's Grand Army was at last over, Poland was to be found on the wrong side.

Now the map of Europe was to be re-drawn again, this time by the victorious allied powers at the Congress of Vienna. They declared their intention was to restore all the dethroned monarchs and to return territory seized in the twenty-five years of fighting. There were to be certain exceptions. The story goes that Tsar Alexander of Russia placed his hand over Poland on the map. "C'est à moi!" he declared—and it was difficult to deny him. Prussia and Austria made the best of it by claiming their 1795 Third Partition territories. The remainder was shaped up into a new Kingdom of Poland—with the Tsar of Russia as hereditary King. It was called the Congress Kingdom. After fifty years of struggle and intrigue, the great powers had their way and free independent Poland had ceased to exist.

CHAPTER TWO
Living Through the Partitions

FOR the next one hundred years the history of Poland was no more than an aspect of the different histories of Russia, Prussia and Austria and the quality of life depended on the character of the occupation. Possibly the Austrian yoke was the easiest to bear. The Hapsburg Empire, like Poland, was basically Catholic, so there was a religious sympathy which was felt by neither of the other occupying powers. Yet the Austrian Empire, sprawling across central Europe, included Germans, Poles, Czechs, Magyars, Croats and Jews, with a diversity of languges and a variety of religions. The bureaucrats in Vienna, seeking a quiet life above everything had no wish to stir up trouble among the disparate groups, either by undue favouritism or unfair discrimination. The Poles in Austrian Galicia were left in peace for years at a time. But the whole Hapsburg Empire was economically backward so equally nothing was done for them—no investment in roads or railways, no industrialization, not even new methods of farming or systems of land holding. The Leja family, like the other people of the region, were locked in a trap of rural poverty and deprivation, with few chances of escape through education or enterprise. When such opportunities came, they had to be seized with both hands—and that is what the family did.

The Protestant Prussians despised the Catholicism of the Poles and looked down on the Poles as an inferior race. After 1871 when the Empire of Germany was created out of a union of Prussia and the medley of German states, the Poles became an insignificant minority in a forward looking self-confident military machine. Yet because Prussian—or German—Poland included busy towns that were centres of trade, as well as good agricultural land where new farming methods were encouraged, this area was reasonably prosperous and some Poles, at least, could enjoy a comfortable standard of living.

The Russian domination was the harshest and the most complete, perhaps the most resented and the most fiercely resisted. After fifteen years numbed by shock, Poland was inspired by a new revolution in France in 1830, and rose in rebellion. It took Russia a year to crush, but at last it was put down with an iron hand. Hundreds of Poles were executed, hundreds of thousands sent in chains to the Russian occupied zone in the east—Siberia. They were the first of many gloomy convoys of such unhappy exiles, which later included Janek and his companions.

After the first uprising, the participants were sentenced to a number of years penal work in Western Siberia, with the hope that if they survived they could return to their families in Poland. Later whole families were deported, their property was confiscated and given to Russian officers and government employees. Before the construction of the railway to Vladivostok the deportees were sent to Siberia in convoys of prisoners chained together. They had to walk the whole way, though their families were allowed to ride on carts or sleighs between the stage posts. It was a journey that took many months to complete. Prisoners who finished their sentences and survived were forced to settle in Siberia along with their families. Cut off from other Polish families, their descendants integrated with the local population in two or three generations. After 1831 all Polish institutions were suppressed and the country was governed by Russian decree. "So this is the end of the Poles," said England's statesman Lord Palmerston. "I am heartily sorry for them, but their case has become for some time hopeless."

January 1863 saw another rising against Russia. Many Polish exiles came home to fight, but to no purpose and the struggle only led to a more brutal and determined crushing of every possible vestige of Polish life and culture. For the next fifty years Russian was to be the official language in administration and education. Poles were dismissed from official positions, Russian teachers and policemen and bureaucrats poured in. The Universities of Warsaw and Vilna were suppressed; Polish intellectuals wanting higher education had to go to St Petersburg or Kiev. The Catholic Church was persecuted and discriminated against. Even the name Poland was not used—the territory was the Vistula Province of Russia and 300,000 Russian troops were garrisoned upon it.

In Austrian Galicia there were a series of uprisings against the occupying powers. A rebellion in 1846 was crushed and the Austrian governor decided to buy peace by offering the peasants possession of the land they had previously leased from landlords. He hoped this would deter them from taking part in future uprisings. The peasants as new landowners had their property in narrow strips seven or fifteen metres wide running at right angles to the axis of the village road. The practice of subdividing land among all the children of a family, resulted after a few generations in strips of land as narrow as seven metres, but extending up to three kilometres. Marriages and dowries complicated the situation still further so that families frequently owned strips of land, and often only small portions of strips, which could be scattered over a distance of fifteen to twenty kilometres. Obviously this made productive farming difficult and exceedingly inefficient.

This is the Poland that Janek remembers. He came from peasant stock and his grandfather Jan Leja, after whom he was named, owned a four hectare farm in the village of Grodzisko, near Przeworsk. The Leja's house was in the part of the village called Zaborcze which means "behind a grove of trees". There were only about fifteen houses in this section, which overlooked a small ravine, curving eastwards from the main road. The adjoining part of the main road about eight hundred metres away was the commercial centre of the village, with a few artisans and tradesmen. It was occupied by landless people, mostly Jews engaged in commerce who like many of the Jews in Poland, lived their own separate life in their specific quarter. They dressed differently, spoke Yiddish, and observed their own customs. In the centre were several cloth shops, a couple of bakeries, an elementary school and a synagogue. At the two ends of this townlet were an inn and post office at the north and a Catholic church at the south with the doctor's house and pharmacy. The combined population of townlet and village was some six thousand.

Janek's grandfather, Jan Leja had two brothers and five sisters. All his sisters became nuns. In the second half of the nineteenth century in a deeply religious country like Poland, life in a religious order was the only alternative to marriage for a girl, for daughters needed a dowry in order to marry. A photograph of the five nuns hung on the wall of the Leja home, all other pictures and ornaments in the house were solely of a religious nature. One of Jan's brothers stayed in Grodzisko and opened a general store, the other moved to Zolynia, fifteen kilometres to the west.

In 1883 Jan's first son Josef was born, followed two years later by the birth of brother Franciszek, known as Stryj in later life—the uncle. There were also three sisters, who later married farmers in the neighbouring villages. Kate's husband Danak came from the nearby village of Tryncza. They had one son, Stach. He was executed by the Germans in reprisal when the Home Army blew up a railway bridge near Tryncza. Stach's orphaned son, Romek Danak, was then adopted by Stryj and Stryjenka and brought up by them after the war in Kraków. But it is the brothers Josef, Janek's father and Franciszek his adopted father, who are closely connected with this story.

Like all farmers, their father Jan Leja struggled to make a living from the land. But he had the imagination to appreciate the value of education. He knew this was the only means of providing his children with an escape from the poverty gap. There was no thought of making provision for his daughters and he could only afford to educate one of his sons. Josef chose to stay on the farm and so it was Franciszek who was given the opportunity to go to school, even though he was the younger son. Secondary schooling was only available in Jaroslav, thirty-five kilometres away and so it involved long absences from home. Franciszek was given the chance to go to school on the strict understanding that he became a priest. Problems arose when he realized that he had no vocation, his ambition was to study mathematics. Fortunately an enlightened parish priest intervened. He was responsible for administering a bequest to gifted pupils from Grodzisko and this gave Franciszek the opportunity to continue his studies. Even so, his allowance was meagre and it had to be supplemented. Fourteen-year-old Franciszek started giving lessons, just as Janek would do when he was only slightly older in order to supplement his income. Still benefiting from his bequest, Franciszek was able to continue his mathematical studies at the University of Lwów. After graduating, he went on to study at Kraków and Paris. But before then, when he was sixteen, he joined a secret organization which aimed at preserving Polish national awareness. It was led by Józef Pilsudski.

CHAPTER THREE

Pilsudski, Father of Modern Poland

THROUGHOUT Poland's long and beleaguered history, the flame of national pride and patriotism was always kept alight. In the nineteenth century there was a split between those who believed the only way to keep the name of Poland alive was to flee abroad and those, like Józef Pilsudski, who preferred to stay and fight. Suppression of national identity was so complete that many of the political, intellectual and artistic élite felt that escape was their only means of survival. They left their mother country and made new homes, mostly in France, where some found fame and honour. The exiles believed that their achievements on the international stage helped to preserve the spirit of Poland.

Frédéric Chopin, who was famous worldwide, was recognized as the voice of Poland. A child prodigy, talented and sensitive, he loved the Polish landscape and the music of its folk songs. But soon he was faced with a terrible choice. He knew, and so did his family and friends, that he had a great musical talent. Yet what future would he have if he stayed in Warsaw, regarded as a Russian provincial town, cut off from the rest of Europe? In 1830 when he was twenty years old, Chopin left Poland, never to return. Stories of his fame came back from Vienna, from Paris, from London. He seemed to pour his heart into his passionate melodies with a nostalgic longing for his native land. Whenever people spoke of Chopin, they spoke of Poland. He died an unhappy exile, when he was only thirty-nine and he was buried in Paris. By his own wish, his heart was sent back to Warsaw to be buried. Above it were the words "Where thy treasure is, there shall thy heart be also".

In 1891 the twenty-four-year-old Marya Sklodowska left Warsaw to become a student at the Sorbonne. Seven years later, married, with her name in the French style, Marie Curie and her husband discovered a new chemical element, unknown to science. They called it Polonium, in honour of Marie's country of birth. But in fact her greatest achievement, which earned her worldwide fame was her subsequent discovery of Radium.

Some Polish exiles chose Britain as their second fatherland. These included Teodor Josef Konrad Korzeniowski who made his name as the writer Joseph Conrad. His life was shaped by the sufferings of Poland. His father was exiled to Russia for his part in a Polish uprising, so Josef spent his early years in Russia. His mother died and father and son returned to Austrian Galicia. But when Josef was only twelve years old his father died and so, like Janek Leja sixty years later, he was adopted by an uncle and educated at Kraków. His great dream was to go to sea and when he was seventeen he set off alone for Marseilles. He qualified as a ship's master and sailed to Britain. Then in his new language English, he began writing under the more accessible name of Joseph Conrad. Books like *Outcast of the Islands*, *Lord Jim*, and *Mirror of the Sea*, written in a language that was not his own, were a sensational achievement. They increased the admiration and sympathy the Western world felt for Poland.

In addition to the politically-induced emigration, many peasants after their emancipation, emigrated from the over-populated areas in central Poland and Galicia, to the United States, Canada, Brazil and other countries. According to one estimate, some 3·6 million left Galicia between 1870 and 1914. 100,000 volunteered to go to Brazil in 1890 alone. The legend grew that each of these exiles carried away a handful of Polish earth to be buried with them. It seemed that many left a piece of their hearts behind in Poland. There were also the Poles who believed they could keep the flame of resistance alive by staying in Poland and forming political parties or printing underground newspapers. In a country where all political opposition was banned and where all books and newspapers were heavily censored, this was highly dangerous.

Though the Russian domination of Poland was harsh, there were some advances as the industrial revolution swept across Europe. Railways and factories were built, mines and steel mills were opened up. The new industrialization created an urban working class, new to the country and looking for political expression. Roman Dmowski led the National Democrats. He believed in a small compact Poland with fewer Jews and no minorities. He saw Germany as the main enemy and was in favour of cautious co-operation with Russia.

Józef Pilsudski always regarded Russia as the great enemy. He was born in 1864 from a landowning family and his childhood was passed in the cruel aftermath of the 1863 uprising. As a young conspirator, he was arrested for playing a small part in the 1887 rebellion and spent five years in Siberia. Back in Poland, he joined the embryo Polish

Józef Pilsudski.   *Hulton Picture Company*

Socialist Party, known as the PPS. Courageous, resourceful, a natural leader, he soon dominated the movement, though his Socialist principles were less than orthodox. He was responsible for a clandestine newspaper called *Robotnik*—The Worker—which had a wide underground circulation. Pilsudski and the PPS relied on the great power and endurance of the growing class of urban workers and the strength of the peasants. The party aimed to link these qualities to the patriotism and idealism of Poland's landowners and intelligentsia. But Pilsudski had another goal. He wanted to create a new Polish army, a phoenix to rise from the ashes to reflect the patriotism of his fellow countrymen. With the limited approval of Austria, he formed Riflemen's Associations in Galicia. They had very few rifles, but there was growing enthusiasm for a cause that saw Poles meeting and drilling together. The first years of this century seemed not entirely without hope.

Young Franciszek Leja supported Pilsudski wholeheartedly and when he was only sixteen he joined the secret organization formed to preserve national awareness, which Pilsudski inspired. Pilsudski believed that the only hope of Polish independence lay in disagreement and war between the occupying powers. But there was no sign of this. Right up to 1914, few Poles thought that there was any chance of gaining independence. Then the First World War erupted and Europe was divided into two hostile alliances. With the inevitability of a domino effect this led to the involvement of all the great powers; Austria and Germany were at war with Serbia, Russia, France, Belgium and Britain. The years between 1815 and 1914 had been a century of Polish patriots and exiles. 1914 saw the Polish pawns on the European chessboard deployed against each other, forced to serve with the opposing great powers. Germany and Austria were allied together against Russia and with the prospect of Pole fighting Pole, the outlook was bleak.

When war broke out, Franciszek Leja, who was by then twenty-eight was spending his summer holiday in the family village of Grodzisko. He hastened to join Pilsudski's Riflemen's Association, along with thousands of other Poles, who believed this was the only way of having a say in their country's future and fighting against Russia in the Austrian-backed militia.

Soon they became the Polish legions with Pilsudski at their head, taking part in a number of actions against Russia. Then the legionnaires were called upon to take an oath of allegiance to Germany. Franciszek Leja, a member of the Eastern Legions, refused along with most of his comrades. Pilsudski supported them. He also demanded that the legions should not be used on the Western front against Britain or France, but only against Russia. The legions were hastily disbanded and Franciszek returned to his mathematical studies. Pilsudski was seized by Germany and imprisoned in the fortress of Magdeburg.

Now events were moving fast. Russia was the first of the three empires to collapse. The Russian army was totally demoralized, the workers staged a revolt and under intense pressure, the Tsar abdicated. This all paved the way for the Soviet revolution of 1917. Germany decisively influenced the course of the Bolshevik revolution by sending Lenin in a sealed railway carriage to Russia at a critical moment. The revolution removed Russia from the war and virtually eliminated the Eastern front. Before long, Germany was also on the point of collapse. Alarmed by the unpredictable policy of the new Bolshevik state, they desperately wanted a buffer to separate them. Despite the longstanding policy of denying Poland independence, Germany ventured a last desperate fling before surrender. Pilsudski, still in the fortress of Magdeburg, was suddenly released and sent by train to Warsaw. Backed by the army and supported by the majority of Poles he declared himself head of the state. Within months the Hapsburg Empire had broken apart and together with Germany, was looking for surrender terms from the allies.

The Allies, with victory in their grasp, began to talk of a free Poland with access to the sea and this became one of the fourteen points on the agenda of the peace conference at Versailles. So came the pivotal year of 1918—the year of Janek's birth. For Western Europe, it marked the end of the First World War and both victors and vanquished were too exhausted to feel anything more than a bitter relief. For Poland two years of fighting lay ahead. Yet there was a scent of freedom in the air when a Polish delegation was invited to attend the peace conference. The delegation, however, found few friends. The liberal establishment was suspicious of a country whose unity was so clearly associated with Catholicism and the allies, ignorant of Polish history were disconcerted by the Poles' apparent lack of gratitude for their newfound independence.

However, the new Poland came into being and after one hundred and twenty-three years the Third Partition was at an end. Ignacy Jan Paderewski, a famous Polish pianist was the unlikely choice for Prime Minister. He was an extremely patriotic and eloquent man and he had become recognized as the international voice of Poland, after a speech he made at the Chopin Centenary celebrations. With the backing of the Allies, he was invited to lead the independent state of Poland. As soon as he believed he had out-lived his usefulness, he returned to the world of music.

1918: Poland after the Versailles Peace Treaty.

It had seemed on gaining independence that a long-held Polish dream had become reality. But all too soon the cracks began to appear. The Treaty of Riga, signed in 1921, failed to set Polish boundaries far enough to the east to include the old Polish lands. They included many minorities, resentful at being split from their co-patriots. The worst mistake was to divide the Germans from their fatherland. This was done to create a Polish corridor which would give the new independent state access to the sea, but it was to prove a recipe for disaster. At no point did the Soviet government in Moscow accept the Treaty of Versailles. As soon as they started to recover from the chaos and turmoil of the Revolution, they attempted to regain the lands of the Tsarist Empire. When German troops were forced to abandon lands they had occupied, the Soviets seized their chance. In 1920 the Red Army invaded Poland and the Poles were called on to support the Socialist cause. The Bolsheviks believed they could sweep across Poland and carry world-wide revolution westward into Europe.

The plan failed. The nationalism and Catholicism of the Poles meant more than the International Socialism of the Soviets and they hastened to rally behind Pilsudski. On August 15, 1920—the Feast of the Virgin—Polish troops inflicted a crushing defeat on the Red Army. This dazzling victory, known as 'the miracle of the Vistula' was one of the decisive battles of the century. The Polish triumph was largely due to the courage and brilliance of the cavalry and this had a long-term effect on Polish military thinking, which was ultimately disastrous. The Battle of the Vistula was followed by more Polish successes, and this ended any hope of Russia regaining Poland or carrying revolution into Western Europe. Like Jan Sobieski before the walls of Vienna, almost two hundred and fifty years before, Poland had not only saved herself but had saved Europe from invasion from the east. It remained to be seen how grateful Europe would be.

CHAPTER FOUR
Janek's Early Life

J ANEK Leja's birth in 1918 coincided with Poland's emergence as an independent nation, free at last from the yoke of foreign domination. His father Josef had continued to work on the farm while Franciszek pursued his mathematical studies. In 1908 Josef married Aniela Pawlik. Their farm consisted of about ten acres, arranged in two strips. One extended from the house, three kilometres towards the Lezajsk-Przeworsk railway line and the other strip was further north about one kilometre away and represented Aniela's dowry. Parts of each strip belonged to other relatives so it is not surprising that this land provided only bare subsistence to Josef, Aniela and their six children. Their eldest child was a girl, Maria born in 1910. The rest were boys, Stanislaw (Staszek) born in 1912, Jan (Janek) born on May 27 1918, Franciszek (Franek) born in 1920, Wincenty (Wicek) born in 1923, and finally Feliks (Felek) born in 1925. Janek remembers that the only time he had enough to eat was on Christmas Eve—*vigilia*—at the traditional celebratory meal. At other times food was scarce. Lack of fat and meat was normal and potatoes were often eaten without salt in the early spring. Janek can remember his father splitting matches into two or even four to make them last longer.

Shortages and poverty were universal. Economically the twenties was the worst time for the newly independent Poland. The country united to withstand the Bolshevik invasion of 1920, but when peace was restored the Poles found their problems had only just begun. The Partitions left a legacy of chaos and confusion, which soon led to conflict. The major problem was trying to establish a national pattern among the three reunited fragments of Poland. Not only was there a variety of currencies in circulation—roubles, marks, Austrian crowns, even dollars and English sovereigns—each part had its own laws, education system and economic structure. To make matters worse, traditional trading markets had ceased to exist. The railways typified

The house where Janek was born in Grodzisko.

the confusion; the gauge in Russian Poland was wider than in the other two parts and all three had incompatible signalling and braking arrangements. What was needed was a central authority strong enough to avoid the old dangers of the elective monarchy and the free veto, yet a structure that would accommodate the demands of the new infant democracy. The idea of political parties, legal for the first time, was so exhilarating that ninety took part in the 1922 election—a situation that could only lead to political anarchy.

Pilsudski stood head and shoulders above the other politicians, unchallenged as head of state after his victories, but his rivals were afraid to make him president with wide sweeping powers. Pilsudski, a soldier and a leader had no taste for party politics. As soon as Poland was independent and at peace he retired into private life. This did not last long. He became so impatient with the ineptitude of the squabbling politicians that in 1926 he seized power again. This caused some of his closest followers to break with him, feeling bound by their oath of loyalty to the constitution. They included Sikorski, an army commander in the 1920 campaign and briefly Prime Minister after 1922, Wladyslaw Anders and Kazimierz Sosnkowski, who had been

Josef Leja, Janek's father, in his apiary.

imprisoned with Pilsudski at Magdeburg.

One of Pilsudski's great admirers was an impressionable young French staff officer, named Charles de Gaulle who had been attached to the Polish Army in 1919. Years later his own political career echoed Pilsudski's, and he used the constitution Pilsudski created for Poland which was adopted in 1935 as his model when drafting a constitution for France.

One of Janek's clearest childhood memories is finding a clip of cartridges—a souvenir from the First World War. Showing an early taste for experiments, he removed the cartridges from the clip and placed them on a millstone which stood at the door of the house. Surrounded by a group of interested brothers and other children, Janek hit the cartridges with the blunt end of an axe. He remembers how difficult it was to lift, as the axe was almost as tall as he was. He finally succeeded in hitting the "right" part of the cartridge. The resulting explosion blew the axe from his hands, the door of the house open and scattered the children. His mother rushed from the house and administered a beating and his father ran home from the field to give him another. No one else was hurt and Janek's enthusiasm for

Stryj (3rd from left, second row) with the orchestra he helped to form in 1912.

experiment was not diminished. Finding leftover explosives was a hazard for several years after the end of the war.

Janek's uncle Franciszek, whom he knew as Stryj, had returned to his academic career after the Eastern Legion was disbanded. In 1923 he was appointed Professor of Mathematics at the Warsaw Technical University. A year later he married Janina Mizerska. Stryjenka, as she was known, had one child who died in infancy. Despite his success in the academic world, Stryj remained very attached to the family home in Grodzisko. Every year he and Stryjenka spent their summer holidays there, living in a small log cabin in his brother Josef's garden, so he got to know his nephews and niece well. Stryj also retained his links with the local community and was instrumental in setting up a co-operative dairy shop and a local brass band.

Janek has no idea why he was chosen for adoption by Stryj in preference to one of his brothers. Staszek as the eldest would have been the more likely choice. Perhaps it was Janek's willingness to run errands, for which he remembers receiving treats. But Stryj probably recognized a scientific talent in the nine-year-old boy, which he thought should be developed. Staszek also showed a lot of academic promise and he was sent to the secondary school at Lezajsk. After some three years, his parents told him they could no longer afford to pay for his schooling and lodging but Staszek was saved by discovering a little seminary — a secondary school maintained by the Church in Przemyśl. It was for boys from the surrounding villages who intended to become priests. He got a place and stayed there for the next five years until he completed his schooling, earning his keep as a tutor. On graduation only a proportion of the boys continued through the seminary, the rest became clerks or went to the University at Lwów which is what Staszek did.

Janek's official adoption papers had to be signed in Lezajsk and Stryj, Stryjenka, Josef and Janek travelled to the courthouse by the family cart. Janek remembers his mother made him a green corduroy suit with a stiff white collar for the occasion. He cannot remember the legal proceedings but he still recalls the great feeling of relief when it was over. Two weeks later all four left in the same cart to go to Przeworsk railway station to take the train to Warsaw where Janek's new life was to begin. It was an incredible upheaval for a nine-year-old boy. He had to learn a whole different set of customs, which included new eating habits and behaviour more suited to life in the capital. At his new primary school, which was about one and a half kilometres away, his country dialect was not understood, so he had to learn to speak a more literary Polish. The changes delayed his expected educational progress and also created problems with his brothers when he returned to Grodzisko. Stryj was more than sympathetic for he had had to surmount these same difficulties when he left the family home at Grodzisko almost thirty years before.

A year after settling in Warsaw, Janek attempted the high school entrance exam. He failed, no doubt due to problems of adjustment. So it was not until 1929 that he was able to enrol in the secondary school Gimnasium Staszica just outside the campus of the Technical University of Warsaw, where Stryj had his flat in a Faculty Housing Block. There were three different types of secondary schools: one which prepared pupils for scientific studies, one devoted entirely to philosophy and classical languages and a third which was a mixture of the two, combining Latin with either German or French and science. Janek went to a science orientated school and also received a good deal of mathematical tuition from his uncle. He was therefore able to absorb the mathematics taught at school with great ease and helped many of his fellow pupils with mathematical problems. Curiously, he later lost this mathematical ability entirely as a result of his experiences in Russian prison camps.

While attending secondary school Janek joined the Boy Scouts *Harcerstwo*. In 1932 he spent his first summer outside Grodzisko at a camp in the south-eastern Carpathian mountains in Bukovina, near the Romanian border. The whole countryside was still full of war

Stryj, Stryjenka and Janek's father Josef.

relics, trenches, barbed wire barriers and other debris spread across some of the most remote uninhabited hills and valleys, which were visited by the scouts. Janek spent a second summer camp in 1934 on the shores of lakes by Dvina. These camping experiences in isolated, rugged conditions contributed immensely to his survival in the tundra near Vorkuta in 1940.

He also went on a two week skiing camp with the scouts in 1934-5. The highlight was a skiing trip from Zakopane to Kraków, with two other scouts. The objective was to gain experience in cross-country skiing and to produce a report describing the geography en route, the people and folklore. Leaving Zakopane, Janek and his two friends decided on a detour via a mountain called Turbacz which would give them a long downhill run to Rabka. Janek broke a ski halfway down and had to make his way through the snow which was so deep in places that he sank up to his midriff. He finally rejoined his companions in Rabka, half-frozen, around midnight.

The result was that in February he was laid low for five months with rheumatic fever. For weeks he lay immobilized, incapable of even feeding himself. He listened to the radio and Stryj, trying to keep him entertained, provided him with a series of mathematical Calculus problems. The result was that by the time Janek recovered, he had completed a first year course in Calculus. Stryj was later to publish a text book on Calculus for Polish students. This proved to be a definitive work and it ran into thirteen editions by 1976.

A signal moment during this period of convalescence was when Janek heard on the radio that Pilsudski was dead. It was May 12, 1935. A few days later Janek, still lying in bed, watched the funeral procession from his window as it passed along Nowowiejska Street. The cortége was followed by many distinguished European figures, including Field Marshal Hermann Goering, Commander of the Luftwaffe that was to destroy Poland just a few years later. For several days the only music played on the radio was by Chopin and his funeral march was heard repeatedly. All Poles mourned Pilsudski, knowing they had lost the father of their country, the man who, beyond all others, had created the new independent Poland. His body was carried from Warsaw to Kraków, to be buried in the cathedral alongside Poland's kings. The streets were lined with weeping bystanders. They did well to weep—Poland had little more than four years of freedom left.

While Poland had been struggling towards a new democracy, neighbouring countries had taken a different direction. Germany and Russia, two of the mighty empires destroyed by the war, had not attended the peace conference at Versailles and had never freely

Stryj and Janek in Kraków.

accepted its terms. Adolf Hitler and the National Socialists in Germany had created a new state, a ruthless military power, determined to reclaim all the territory Germany had lost at Versailles. They vowed to bring back every separated German citizen and create one nation in one empire, ruled by one Fuehrer. The USSR had forced its way through the chaos that followed the 1917 Revolution and under Stalin a tyranny more absolute than anything the Tsars had known was brought into being. A rigorous Secret Police controlled the lives of Soviet citizens, while the powerful Red Army stood poised to regain the abandoned lands of the old Russian empire. Shadowed and menaced once more by two mighty neighbours, after Pilsudski's death Poland stood once more in danger of partition. A non-aggression pact Germany had signed with Poland in 1934 gave little sense of security, even to the most optimistic. Only the unbroken hostility that divided National Socialism and Communism gave some hope that neither power would allow the other to gain an advantage.

As Janek grew up he became increasingly conscious of Poland's vulnerability. Living with his highly intelligent uncle, he was always well informed of the political situation. Though after missing five months of school through his illness, Janek's first concern was to try to pass his exams on schedule. He managed this and started what was to be his last year at the Staszic Secondary School for in 1936 Stryj was appointed Professor of Mathematics at Kraków University. This meant a move to Kraków and a change of school for Janek. It was his last year before taking the vital *matura* examination and problems arose when he was transferred to a different type of school. Mathematics and science were completely neglected and Janek had to study a great deal of Latin, which he found especially difficult. He managed to pass the necessary exams and went on to take another more specialized entrance examination for the Akademia Gornicza, a Mining and Metallurgical Academy.

Polish Universities were run differently from those in the West. The courses were listed in a special booklet called an Index and students had to have their attendance recorded separately from marks awarded at examinations. As a result it was customary for courses to be attended intermittently for as long as fifteen years before an exam was attempted. Janek remembers one student of fifty-five years of age. When he started his degree course in 1937, aged nineteen, Janek helped out one of these mature students. Zenon Krzekotowski was a prominent figure in the metallurgical industry with exceptional experience but he had no degree. He worked 120 kilometres away in Silesia and so he could only attend the University at weekends. Janek filled in the gaps with special tuition and after two years of study they both passed the exams with high marks. Janek used the money he earned from Zenon to buy a bicycle for his brothers in Grodzisko and much to his family's surprise, he was able to step in when Stryjenka's brother needed a loan to buy a house.

Janek was showing great promise as a student. He got his half diploma unusually early and was looking forward to completing his studies. Events on the international stage were moving fast, but few could anticipate the shattering effect of the rising tide of Nazism in Germany.

Since 1935 Poland had been governed by army officers incapable of giving the country strong government and equally unable to satisfy the demand for democracy. The leaders tried to follow the traditional policy of balancing Poland's interests against their two powerful neighbours as Pilsudski had done, but events moved faster and faster out of their control. Disillusioned by the military rule, which seemed a poor substitute for the hoped for democracy, Poles watched helpless as Germany snatched back more and more territories that had been taken away by the Treaty of Versailles. Perhaps there was a kind of ironic satisfaction, particularly among the peasant farmers of Galicia, when in the spring of 1938 German troops invaded Austria and declared a union of the two German speaking nations—the Anschluss—for this meant that Austria, remnant of the all-powerful Hapsburg Empire, had ceased to exist. Any satisfaction was short-lived.

The compromise of Munich, in the autumn of 1938, saw Britain, France and Italy signatories of the Versailles treaties, appeasing Hitler by agreeing to the dismemberment of the new Versailles State of Czechoslovakia. The Czechs were not invited to share in their deliberations and their agreement was not sought. The next March, Hitler went further than the ultimate aims he had proclaimed at Munich and took over the remaining territories of Czechoslovakia, no longer defensible since the loss of Sudetenland at Munich. This last encroachment was inevitable, but it was too much. The people of Europe had mostly gone along with the politicians, seeking peace at any price. But a shocked realization of the price that Czechoslovakia was being forced to pay, gained ground after the terms of Munich were made known. Now the price seemed too great and by a kind of groundswell of public opinion, it was agreed that Czechoslovakia must be Germany's last undefended victim.

The next intended victim was obviously Poland. Hitler in a crescendo of insistence demanded Danzig and the destruction of the Polish corridor, the strip of land that the Versailles conference had decreed should separate East Prussia from Germany, and give Poland

Soviet Foreign Minister Vyacheslav Molotov signs the ten year non aggression pact with Germany on August 23, 1939 in Moscow, while German Minister for Foreign Affairs Joachim von Ribbentrop and Marshal Jozef Stalin look on.

Imperial War Museum

access to the sea. In March 1939, in the face of these threats, France and Great Britain guaranteed Poland's frontiers, undertaking to give military assistance if Poland were invaded. They hoped that the threat of war immediately following invasion of Poland would cause Hitler to stay his hand. But they had waited too long and done too little on other occasions to be taken seriously now. Their threat was no deterrent, and the summer of 1939 was overshadowed by renewed threats against Poland.

Once more—as in the Munich days of 1938—the peace of Europe was balanced on a knife-edge. Britain and France made overtures to Russia, hoping that an ally in the East might make it possible for them to resist Germany's claims more effectively, but these came to nothing. Then, on August 25, an announcement was made that shook the world in its cynical disregard for all previous policies and beliefs. Germany and Soviet Russia had signed an agreement, called the Nazi-Soviet Pact of Non-Aggression, the Ribbentrop-Molotov Pact, after the Foreign Ministers who had pieced it together. The world was

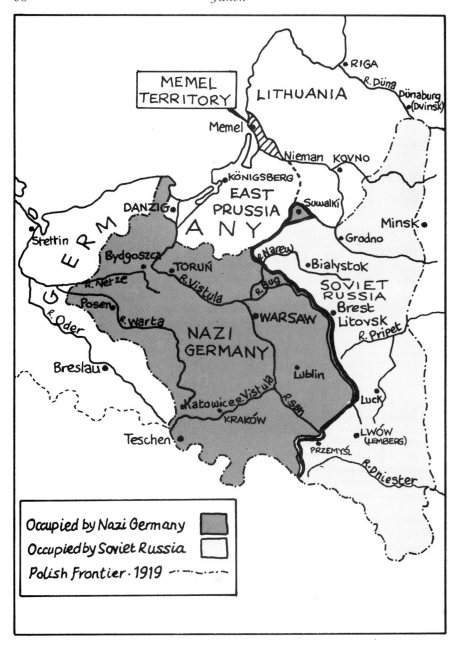

Fourth Partition of Poland: 1939.

appalled and horrified. The ideologies of Nazi Germany and Soviet Russia, hateful as they might appear, seemed at least deeply rooted and sincerely held. For nearly twenty years it had been claimed that the chief foundation of each creed was an undying hatred for the other. Now this was blown away in ruthless self interest, as it appeared that Soviet Russia was prepared to stand by as Germany invaded Poland.

Yet there was more. The full depth of infamy was not revealed until later. The Non-Aggression Pact contained a secret clause: *"In the event of a territorial and political re-arrangement of the area belonging to the Polish state the spheres of influence of Germany and the USSR shall be bounded by the lines of the rivers Narev, Vistula and San. The question of whether the interests of both parties make desirable the maintenance of an independent Polish State and how such a State should be bounded can only be definitely determined in the course of future political developments. In any event both Governments will resolve this question by means of a friendly agreement."*

Similar clauses "gave" the Baltic States and Romania's Bessarabia to the USSR. Germany renounced her 1934 non-aggression pact with Poland.

By this Nazi-Soviet Pact of Non-Aggression, Germany and Russia had set up everything they needed for a new partition of Poland. Janek Leja's growth to manhood had coincided with the twenty-one years of Poland's independence. Now Poland was to suffer a new partition— the most violent and horrific one of all—between Nazi Germany and Soviet Russia. This partition, which lasted for six years mostly under German occupation, was to have a profound effect on the future of all Poles, including the Leja family. The spectacular savageries of the German occupation have been often described and have perhaps overshadowed the less well known brutality of the Soviet occupation. This only lasted twenty-one months, until the Russians were driven out by the invading Germans but the attempted destruction of the Polish nation, especially its potential leaders, exceeded anything that had been perpetrated during the whole of the nineteenth-century occupation under the Tsars.

With the freedom granted by the pact, without any declaration of war, Germany invaded Poland on September 1, 1939. Janek's story is the account of how one Pole, among millions, was affected by the "non-aggression" pact, the war, and the partition.

CHAPTER FIVE

September 1939

AT the end of August 1939 Janek returned to Kraków after two months practical work at the Ostrowiec Swietokrzyski steel plant. He rejoined Stryj who had just come back from his regular holiday in Grodzisko. Rumours of war were rife and the whole of Poland could do no more than await the inevitable. On August 28 the army was ordered to mobilize. Almost immediately this was cancelled following pleas by Great Britain and France who believed it would provoke Germany to an immediate declaration. Then on September 1 at 5am the Germans started bombing Kraków near the railway station. All hopes of averting war were over and the music of Chopin was played on the radio throughout the day as the bombs fell.

Germany made no formal declaration of war and this unprecedented act emphasized how different the course of events were to be from any previous European war. The month that followed was a total contrast to the slow war of attrition and the grim stalemate of the trenches that characterized 1914-1918. Germany had devised a new kind of warfare—blitzkrieg. It was a war of movement, lightning war they called it, and it left non-combatants, whether they were men, women or children, completely vulnerable.

When the bombing started in Kraków, Janek's first concern was that his uncle should return to the peace of Grodzisko. With his friend Kazik Hozer, a nephew of Stryjenka, he spent the morning organizing this and at 1pm they took Stryj to Kraków railway station. The same afternoon Kazik Hozer received his call-up papers and Janek accompanied him to the station at 11pm. The station was in chaos and they found Stryj still waiting for his train.

Warsaw and Kraków were both under attack and before long the bombers switched their targets to the long straggling lines of refugees, trying to find greater security in the countryside. On the night of September 1 German tanks, launched from the newly acquired territories of former Czechoslovakia, thrust forward into Poland. It

Janek (centre) in Kraków 1939.

was said that there were three thousand German tanks; Poland had just three hundred. The Polish armed forces fought with desperate bravery at first, afterwards with dogged obstinacy as it became clear that the German attack was not to be beaten off. Cavalry units re-formed themselves and charged the columns of tanks. Efforts were made to position horsedrawn artillery for stands to hold up the advance. Resistance in Warsaw and the cities was undertaken by civilians and soldiers side by side, but the advance continued.

The Poles did not consider they were on their own. They had guarantees from Britain and France pledging that they would come to the aid of Poland if it was attacked, and indeed these promises were honoured. On the morning of Friday, September 1 both countries handed Hitler an ultimatum, stating that unless German troops were withdrawn within twenty-four hours, the two countries would consider themselves at war with Germany.

For Janek, who had stayed behind in Kraków, it was now imperative to join the Polish Army. University students had to serve one year's military service after graduation. This could be reduced to six months if they underwent intermittent training. Janek had chosen

Shattered armoured vehicles mark the flight of the defeated army, showing the devastating results of the blitzkreig.
Hulton Picture Company

this option and on the third day of the war he joined two fellow students Leszek Palasinski and Karol Kotlarczyk and set off eastwards on foot to find the call-up point for the Polish Army. They had been told to go fifteen kilometres east of Kraków to register with the Legia Akademicka. En route they were strafed by German planes. Everyone on the road fled to the ditches and fields and the returning planes machine-gunned them as they tried to take cover. When Janek and his two companions reached the call up point, it was deserted. A note had been left stating that military personnel had retreated further east. They spent the night at Zlotniki. One of Janek's friends had cousins living there, who took them in and gave them food. Later that night about twenty members of the family who had fled from Kraków, were also given shelter. As the situation worsened droves of people arrived from Kraków believing the Germans would soon occupy the city. They were entirely dependent on the kindness and hospitality of those living in the country.

On the same morning, Sunday, September 3, that Janek left Kraków British Prime Minister Neville Chamberlain made a radio announcement. He said that as the Germans had not withdrawn from

Poland, Britain was now at war with Germany. On the same day France also declared war on Germany. So Poland, who had so often stood alone, at last had allies. But what could they do? There was a melancholy Polish proverb: "Poland has two allies, God and France. And they are both a long way away." And certainly Britain was no nearer. So while Britain and France slowly moved into a war gear and took up defensive positions on the Western front to guard against a German attack in that quarter, the blitzkrieg against Poland continued.

On September 4 Janek and his two friends decided to move east in a bid to find the new call up point. It was suggested they would make quicker progress if they commandeered a boat. On the Vistula the only boats they could find were large metal barges. A number of people were already trying to manoeuvre one of these midstream and Janek and his companions were welcomed as additional manpower. They set off along the Vistula, sleeping on the barge at night. But as they passed under a bridge near Szczucin, they were shot at by the Germans. They abandoned the barge on the right bank and set off on foot using the bushes as cover. The Germans continued to shoot for some time until eventually the sound of shooting became more distant as they continued their journey. When the food given to them at Zlotniki was exhausted they stopped at a peasant's cottage. They were just ahead of the mass exodus of refugees from the towns and were treated with great kindness. There was water in the well and they were given potatoes, eggs and tomatoes. As the three continued eastwards they were constantly surprised by the generosity of the local people; despite their poverty they were willing to share anything they had.

When they first left Kraków they had been walking with a column of refugees but the German planes were quick to see these as targets so Janek and his companions took to minor roads where the groups of refugees were fewer and more spread out. They stopped at a barn which was full to capacity with refugees. They managed to find a space to lie down and early next morning Janek woke to see a file of rats enjoying a half full jar of jam on a beam above him. Soon they came to an area where the wells had run dry and the local population had no food left to give away. They had literally been engulfed by refugees. A week after leaving Kraków Janek and his friends reached the River San bypassing Grodzisko which was some sixty-five kilometres to the south. The bridge over the river at Rozwadow had been bombed and was lying in the water. But part could still be crossed on foot, with a twenty foot gap that had to be swum. German planes were strafing anyone who attempted to cross, but choosing their moment Janek and his two companions succeeded in reaching

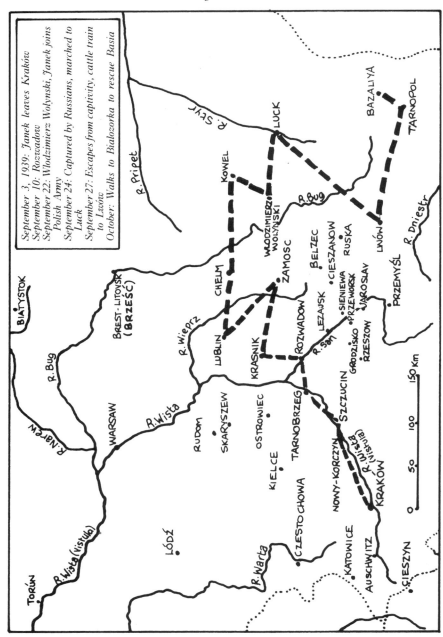

September 3, 1939: Janek leaves Kraków
September 10: Rozwadow
September 22: Wlodzimierz Wolynski, Janek joins
   Polish Army
September 24: Captured by Russians, marched to
   Luck
September 27: Escapes from captivity, cattle train
   to Lwów
October: Walks to Bialozorka to rescue Basia

Janek's journey to join the Polish Army.

the other bank. They found the place where army volunteers were being enrolled and were given half a loaf of bread between them and told that uniforms and arms would be supplied the next day. They spent the night in a barn and in the early hours they were disturbed by a commotion outside. They decided to stay where they were but in the morning they discovered that the Germans had passed through the area and the Polish recruiting team had again disappeared.

Once more behind the German lines, they set off eastwards, sticking to minor roads. The biggest problem was trying to find out whether the German lines were in front or behind them. They received conflicting advice from the locals and often unwittingly crossed the line during the day, only to be leap-frogged by the Germans during the night. The towns and villages they passed through have become a blur to Janek. Their main concern was to find out if the Germans were in control before they entered a town. Their route from Kraków took them via Zlotniki, Novy Korczyn, Szczucin, Mielec, Tarnobrzeg, Rozwadow, Krasnik, Piaski, Chelm, to Kowel— a distance of about five hundred kilometres. Janek's only recollection of Kowel was knocking on the door of the prison to see if they could sleep there but the guard at the gate would not accept them as they were not prisoners. They walked another fifty-five kilometres to Wlodzimierz Wolynski where they found the Polish recruitment point and at last signed on as soldiers.

The unit Janek joined was given the task of defending Wlodzimierz Wolynski from the approaching Germans. On September 24 they were deployed in dugouts facing the direction of the anticipated German advance. Suddenly they were being shot at but it was difficult to find out from which direction the bullets were coming because the whizz of the bullet was audible before the report of the gun. It soon became clear that the shots were coming from behind and it was the Russians who were firing. The Polish soldiers assumed the Russians had come to their assistance to halt the German invaders. It was not until they were surrounded, ordered to lay down their arms and then taken prisoner, that they finally realized that the Russians had come not as friends but as allies of the Germans.

When the Germans first invaded Poland they invited Russia to join them in accordance with the secret protocol of the Soviet-Nazi Pact. But Stalin preferred to wait until the Polish army had been destroyed. On September 9 the Germans forecast the fall of Warsaw within a week. In a communiqué on September 16 they announced that the city had fallen. The next day Stalin invaded eastern Poland—only to discover that the communiqué was false and the Red Army was committed to unnecessary sacrifices. The amazing defence of Warsaw

A village catches fire after bombardment, September 1939.

Hulton Picture Company

continued and the city managed to survive until September 27. Even then there was no thought of surrender. The Polish government, with the Commander-in-Chief's headquarters at Brest Litovsk, trapped between the German and Russian troops, managed to escape to Romania on September 18. Russia and Germany put such pressure on Romania that these Poles were interned. The President managed to get out a resignation statement to leave the way clear for a successor to be appointed. General Sikorski got to Paris, and there the Polish ambassador invited him to command the Polish armed forces. A Polish Government in exile was established, recognized by Britain and France, and before long by the United States. There was never a Polish puppet government or a Vichy type of compromise in Poland.

Janek was now a prisoner of the invading Soviets. His first feeling was one of resentment when he was ordered to hand over an excellent spring knife which had belonged to Stryj. He was among several hundred Polish soldiers who were marched in columns by Russian troops, carrying fixed bayonets. The journey to Luck military barracks, some fifty-five kilometres away took three days and two nights. At night they slept on the road and it was then that the first rains came. Poland had been praying for rain since the war started in the hope that muddy unpaved roads would slow down the German armoured units. Until then the weather had been exceptionally fine.

When they reached Luck barracks they were given their first meal. As an act of mockery to their "bourgeois" prisoners, the soup was served in chamber-pots. The Russians were preoccupied with seizing everything they could lay their hands on and consequently neglected to guard their prisoners properly. While they were attempting to commandeer some race horses from a local stable, they left the main gate of the garrison open. Janek and his two friends seized the opportunity and escaped by slipping out of the main entrance. They were shot at, but managed to get away keeping under cover until they found a hiding place beneath the floor of the local school. That evening, locals brought them food, civilian clothing, and gave them shelter. The next day they investigated the possibility of going to Lwów by cattle train and eventually arrived there early in the morning on September 29. Janek's brother Staszek had a flat in Lwów and the three made their way there. Staszek had graduated at Lwów University in 1938 and had been a lecturer at the Technical University. He had been called up in August and after a brief spell with his unit he had also been captured by the Russians. Like Janek he had managed to escape.

On the same day as Janek arrived at Lwów, General Anders was taken into imprisonment in the city. He had been wounded and captured by the Russians at Jesionka Stasiowa just south of Lwów, attempting to hold a bridgehead to allow Polish troops to escape into Romania and Hungary but their guns had fallen silent after running out of ammunition. Now, by the end of September, all organized resistance in Poland had collapsed.

Within four weeks the modern German forces had wiped out the old fashioned, ill-equipped, tragically heroic Polish army. Ribbentrop and Molotov met once again to amend their secret protocol so that Lithuania should be awarded to the USSR and the provinces of Lublin and Warsaw should be under German control.

It was now that isolated individuals or groups from the scattered armed forces began to leave Poland, trying to get through Romania or into Hungary to join Polish units that were forming in France and Britain. Janek's two friends decided to return to Kraków but Janek was determined to join the resistance abroad. The long standing desire to fight for Poland and Poland's freedom, was as strong as ever and fifty thousand Poles joined up. Others, like Janek, initially found the obstacles overwhelming and it took years of effort before they could join the ranks.

CHAPTER SIX

Last Months of Freedom

On the night of September 29, 1939 Janek and his brother Staszek sat up discussing the appalling happenings of the last four weeks and trying to guess the course of future events. Both had been taken prisoner by the Russians and managed to escape, but they knew any attempt to join the Polish resistance would put them in immediate danger of recapture. Staszek, with considerable insight, said he believed the only people who would be safe under Russian occupation would be the uneducated and illiterate. Following the defence of Warsaw, the occupying forces were determined to crush the Polish people once and for all. Staszek was convinced they would see the educated classes as their biggest threat. As he was a university lecturer and Janek was a university student, they were obviously in the front line. This conversation proved to be crucial when Janek was later under Russian interrogation.

Staszek was very worried about his wife Basia, who was teaching at a primary school in Bialozorka, near the Russian frontier. They had been married only six months and Staszek had had no news of her since the outbreak of war. Janek wanted to join the resistance abroad but he offered to go and find Basia and bring her back to Lwów, before he made his plans. First he went by train to Brzezany to contact an old friend from the Academy, Karol Weiss. He hoped Weiss could give him information about escape routes from Poland to France via Romania, Czechoslovakia or Hungary. Brzezany lay close to the border with these countries.

In early October, Janek started his journey to Bialozorka. Leaving around midnight he went by rail to Tarnopol travelling on the step outside the engine. The train got as far as the bombed-out bridge near Tarnopol and Janek then walked sixty-seven kilometres to Bialozorka, which is two to three kilometres from the pre-war border with Russia. This was the longest distance he walked in one day. He was trying to avoid the Russians who were pouring into Poland along the main roads, so he kept to the minor roads managing without a map. He had a narrow escape when a Ukrainian vigilante group intercepted him en route, asking to see his identification papers. Two went to fetch an interpreter and left him with only one guard. Janek saw his chance and escaped. That evening, sleeping by the side of a cart-track in a field, he awoke to the sound of Polish voices. When he asked a cart driver the way to Bialozorka, the driver offered him a lift for the seven remaining kilometres. It turned out that the driver's children were taught by Basia and so Janek was taken straight to her.

Basia was horrified by Janek's condition after his long journey. He was in terrible pain with his feet and when he took his socks off the skin from his heels came away in one piece. It was therefore a day or two before they were able to set off for Lwów, even though they knew it was dangerous to remain at Bialozorka. As Staszek had predicted, the Russians were cracking down on education and it was clear that Polish schools would soon be closed. Basia's friends organized transport to a village twelve to fourteen kilometres away. From there they were taken by another cart for fifteen kilometres. In fact, they made the whole journey back to the bridge near Tarnopol in a series of cart rides.

By the time Basia was reunited with Staszek, snow was beginning to fall. The Russians in Lwów started to register all the inhabitants to weed out refugees from permanent residents. The plan was to organize an election to install Communists in control. This election was held on October 21 and was supervised by Krushchev, later a successor to Stalin. Six days afterwards, the resulting West Ukraine National Assembly, predictably compliant, voted for incorporation into the USSR as did the similarly formed White Russian Assembly at Bialystok. The independent state of Poland had officially ceased to exist. On the last day of October 1939 Soviet foreign minister Molotov said: "After one quick blow, first from the German and next from the Red Army, nothing remained of the mis-shapen monster created by the Treaty of Versailles."

As an unregistered inhabitant in Lwów, Janek needed to move before he was caught again. He was also anxious to find out what had happened to other members of his family on the German side of the demarcation line in Grodzisko. He decided to cross the line and go to Grodzisko before trying to join the Polish Army which was being formed under Sikorski in France. He left Lwów later in October, travelling on foot and by cart via Rawa Ruska, Wiazownica, Cieszanow, to Zamość and then by train to Lublin, and Warsaw. This was his first sight of Warsaw under German occupation. He remembers All Souls Day, November 2, and the local people placing candles on the temporary graves in the streets, marking those who had died in the valiant defence of the city. Janek stayed with some of his friends from his former secondary school who were also planning to escape through Romania or Hungary to join the Polish Army in France. Active plans were being made for surreptitious crossing of the Russo-German demarcation line in both directions but Janek felt he had to check on his family before making his escape. He travelled by train to Rozwadow and was then able to reach Grodzisko where he found his parents and his younger brothers Wicek and Felek in good health.

Stryj had returned to Kraków after a brief stay in Grodzisko and on November 6 he was invited along with other university professors, to attend a lecture organized by the Germans, prior to the official re-opening of the University. The subject was "The Attitude of the German Authorities to Science and Learning" by a Dr Meyer. When the professors were gathered, Dr Meyer revealed himself as the Gestapo chief and instead of the expected lecture, the University staff were accused of opposing the new authority. They were all arrested and taken to the concentration camp at Oranienburg near Sachsenhausen which was to become one of the most notorious under Nazi control. Stryj, in his mid fifties and a highly respected Professor of Mathematics was reduced to a day by day fight against cold, hunger and other terrible deprivations.

Janek was growing increasingly restless in Grodzisko. The daily evidence of increasing retributions by the occupying powers made normal life impossible. When he saw the Germans enforcing requisitions of pigs and cattle on his father's and neighbour's farms Janek decided the time had come to act. In December he returned to Warsaw by a different route, through Skarzysko and Radom, to find out what was happening in the resistance movement. In the first months of the war there was a spontaneous outburst of conspiratorial activity in Poland. For much of the population this was a return to the kind of behaviour that had been normal when under foreign occupation twenty-one years before. It was typified by a contempt towards authority, an integral part of the Polish character evolved during the long years of Partition. Consequently the underground movement was to become extraordinarily well organized and significantly, Poland was the only Nazi-occupied country that did not provide a collaborationist quisling regime. As the war progressed the underground operated schools and even universities as well as maintaining an entire legal system with underground courts. The Home Army, which was to become famous in the ill fated Warsaw Rising, even succeeded in capturing and dismantling all the working

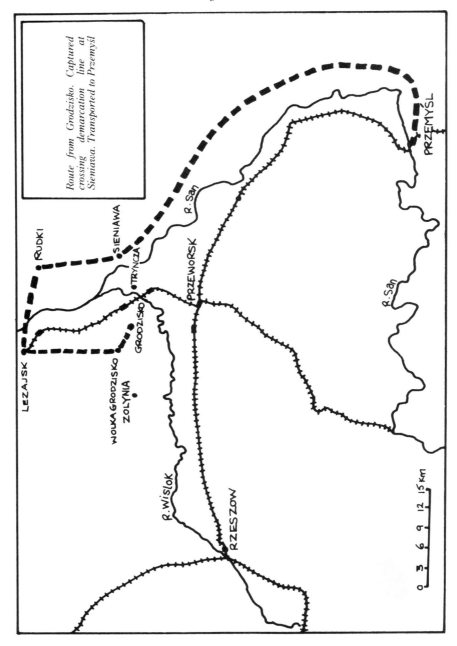

Janek's capture and journey to Przemyśl Fortress.

parts of a German V2 rocket and delivering them to London. The underground state, which Janek saw in its early stages, owed its allegiance to Sikorski's government in exile. This was growing in strength and included a number of political leaders who had evaded capture by either the Russians or the Germans. One of these was Stanislaw Mikolajczyk, a leader of the Peasant party who joined Sikorski in Paris at the end of November after escaping from Poland via Hungary.

Janek made journeys to near Przemyśl and Jaroslav by bicycle to reconnoitre possible crossing routes of the demarcation line. It was at this time that an older friend from the same village, Wojtek Szklany, a fourth year seminarian student, came from Przemyśl to spend Christmas with his mother in Grodzisko. He was also determined to join the resistance abroad and on January 8, 1940 Wojtek and Janek set off using a horse and sleigh to visit a priest in Tryncza, twelve kilometres away. Wojtek wanted to persuade the priest to come with him and another friend, Kazik Markocki, to Romania. Kazik, son of Grodzisko's postman had escaped from the Germans after being involved in the defence of Warsaw. He had come direct from a prisoner-of-war camp to his parents' house. The priest could not make up his mind and as he vacillated, Janek decided on the spur of the moment to take his place. They left the next morning at 5am. Janek's father was dead set against the plan and when words failed he tried to prevent his son from going by hiding his coat. Janek was determined, and despite the intense cold and snow, he set off without it. He had arranged to meet Wojtek and Kazik at his sister Maria's house. In fact his mother had been there all night looking after her daughter in childbirth. The baby Helena was born in the early hours of January 9 just before Janek left. At the last minute his father relented and sent his youngest son Felek with Janek's coat. Felek was only fourteen years old but already he was adamant that he should be allowed to join the army. After farewells the three army-volunteers went to Lezajsk, and around noon had a last drink together in the local bar. Janek was not to see most of his family again for thirty-three years.

Janek, Wojtek, and Kazik needed to find the best place to cross the demarcation line. They heard that it was safest at Rudki near Sieniawa and at 4pm they reached the arranged crossing point. They were met by someone introducing himself as a courier and were told to attempt their crossing at 10pm. The demarcation line was supposed to run through the middle of a clearing in the wood and at the appointed time the three started to make their way across. Suddenly a shot rang out and a Russian voice ordered them to stop. It was only then they realised the courier had betrayed them. They were surrounded by

Russian soldiers, who appeared almost invisible in the snow with their white hats, white clothes and white boots. A soldier was detailed to escort the new prisoners away, while his colleagues awaited further unsuspecting victims. Eventually they were joined by another twenty-five prisoners all caught in the same way.

None of them realized how seriously the Soviets regarded the offence of crossing a frontier. To the Poles it was merely an artificial demarcation line in their own country, and they had no idea how severe the penalties would be. From then onwards, Janek was in Soviet custody, and as far as he and his fellow Poles were concerned, they were on Polish territory under enemy occupation. With this dramatic change, it is appropriate that Janek's experiences as a prisoner of the Russians should be told in his own words.

PART II

CHAPTER SEVEN

A Prisoner of the Russians

W E were questioned immediately and remembering my brother Staszek's advice, I said I was unable to read or write and could only sign my name with a cross. I gave my correct name but I said that I had been captured by the Germans and had escaped from their prisoner of war camp. I told them I had been making my way to my village which was near Tarnopol. Kazik and Wojtek gave equally misleading stories, which we all compared when we were reunited. We were kept in a room at Sieniawa for three days and then on a bitterly cold winter's day we were taken on an open truck to a temporary prison in Przemyśl. A week later we were marched to the local fortress prison where we were to be incarcerated for the next two months.

The military fortress-prison at Przemyśl had been built by the Austrians who had defended it against Russian attacks during the 1914-18 war. When I first saw the prison, there was a central group of buildings surrounded by the remains of thirteen enormous forts which radiated from the central block. Some of these forts had been destroyed and many others badly damaged by Russian shells in 1915, an onslaught which also resulted in many casualties. Later in the war the Austrians demolished more of it when trying to recover metals that were becoming scarce. This destruction continued after Poland became independent, when private contractors moved in. Much later I heard a curious story of a lone survivor who emerged from the underground cells in the fortress, when its remnants were cleared in 1923. In 1914 two Russian officers, prisoners of war taken by the Austrian army, were imprisoned in an underground cell in the Przemyśl fortress. They became trapped in 1915 when Russian shells demolished the structures above ground. Polish contractors clearing the rubble in 1923 uncovered a massive metal door. When they broke through, they found steps leading down. The first man entering with a flashlight was heard yelling hysterically and fell unconscious on the

Przemyśl Fortress.   Polish Institute and Sikorski Museum

steps. His friends rushed to his aid and saw a semi-naked skeletal figure with a white beard down to his knees. He was completely incoherent and inarticulate and died shortly afterwards in hospital. In the underground maze of storerooms and cells a box was found with old snapshots and an exercise book filled with writing, clear at first then gradually less and less legible. This diary of the survivor related how the two Russian officers survived the 1915 shelling and had then discovered stores of food, clothing, water, and candles. The writer had constructed a water clock—a barrel with a small hole which took thirty-six hours to empty, taking his pulse as seventy per minute as a reference. His diary ran through over one thousand barrelfuls when his last candle expired. His companion became depressed, drank all the liquor he could find and took his own life. The survivor, alone in the darkness, must have spent over eight years in the demolished fort.

I was now incarcerated in this depressing place. I was separated from my companions and was allotted to a cell with complete strangers. My first experience of rigorous interrogation now took place. I was accused of being a German spy and the NKVD interrogator tried to intimidate me by firing shots close to my head.

The interrogation cell was some six to seven flights of steps underground and the door and walls were covered with thick layers of sound-deadening material, so I feared there would be no witness to any "accident" that might befall me. My morale was very low at this stage. Within a remarkably short space of time I had lost my freedom, I was accused of being a spy and I was in fear of my life. The hardest thing to bear was being separated from my friends from Grodzisko. There was no one in the cell among the twenty-five or so occupants whom I could trust, even though I desperately needed to talk to someone. In the first two weeks in detention, the three of us from Grodzisko talked only to each other. We quickly learned that informers—"stool pigeons" were always in a cell among the inmates.

Communication with fellow prisoners in other cells was forbidden, but it took place in the way that has become familiar to all who have read Alexander Solzhenitsyn—by tapping signals on the wall or leaving written messages among the scribbles on the lavatory walls. As an inexperienced inmate I wrote a message to Wojtek Szklany using his initials. In Polish the initial S is different from the single letter in Russian that replaces "SZ" (C), so the Russians were unable to discover who the S represented as there was no prisoner who matched with this initial. By this time I had discovered that Wojtek was in an adjoining cell so by tapping at first, we agreed to talk more directly later that night, using an air vent at the top of the dividing wall. In order to reach the vent I had to stand on another prisoner's back. By this time most inmates were lying down on the floor for the night. But I did not realize that I was making myself visible to the guards in the courtyard below who could see through a narrow crevice in the wooden blind covering the outside of a window. Suddenly a shot rang out, ricocheting from a bar in the window, inches from my head. The shock made me fall to the ground, but when the guards came in to find the body, they could not find their victim. Not one of my fellow prisoners would admit to hearing a shot and they pretended to have no idea what the guards were looking for. Each prisoner was interrogated separately but nobody gave me away.

The two months I spent at Przemyśl gave me my first experience of prison life and I learnt the ways prisoners developed to counter some of the rigours to which we were subjected. The most important precaution was to be circumspect in all dealings with fellow prisoners until by careful observation, a trustworthy companion could be isolated. As a supposed illiterate, I had to act accordingly and not betray myself with the use of literary expressions. The best course of action was to keep silent, whenever possible. I also had to remember not to recognize written words or numbers, not only during

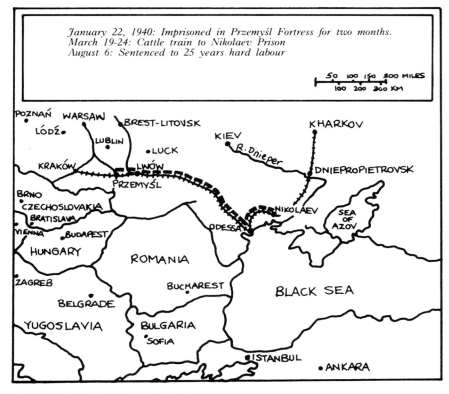

January 22, 1940: Imprisoned in Przemyśl Fortress for two months.
March 19-24: Cattle train to Nikolaev Prison
August 6: Sentenced to 25 years hard labour

Journey from Przemyśl to Nikolaev.

interrogation but at any other time when I was among other prisoners. If I talked to someone I trusted, I learnt to do so in a hushed voice, out of anyone else's hearing. Whenever possible, I walked in the cell alone. The distance was only three to five steps but I kept my mind occupied by silently repeating any song, poem, prayer, or conversation that I could remember or invent.

On March 19 I was transferred with fellow prisoners in cattle trucks to Nikolaev, seventy miles north-east of Odessa on the Black Sea. The journey took five days. As we were passing through Lwów I threw a piece of paper with a message describing my fate, on to the side of the railway track. I learnt later that this found its way to my brother Staszek. After this attempt to contact my family, I saw a few last glimpses of my homeland which I was not to see again until 1973.

When we arrived in Nikolaev, a naval base at the mouth of the River

Southern Bug on the Black Sea, the prisoners were separated and interrogated afresh. This was the customary procedure. I found myself sharing a cell with a chemical engineer who had worked in a sugar factory. After a few days of careful scrutiny, I had picked him out as a trustworthy companion. Boris Gumenuk was of Byelo-Russian origin and his family had emigrated to Poland after the Russian revolution of 1917. He was two years older than me, a recent graduate of chemical engineering and we got on very well, exchanging observations, sharing knowledge and experience. As a result I learnt a great deal about the manufacture of sugar from sugar beet and in turn I described some aspects of steel production that I had learnt during the summer of 1939 from my time at the steel plant. This exchange continued intensively every night until it was Boris's turn to be interrogated. I was horrified to see his rapid deterioration after each session of questioning, which started at 11pm and went on until the early hours of the morning. These interrogations were not allowed to interrupt the normal routine of the prisoners and so those who had been interrogated were forced to stay awake the following day. Sleep deprivation caused by continuous night sessions of interrogation was a serious factor leading to despair. After only two nights Boris was imbued with fear. He became less coherent with rambling self-accusations about spying and he died within a week. This was a terrible shock to me. I had not realized until then how a psychological assault could kill a healthy young man so quickly.

I was fortunate that my original claim to be an illiterate was accepted so I only had to undergo interrogation twice. My main problem was to remember my cover story which had to be repeated in all its detail at the start of every interrogation session. I also had to make sure that I was not caught reading or trying to decipher notices. If I went into an unfamiliar room where there was a choice of doors I had to remember not to automatically head for the one marked EXIT in Russian. I still recall the satisfaction I felt when I damaged their pens by digging the nibs clumsily into the paper when I was asked to sign each page of the interrogation report with a cross.

I made friends with Wlodzimierz Gorzecki, a prisoner in his late fifties from Silesia in Western Poland who had been a government worker. After the war he met my aunt Stryjenka and was able to give my family some news of me. Life in Nikolaev prison differed from Przemyśl. In Przemyśl inmates had comprised Poles, Jews and Ukrainians from every walk of life. There was a sprinkling of the criminal element and a large number of speculators who had attempted to make money from goods going across the demarcation line. In Nikolaev the prisoners were drawn from many nationalities of the Soviet Union and its neighbouring countries. They included occasional long-timers of five or six years under interrogation such as *kulak* peasant farmers, coalminers from Donbas, Czechs, Romanians, Slovaks and many others. The criminal elements in the Przemyśl group stood out by their adherence to their own code of behaviour. They kept together, they maintained order and did not exploit the rest of the inmates, nor did they cheat at food distribution. They usually defied the guards and the prison authorities. I believe it was a member of this group who let me stand on his shoulder in Przemyśl when I tried to talk to Wojtek Szklany through an airduct in the wall. Other groups, who kept together through nationality or profession were never so unified and were frightened by officials. But the *blatnoys*— Russian criminal groups—that joined the cells in Nikolaev were far from helpful to other prisoners. They were demanding, ruthless, vicious, and fearless in relation to the guards. They did not attach any value to their own lives or the lives of others.

All inmates suffered infestation of lice and bedbugs, although there were never any beds in the cells. Prisoners slept on the floor, the more privileged occupied floor space away from the obnoxious *parasha*—a dustbin type container serving as a communal lavatory which stank to high heaven and was usually overflowing in the early morning. Once a day, irregularly, we were let out to a lavatory, waiting our turn in queues. If the water supply was not exhausted, we were able to wash our hands and faces. There were no towels except shirt tails. Nobody had any handkerchiefs, these were confiscated fairly soon after incarceration as an example of "capitalist prejudices". Spitting on the floor and cleaning noses by hand on to the floor were common until the criminals introduced a no spitting rule to keep the floor reasonably clean for sleeping. This was an example of how order was maintained in the cell by the criminals rather than the cell leader. Whole days were spent walking up and down the cell or lice hunting— systematically going along all seams, crevices and joints, and killing the beasts. Everybody became an expert as their stay in prison lengthened. Opportunities for baths, either showers in prison or bowls of water in the camps, were restricted to two or three occasions in every six months. These, even with the steam treatment of all clothing were ineffective in eradicating the lice. They were reduced for the few days immediately following a steam bath, but multiplied with a vengeance within a week.

The daily routine was to be woken by the guards at 6am and then rations of heavy and moist bread were distributed. *Kipiatok*, hot water, or coloured water substituting for tea was also handed out and on rare occasions we were allowed sugar. The next meal, not until evening, consisted of soup, served in dishes that were always too few for the number of inmates. Those without dishes had to wait until the first group had finished and this included a thorough licking of the bowls, before they were passed on. At night the cell light was left blazing from the ceiling and the call up for interrogation would start. The grating of the heavy lock in the door would announce its opening. Then two or three NKVD men with some files would call out: "Who is here whose name begins with a K or a W?" And the inmates would respond. One of them would be told to go out, a few minutes later another group of NKVD men would come in and repeat the performance. Towards the morning the interviewees would start being readmitted to the cell, some as late as midday. Every few days all the inmates of a cell would be called out and surrounded by guards with guns and bayonets. A group of NKVD men would go through the cell looking for hidden knives, needles or any other evidence of escape plans. Every prisoner would then undergo minute inspection before being slowly readmitted to the cell. Occasionally the whole group would be transferred to a new cell and mixed in with other prisoners.

There were times when we did not receive our regular food rations and despite prisoners complaining and banging on the door, there were no official reprimands. But as soon as prisoners refused to accept food, all hell broke loose. Squads of armed NKVD would appear with the prisoners' manager and his subordinate and they would attempt to restore peace. I remember one occasion when a *zek*—prisoner was given a bowl of soup. He found a long object in it which on closer inspection proved to be the tail of a rat with one hind leg still attached. He showed it to the rest of the cell and we all stopped eating. Our shouts of outrage brought an NKVD officer to the scene. The *zek* showed him the rat's tail, keeping the leg hidden in his palm. The officer immediately berated us for our lack of knowledge and culture. He said in the Soviet Union there were all sorts of unusual specimens including a big fish that had whiskers, just like the one the *zek* held in his hand. He pointed out the trouble the prison authorities took to provide such exotic food. The *zek* then opened his palm and asked how a rat's leg came to be attached to a fish's whisker? The officer left, but in a few minutes a more senior officer appeared and accused us of counter-revolutionary agitation and resistance to lawful authority. We were subdivided and transferred to the lavatory block and the cell was searched. We were all subjected to inspection and interrogated to find the instigator of the hunger strike. Later that night gruel was issued and everything gradually died down.

The Nikolaev prison left one indelible mark on my mind. Two or three weeks after I arrived, I was moved to a cell at a corner of the prison building which adjoined another wing at right angles. In this adjoining wing were the cells for women prisoners and children. The children were separated from their mothers and I had to listen to the constant sound of children and babies crying. The guards shouted and cursed but the noise, though varying in intensity, never died out. For over two months those cries were always in my ears and there was nothing that I could do about it. When I had children of my own I could never bear to hear them cry—a reaction which dates from that time.

The regular routine of my life was suddenly changed on Tuesday August 6, 1940 when I was called out from my cell with many other prisoners and we were given our sentences. As we were prisoners of war, there was no justification for putting us on trial or handing out jail sentences. But we were told our sentences were administrative as distinct from court sentences, which had some logic as there were no trials and not even the pretence of a court hearing. The sentences were entirely arbitrary, ranging from three, fifteen or twenty-five years. All the sentences had the annotation *Katorga*—hard labour. I was given twenty-five years. I met up briefly with my friends from Grodzisko whom I had not seen since we were taken to Przemyśl prison in January. I discovered that Kazik, a corporal, had received three years and Wojtek a seminary student was sentenced to fifteen years. There was no rhyme or reason to the length of sentence, it was as though some quota had to be completed. The newly sentenced prisoners were separated yet again, into different groups. We were put into cells and next day each group was taken for a medical examination. We were told to undress and two women dressed in white came in with the NKVD officers. Names were called and we had to stand naked in turn between the women who were seemingly doctors or *vrach*—medical orderlies. They looked at each inmate from the back and front and then pronounced them *khorosho*—good, approved for physical appearance. One of the Russian *zeks* asked where they were going to be sent. One of the women replied, using a vulgar Russian expression: "I don't know but don't worry. You may live, but you'll never want sex again." The complete medical examination of forty to fifty prisoners took ten to fifteen minutes.

Three days later on August 9 the group of prisoners I was with left Nikolaev by cattle train for Kiev. This is the third largest city of the USSR after Moscow and Leningrad and as the capital of the Ukraine it had once been part of Poland. We had no opportunity to see Kiev but were taken on to Kharkov, where we spent two weeks in an outer courtyard. Next we were loaded on to a train which contained the famous Stolypin cars. The original cars, built before 1911, were named after Russian premier Stolypin. They were fourth class compartmented passenger cars re-equipped with double-gratings on the windows, and taking five per compartment. By the time the Soviets took them over, they were further altered so that the windows were completely blocked out and the doors were replaced by sliding iron diagonal bar gratings, so that they looked like animals' cages. We continued the journey to Archangelsk via Moscow, in one of these. We could only see through cracks in the boarded windows, and we had to wait on a railway siding for about two days, before the engine was attached. We were packed like sardines and most of the prisoners in the Stolypin compartment with me spoke Russian or Ukrainian. After a day I noticed another prisoner who was keeping very quiet and he proved to be a Pole. We managed to manoeuvre ourselves so we could settle side by side where we could talk quietly in Polish. The other prisoner was Adas Skrzynski from Warsaw, a student at the Politechnika Warszawska who had taken lectures from Stryj a few years back. His father was a former ambassador of Poland to the United States and Adas had spent two or three years in Washington before his father was recalled to Warsaw after Pilsudski's death in 1935. Adas painted a dream-like picture of life in the USA and I was determined that one day I would go there. But mostly Adas and I talked of the things we had in common, our Polish families and our mutual acquaintances from Warsaw. That kept us going throughout the journey and during our stay in the transit camp in Archangelsk where we spent a few days in October. Archangelsk is the major port on the North Dvina delta fifty-two kilometres from the White Sea and is only ice-free for six months of the year.

One of the worst things about my imprisonment was having no knowledge about what was going on in the outside world. It was only through talking to Adas that I realized France had fallen three months previously and Britain's predicted occupation was imminent. He was convinced that the United States would never allow Europe to become a Nazi empire. We were separated during the forthcoming sea voyage and only saw each other occasionally in the distance. We were not to meet again until 1948 in London.

CHAPTER EIGHT

In Transit

FROM Archangelsk we were loaded on to a coal boat which took us through the White Sea, a branch of the Barents Sea, to Nar'yan Mar. The coal boat was powered by steam and had been converted for transporting prisoners. As soon as we were on board we were led to the aft hatch and descended down a wooden staircase into the bowels of the boat. At levels of approximately seven feet from the deck downwards, the staircase opened out into four foot wide platforms, from which there were corridors running at right angles from the staircase. These corridors branched off every twelve feet or so into other corridors, again at right angles to each other. In effect, the whole ship was a huge maze of criss-crossing corridors with the spaces in between filled with shelves acting as bunks. Each shelf was twelve feet by twelve feet, accommodating two rows of tightly packed prisoners, feet towards feet. There were three tiers of shelves accessible from each side of a corridor and each twelve foot shelf had ten prisoners in a row. It was so crowded we all had to lie on the same side and could only turn over by mutual agreement.

The loading of prisoners started from the bottom of the hold upwards. When it came to my turn, I was put in one of the tiers at the second level below the deck, very close to the staircase. This turned out to be a very favourable position, with air and light getting through from the hatch. Even so the light was so dim that I could not see from the platform on my second level down to the fourth or fifth level. A hum of voices and an occasional shout indicated a multitude of people. A similar staircase existed in the forward part of the ship. When loading was finished guards were posted at all levels, at all the staircases and at the crossroads of long corridors to make sure that all prisoners stayed on their shelf bunks. When evening came, temporary lights were strung along the staircase and at the first corridor of each level where the guards were stationed. Once a day groups of prisoners were allowed on the deck, under guard, to use the lavatories. These

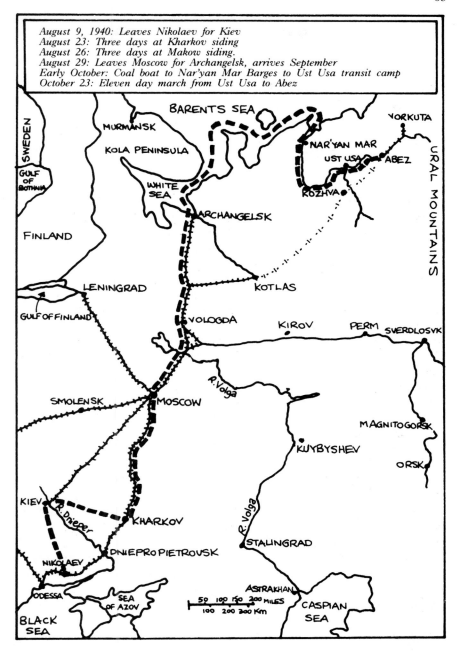

August 9, 1940: Leaves Nikolaev for Kiev
August 23: Three days at Kharkov siding
August 26: Three days at Makow siding.
August 29: Leaves Moscow for Archangelsk, arrives September
Early October: Coal boat to Nar'yan Mar Barges to Ust Usa transit camp
October 23: Eleven day march from Ust Usa to Abez

Journey from Nikolaev to Abez.

were rickety wooden contraptions overhanging the edges of the decks on both sides. The rest of the deck was packed full of boxes, presumably provisions for the guards and prisoners. Adjoining the superstructure with the steering gear and cabins for the crew, there was a large wooden shack for the guards.

Once the engines started, the whole ship began to throb and groan. We learnt that we were on our way to the Pechora *katorga lager*, though we had no idea where that was. In fact the route took us via the White Sea, passing by the Kola Peninsula with Murmansk and then turning east and skirting Novaia Zemlya Island and proceeding towards the northern Urals. Prisoners were able to talk to each other from the various bunks and even between the different levels. At night surreptitious movement between bunks on the same level was possible. On the second day there was some muted scheming to overpower the guards on the various levels, timed for when the boat would be steaming past the Kola Peninsula. The plan was to rush the deck and the steering superstructure and force the captain to turn westwards towards Norway. However towards the end of the third day the weather started to deteriorate. The throbbing of the engines became more and more laborious and gradually, one by one, the prisoners and the guards on duty became ill and general seasickness took hold of everyone. The routine of going on to the deck to the lavatories was abandoned. At the end of the first week a storm hit the ship, swaying it from side to side and tossing it up and down. The waves started to splash seawater over the lip of the hatch and down the staircase. The hatch was battened down except for the last couple of planks, so that you could still squeeze on to the deck and some air could get in. All guards from the staircases and corridors on various levels disappeared because they could not stand. They were scarcely needed as most prisoners were immobile on the bunks.

This storm turned out to be a preliminary warning, for soon the ship was hit by a real hurricane. The deck was awash and seawater poured over the lip of the hatch into the hold. The ship was being tossed about and appeared to mount enormous waves and then the aft part of the ship started to hit troughs between the waves. The propeller raced when it was out of the water and then laboured when the aft part of the ship hit the water. After one of the high uplifts, the aft of the ship hit the water with such force that some of the structures at the lower levels disintegrated, crushing down into the swirling water on the bottom. Yells, shouts and moans were heard throughout the hold. But there was nobody to respond. Most of the guarding troops were seasick and those who were not, did not appear. The storm lasted about a week. I survived without being seasick and when the storm abated I crawled to the gap in the hatch to have a look around.

The deck was clear. There were no tarpaulin covered packages, no lavatories and only a few planks left from the guards' shack. Everything had been washed overboard. There were no guards to be seen anywhere, the ship appeared to be abandoned. But none of the prisoners was in a state to do anything about it. The barrel with drinking water had become contaminated with salt water and vomit, with the result that any prisoner who drank from it developed diarrhoea. As there were no lavatories and no order, everyone relieved themselves in situ under the deck. Guards were finally stationed at the exit from the hatch, threatening to shoot anybody who tried to come on to the deck. The overpowering stench rising from the bottom of the hold from the diarrhoea sufferers eventually made the guards realize that the prisoners were suffocating and finally the hatches were fully opened.

The whole trip lasted two and a half weeks and about one quarter of the prisoners died during the journey. The survivors were led into a clearing near the docks at Nar'yan Mar where we lay exhausted. Nar'yan Mar lies at the mouth of the River Pechora, which flows 1,809 kilometres from the Urals, and it was along this river, the only route available, the next stage of our journey was to be undertaken. But first, the dead had to be carried out by the local prisoners. It took the next two days to clear out the ship and to separate the files and identities of the survivors. As soon as the living were identified and sorted out we were loaded on to river barges.

There were three barges measuring approximately thirty by one hundred and twenty feet. They were taken in line by a tug and started chugging against the current. My barge included a very mixed group of *zeks*, including a few dozen Poles. There was also a number of *blatnoys* who domineered the rest. They played cards and the winner would indicate any object he wanted from another prisoner. The loser would then have to get it for him. This included all possessions of any value and on occasions gold teeth were wrenched out. I lost my jacket to admiring *blatnoys*, but then the Polish group started sticking together. We withstood an attempt to take someone's highly prized cavalry officer's riding boots and that ended the *blatnoys* reign of terror. I had lost track of Adas and my two friends from Grodzisko but I linked up with some other students—Zbyszek from Gdańsk Technical University, Piotr from Warsaw Wawelberg School and Zygmunt from Lwów University. The trip on the barge up the Pechora river lasted a few days. I remember talking with my new companions, but very little of the trip remains in my memory. We were all worn out by the sea journey and we only had the energy to de-louse ourselves and try to recuperate. As the days dragged on, ice floes started passing the barge. At first this only happened occasionally, then during the next days they became more and more frequent. Finally it snowed and after one or two days the tugboat and barges were moored to the bank near a transit camp at Ust Usa. We were kept at Ust Usa for about two weeks, sleeping in tents at night and being taken to the forest during the day to collect timber. This had to be cut to various lengths depending on whether it was to be used for construction or as firewood. At the end of two weeks a column of about two hundred and fifty prisoners was assembled and an eleven day supply of food was issued to each prisoner. This consisted of eleven salt herrings and eleven pieces of dried bread. We were marched in a convoy, with guards stationed every ten yards on each side of the column. They had dogs on leashes and we were warned that if we attempted to leave the column we would be shot.

The first night we slept in a clearing in the snow. Some of us collected bundles of frozen tall grass, which was sticking up above the snow, to act as an insulation barrier between the snow and our clothing. No winter clothing had been issued and the pieces of grass provided some protection, particularly for legs and feet. While we suffered in the intense cold, the guards built four fires to sleep by and to warm themselves while on duty. I remember debating with a group of prisoners whether it was better to take off our shoes or not. We all decided to keep our shoes on, except for one man. That was his last night. Next morning his feet were frozen, his shoes were also frozen so he couldn't put them on. He had to walk in socks, with pieces of cloth tied over his feet. After a few hours he lagged behind the column, incapable of walking. One of the guards stayed behind with him. When we lost sight of him, we heard a shot and a few minutes later the guard rejoined the column.

It became bitterly cold, though there was no wind on most days. Daylight was restricted to two to three hours, the rest of the time it was semi-dark. Nevertheless, we walked for twelve to fifteen hours a day, at first over the ice on the river, then through the forest, and then over the ice again. Only once in twelve days of walking, did we have shelter under a roof and have hot water—*kipiatok* issued. The rest of the time we slept in the snow. We were allowed to have fires, but we had no metal containers to melt the snow. The marching became more difficult and we found it harder each day to drag ourselves forward. The shots rang behind us more and more frequently—two or three prisoners were lost this way each day.

On the twelfth day we arrived at a camp, and were put into a well heated large log cabin and issued with a hot meal. We were told that we were at the supply depot camp at Abez, from which we would be sent to our constructive rehabilitation camps. Next day we were issued with felt boots—*valinki*, for snow, also winter coats and trousers, all padded. It was November 2, 1940. We were told that from then onwards there would be no more free meals. We would eat according to the proportion of work norm that we accomplished. The following day prisoners were sorted out according to length of sentence and the article of criminal or political law under which we had been incarcerated. Socially Dangerous Elements which included me, sentenced under Article 58 to fifteen to twenty-five years, were formed into a colony of one hundred and twenty-five prisoners and marched out of Abez.

CHAPTER NINE
Life in a Penal Colony

ABEZ is not far from the infamous penal camp at Vorkuta, with its coal mines operated by slave labour, and is in the area of the Vorkuta Governing District. In 1940 the only way for supplies to be shipped in and for the coal to be shipped out from Vorkuta was by using the Usa river to Ust Usa and then the Pechora river to Nar'yan Mar. This route was open from June at the earliest, to October at the latest—otherwise routine communication ceased. In 1939-40 it was decided a railway line should be built to supply Vorkuta coal to the industrial belt north and east of Moscow. The construction was started at both ends of the missing link—Kotlas to Vorkuta. The section from Vorkuta to Abez had been started in the spring of 1940, but nothing existed to the south-west of Abez towards Kotlas.

The penal colony of one hundred and twenty-five *zeks* which included me, was given the task of building interim camps for the intake of prisoners who were to undertake railway construction, at the reputed density of one prisoner per metre of railway. Preliminary interim camps were built every ten kilometres or so. Prisoners were settled there with the task of building a connecting winter road for supply trucks. Camps were also needed every three to five kilometres for the prisoners who had to clear the tracks of trees for the railway route, make the necessary cuts through hills, build up the low lying areas and construct bridges.

This was the start of my life in a so-called corrective camp, but which should be more accurately described as an extermination camp. Within two months of arrival there were only nine survivors of the one hundred and twenty-five that started work there. We were a group of mixed nationalities, with only a minority of Poles. It was not until I reached Abez that I learned how meaningless our prison sentences were. The foreman—also a *zek*—who arranged the work rotas, payment and rates told me that nobody ever came out alive from these camps. If you survived your sentence, it was automatically extended.

The usual justification was that the prisoner was a "socially dangerous element".

My colony left Abez on November 3 and marched south-west about ten kilometres. After a night sleeping in the snow, we were organized to clear a site, fell trees, cut timber and construct barracks from rough logs, with their bark still on them. Inside, bunks like shelves were built of thinner trunks, also with the bark on. Badly trimmed branches were frequently used which later proved to be the bane of prisoners who had to sleep on these bunks without any mattresses or blankets. There were no saws to cut the planks or to square up the logs. The first day's work provided housing for the guards. It was not until the third day that everybody slept under a roof. We did not know how long we worked for at a stretch, it could have been eight, twelve or fifteen hour shifts—but in two more days the interim camp was pronounced ready.

The next day the colony was forced to move on. We were marched another ten kilometres or so and after a night in the snow, the whole exercise of camp construction was repeated. This continued relentlessly until we had covered some seventy kilometres, building camps every ten kilometres. By this time the colony was so depleted that construction became increasingly slow and inefficient. It took eight or nine days to build a camp, instead of the original five day period. We then saw another group of about one hundred and thirty *zeks* being led past us, presumably our replacement as our colony was now so few in number and we were so weak and unproductive. When we had finished that particular camp, we were assigned to clearing the forest for a motor road. We were told to uproot all trees along a given width of the forest, cut the trunks into lengths and burn off the branches. The one advantage of this latest task was that we had fires to keep us warm. The snow around the trees was one to two feet deep, but in some areas it was much deeper. Underneath the snow there was a thick layer of moss, sometimes as much as four feet thick.

It was utterly impossible for us to uproot enough trees to fulfil a work norm and thus earn our food ration. In order to survive, we pushed the snow aside to the level of the moss. The tree was then cut with a saw or chopped with an axe and the snow pushed over the stump. The foreman came at the end of the shift to see how much of the "norm" each group should be credited. He had no time to check whether the trees had been uprooted—neither did he care as he was also a *zek*. Once the trees were cleared another colony of *zeks* was assigned to melt the snow in large vats and sprinkle the water over the snow in successive steps to provide a solid foundation for the trucks.

The result of this haphazard construction was that in July 1941 when all the snow melted, numerous ravines were disclosed crossing the winter road. This revealed the extraordinary way that the trees in the ravines had been cut. Trees growing in the deeper parts had been cut high up, while on the slopes the cut-off point varied, marking the level of a winter road. New *zeks* who arrived in July and August from Murmansk labour camps could not understand why or indeed how, the trees had been cut in that way.

One day when I was clearing trees I saw a horse-drawn sleigh trying to cross the prepared winter road, which had snow banks piled along the side. The horse fell and the load spilled out over the snow. Six or seven skeletal naked corpses of *zeks* fell out. The bodies were being delivered to the base camp at Abez for their files to be closed. Each had a name tag attached to his hand. The *vozchik*—driver asked me to help him load the corpses back on the sleigh; then he sat on top of them again and drove off.

Sometime in December a northern snow storm—*purga* hit the camp where the remnants of the colony were working. For three days the cold was so intense and the winds were so terrible that even the well fed and clothed guards did not venture out. The kitchen was closed and the *zeks* were not issued with a hot meal for three days. A spoonful of flour was given to each *zek* straight into his hands. This was eaten raw, very slowly and mixed with snow. But we did not mix the snow until one hand was free of flour, for fear of spilling any.

On the fourth day, those of us that could still move were taken out to work. A horse was found frozen near the winter road, apparently abandoned by the *vozchik* who had left it during the *purga*. As soon as I could absent myself from work, I stole back and tried to hack off the hind leg—the horse was lying on its side. The first blow in the crotch reverberated as if I had struck a tightly stretched drum and the axe flew off into the snow. I recovered it and then with great difficulty I cut some of the frozen meat from the back leg. The axe proved too blunt to chop the meat easily and I planned to come back later. The guards made routine counts of the working *zeks* and as I had disappeared after the first count, I had to be back before my absence was noted. I rejoined my group of three and we divided the piece of meat and each tried to cook our piece surreptitiously at the open fire which had been lit to destroy the tree branches. When one side of the piece of meat was practically burning, the other side was still nearly frozen so we had alternate bites of cold, burnt and raw, hunks. It was difficult with a blunt axe to slice the meat into reasonably thin pieces, but I cut what I could and put some in my pocket for later. I did not feel these few mouthfuls had appeased my hunger and I suffered from much more intense stomach acidity than usual. I started to worry that maybe the horse had not died of exhaustion and cold but had been poisoned. But when the other prisoners returned to the camp, I noticed that only the head of the horse was left. I finished the remaining pieces of meat from my pocket and regretted that I had not taken more.

The terrain that we were working at that time was not very thickly forested. There were occasional open plateaus and shallow depressions, with scarcely any trees for hundreds of metres. If the clearing for the winter motor road happened to encompass one such open space, the allotted group could accomplish in one day enough work to exceed 300-500 per cent of the norm. On one lucky day my group cleared two or three measly looking trees and spent the rest of the day trying to keep warm. But according to the rule we had achieved 300 per cent of the norm for that day and earned an extra piece of fish. However, soon afterwards we paid for it sevenfold by not even achieving ten per cent of the norm. Later we had to mark the sides of the road on such open stretches by planting young fir trees brought from the nearest forested area, so that drivers would keep to the road during snowfalls.

The initial colony of one hundred and twenty-five on November 3 was gradually reduced to about twenty-five by the time Christmas 1940 was approaching. We not only had to contend with the freezing cold, the back-breaking work and near starvation, there were also accidents which happened while we were working. *Zeks* were killed by falling trees. Or even worse they suffered broken legs and then froze to death because there was simply no provision to take care of incapacitated *zeks*. Sickness of any kind, mainly diarrhoea, took its toll. But the swiftest and most alarming cause of death was due to psychological reasons. Anybody who lost faith in survival did not last for more than a day, two at the most. There were several suicides including Zygmunt, the young student from Lwów University, who I had first met on the barge at Nar'yan Mar. We had worked in different brigades but we continued to be friends and slept next to each other in the barracks. One morning he didn't feel well. He complained of swollen legs and could not go out to work. He was left in the barracks and committed suicide by drinking a bottle of iodine solution—one of the only two medicines at the disposal of the chief foreman who acted as medical man. When I returned from work Zygmunt was in agony. He died in a couple of hours.

Everybody suffered from under-nourishment, if not starvation. Infestation of lice, acute stomach acidity and scurvy were common problems. Lice were so numerous that even though we killed dozens and dozens of them before falling asleep at night—it made no difference. Everybody scratched themselves night and day. At one stage I was so frustrated at seeing all the seams of my shirt crawling with lice, I took a dry wooden splinter, lit it from the stove that heated the barracks and applied the flame to the seams of my garment to roast the lice. The result was that most of the lice were indeed burnt, but so were the seams of my shirt. I was left with a few pieces of cloth, only suitable to use for wrapping my feet in place of non-existent socks.

Scurvy also attacked every *zek*. In my case the small cuts on my hands and legs did not heal, but became progressively larger and deeper as all of them invariably became infected and oozed pus. A cut on my knuckles on the little finger of my left hand eventually resulted in a fairly large hole, three eighths to half an inch deep. When the pus was removed, it revealed the sac surrounding the joint. I found a morbid fascination in watching the joint move under the sac membrane. A more horrifying manifestation of scurvy was a progressive retention of fluid in the body. Legs and arms began to swell and movements became restricted and extremely painful, as the joints became deformed and fragile. If a victim knocked against a solid object the swollen limb would fall off. The only mercy was that the sufferer soon died from loss of fluid. My scurvy never reached the swelling stage. But the pus from the infected scratches and cuts, particularly on my legs stuck like glue to the inner material of my padded trousers. The result was that taking off my felt boots became an extremely painful process.

It was Christmas Eve 1940 when the remnants of the colony were ordered to move to camp, nearer to Abez. There was no need for the guards to convoy the group, even though most of the journey took place in the gloomy twilight winter of the Arctic circle giving plenty of opportunities for escape, for the *zeks* were hardly able to walk and were quite incapable of flight. I was walking behind the others and at one point I lost sight of them. I was having difficulty with my eyesight and I could not keep to the beaten path in the snow. I strayed just a few feet from it and started to sink deeper and deeper into the snow. Suddenly I lost my footing and rolled down a snow bank. I could not crawl out from the snow bank on to the path and so I stayed huddled where I was. I lost all sense of time and began to daydream. I felt quite cosy except for a tingling in my toes and fingers. Some time later I heard Russian voices. I started shouting and I was finally answered. The men were the kitchen staff, the last group of the colony who were bringing the equipment from the old camp. They pulled me out from the snow, gave an invigorating rub to my hands and feet and took me with them to the new camp. Without their intervention I would have frozen to death.

In the new camp I shared a head of a fish, bartered for some tobacco from the cook, with another Pole. It was no bigger than three inches at its base—it was our *vigilia*—Christmas Eve 1940 meal. The same evening a *zek* went to fetch water from a hole in the ice at a nearby stream. He was later found frozen to the ice. Apparently he had spilt some water under his felt boots when he was pulling the bucket out. His boots immediately froze to the ice and when he was found only half an hour later, he was already stone cold. We never knew what the outside temperature was, only its effect on ears and noses if they were uncovered for more than a couple of minutes. We also guessed it by seeing whether our spit froze in flight before it hit a solid object or after. That Christmas Eve night was obviously blisteringly cold.

The exact sequence of what happened after the uncelebrated Christmas of 1940 is hazy in my memory. The only thing I remember is that the last nine survivors from the original colony of one hundred and twenty-five were brought in in a state of extreme exhaustion to a dugout which they called a hospital. The date was January 7, 1941. The hospital consisted of the now familiar barrack structure with shelf type bunks of thin tree trunks, still rough from stumps of branches not properly removed. A front hall was partitioned off and a two door entrance to the hall kept the heat in. A small stove heated the hall and its partitioned space for the supervisory *vrach*—medical orderly. There was also a large stove to heat the main barracks with its shelf bunks running along all three walls.

By this stage I was semi-conscious. I was put on a bottom shelf, squeezed in between two fully clothed *zeks*. The next thing I was aware of was one of my neighbours being dragged out. Some time later my other neighbour also died. Another man was put in his place and I vaguely recall seeing somebody with badly swollen legs climbing up to the upper shelf. A passing *zek* knocked against him and I saw a leg fall off, followed by the climber. Later, on a cold windy day a *vozchik*—driver came into the hall to announce that he had brought five *bolnoy*—sick people. He dragged them in one by one, placing them by the small stove in the hall. A few minutes later the medical orderly attempted to establish their identity and found all five were frozen solid. The same *vozchik* was called in to drag them out again.

I spent the next two months in the dugout hospital. It had some sixty to seventy patients at any given time and was run by a very helpful and compassionate woman, Anna Nikolaievna. She was a free worker who had arrived in the Pechora district looking for her imprisoned husband. Everything in outlying regions like the Komi republic was under the control of the NKVD, and prisoners in labour camps engaged in major undertakings such as the Kotlas-Vorkuta railway line were not allowed visitors. The only way Anna Nikolaievna could search for her husband was by collecting information from the roving *zeks*. Officials were silent, unwilling to provide any information. I don't know whether she ever found her husband, but I saw her doing her utmost for the sick prisoners. She would prepare special food—cream of wheat or buckwheat—for those who could not stomach the routine kitchen gruel. She would argue with the kitchen commissioner for better quality or larger quantities for convalescing *zeks* and would spoonfeed the very sick patients who were unable to feed themselves.

At the beginning of March I was sent to convalesce at the base camp central hospital near Abez, before returning to full time labour. This hospital was about three times larger than the dugout and the atmosphere was non-caring and bureaucratic. All employees were *zeks*, but they had no compassion for their charges. In my two week period of convalescence I worked as a shift helper, tending the fire stoves, distributing meals to those unable to walk and removing the bodies of those who died.

The first time I removed a body to a morgue was very frightening. The dead man was Zbyszek, the student from Gdańsk I had met on the barge. The previous evening I had spent several hours chatting with him. I dragged his naked body to the morgue, opened the door and lit the candle that I had been told to take with me. The shelves were already filled with dozens of bodies. I put down the candle and found the only space was on an upper shelf near the far corner. I dragged the body over to the spot and was just lifting it when a gust of wind slammed the door shut and blew the candle out. The body fell on my head, wrapping itself round me. I was so frightened it took some time for me to extricate myself and to gather my senses sufficiently to relight the candle and place the body on the shelf.

The stay in the convalescent hospital at the base camp was noteworthy because I had my first bath since my stay in Nikolaev prison in August 1940. I underwent a thorough delousing and was issued with new clothing. I also encountered the first batch of women prisoners in the labour camps. They entered the disrobing hall of the *bania* to view the naked newcomers and selected mates in the most brazen manner.

The stench that reigned in the dugout hospital must have been beyond imagination, probably approaching that in the hold of the ship at the end of the sea journey, but my senses were too dulled to register this. What I remember vividly is the open countryside in the neighbourhood of the dugout, with a few birch trees and fir trees in the distance. I used to see these whenever I went to the open air lavatory, which was constructed forty feet or so from the dugout, without any fence or wall around it. The view of this countryside in the Arctic zone has stayed in my mind ever since. I often used to look at it and wonder if I would die there and be buried in those parts. Years later I saw that countryside, when I watched the scenes portrayed in the film *Dr Zhivago*. But it is when I hear the *Sinfonia Antarctica* by Vaughan Williams that my memories are truly awakened. Whenever I hear that music I can see the snow covered countryside surrounding the dugout hospital with the wind whistling among the dunes and the distant tree groves—and I remember the work and sacrifice of Anna Nikolaievna. In the late sixties I saw the film *One Day in the Life of Ivan Denisovitch* and it made me think that the life of those prisoners was palatial in comparison with my own experience in the Pechora district.

CHAPTER TEN

Working on the Abez-Kotlas Railway Line

O N Tuesday March 25 I left the convalescent hospital and had to start work again. My immediate problem was to manipulate the system so that I could be allocated to the least arduous task available, particularly while I was still convalescent. I claimed to be a capable draughtsman, my pretended illiteracy was now only needed when dealing with NKVD personnel. This had to be maintained when dealing with them until my release but it was now no longer necessary with the camp management who were all *zeks* themselves. I was able to work as a draughtsman for several days until I was replaced by another prisoner with better connections, though he was not necessarily any better at the job. I then offered my services as an expert soil tester, advising on suitability for railway construction. My ineptitude was soon discovered and I was assigned to a team of loggers, whose task was to provide firewood for the camp stoves. The other members of the team consisted of three citizens of the Union of Soviet Socialist Republics—*Soiuz*, who came from different areas, the Republics of Buryat, Kazakhstan, and Kamchatka. They had no common language between them and so communication was by sign language. I quickly learned from my new colleagues that survival depended upon how successfully the supervisors could be tricked.

One way was to manipulate measurement of the norm, which in this case consisted of the number of cubits of wood that were cut and stacked. The quantity of food we got depended on achieving the norm but it was well known that this was set at an impossibly high level. Even if you reached the norm, the reward was a ration at bare subsistence level. So on the first day we cut about one third of the norm which was all we could reasonably manage. On the second day we cut another third and then moved the first day's wood to a new position so that both were counted. On the third day we repeated the process—the two previous days' wood were moved and included with that day's cut. On the fourth day, we did the same again and when this was counted along with the previous three days' wood we were credited with one hundred and twenty-five per cent norm, and special rations were awarded as for the *stakhanovite* heroes of Soviet mythology. This system was successfully operated for more than a month so that we enjoyed one hundred and twenty-five per cent "norm" credit and an extra meal at noon as our rations, though only cutting one third of a norm each day. The supervisors only discovered how small the total output was six weeks later when the sleighs and *vozchiks* were ordered to collect the masses of recorded firewood and found miserably small quantities.

I found out that the Soviet citizen from Kazakhstan had been sentenced to ten years after he had been caught appropriating the *kolkhoz's*—collective farm money when he was its treasurer. The Buryat prisoner had been sentenced to fifteen years for attempting to cross a border, the same crime for which I had been arrested and the prisoner from Kamchatka had been arrested for killing someone during a brawl. He had the lightest sentence—three years. I learnt this from the only *zek* capable of communicating with all of us, our foreman, Wasyli Nikoforowich. Wasyli had been in prison for over twenty years as a former Tsarist officer and had spent the time in innumerable forced labour camps across the breadth of the Soviet Empire from the West to Kamchatka. He had corresponded with his wife for the first ten years or so of his captivity but she had lost hope of ever seeing her husband again and decided to remarry. By my calculations Wasyli Nikoforowich was approaching the end of his twenty-five years imprisonment—the same sentence I had received. I was horrified that Wasyli had served so many years for I was convinced that I would only be imprisoned for three years. Wasyli just laughed at my claims. He said he was living proof of NKVD justice. He had been imprisoned originally in 1917 and had somehow escaped execution. He was sentenced by the then Cheka authorities to a three year stretch of rehabilitative employment for the glory of the revolution. But when he completed his sentence, it was simply extended for another period. This had been repeated continuously. He said it was only the criminals who were released after serving their sentences. Political prisoners and especially the socially dangerous elements sentenced under Article 58 had their sentences automatically extended, without even the formality of being notified.

I cannot exactly recall when it happened, whether it was in the Nikolaev prison or during the trip in the Stolypin car from Kharkov to Archangelsk, but the firm belief established itself in my mind, that my Russian imprisonment would last no longer than three years—despite all indications to the contrary. My belief in this three year period was so strong that even when I was semi-conscious at the end of my penal colony existence and in the dugout hospital, I never lost faith that I would pull through.

By now I was able to understand Russian quite well and I could speak the vulgar dialect used by the *zeks* in everyday conversation, which was full of swear words and curses. Wasyli's Russian was more refined and literate and I learned a lot from him about the events in the early days of the Revolution and about the European and Asiatic parts of the USSR, where Wasyli had worked as a prisoner. He liked to come around noon to check on my group of loggers. According to Wasyli, we were working twelve hour shifts, we had no real idea as we had no means of telling the time. One day he arrived to find us enjoying an extra meal—a feast not envisaged by the authorities for even the most heroic *stakhanovite*. It was a large dish of horse meat stew. The three native *zeks* in my group had stolen two horses from the *vozchik's* precinct earlier in the winter. They had hidden the meat in the forest under the snow—a most efficient freezer, particularly that year. About two hours before noon, one of the three would disappear from the working crew and when the *stakhanovites* were due to pick up their extra noon meal, he would appear with a blackened gallon tin filled with thick meat stew. When Wasyli discovered us he was invited to join in and he came every day for as long as the supply lasted. His presence was an excellent cover. If one of the guards or the *diesiatnik*—evaluator who assessed the day's work, appeared unexpectedly Wasyli would start berating us for laziness and lack of effort. Apparently it was the *diesiatnik* who later had his sentence extended for failure to correlate the production of firewood with the recorded figure.

The three native *zeks* were not much interested in my talks with Wasyli, perhaps because they could not follow his Russian. But they were kind men. When they found out that I was struggling with my eyesight and had developed night blindness, a symptom of lack of vitamins, they saved all the pieces of liver and other special pieces of meat for me and led me by the hand when it grew dark.

A few weeks after the fiasco with the firewood we were involved in setting up a telephone line from Abez towards Kotlas along the winter motor road. I was among a number of *zeks* who were given the job of planting telephone poles into the frozen ground. In a region with widespread permafrost, where the ground was frozen even at the height of summer, we soon discovered how hopeless this task was—especially when viewed against the established norm. It did not take us long to limit our digging to the layer of moss, which was easy to cut, even using a blunt spade. We then set the pole in its hole and poured some water from melted snow around the pole. The water froze in seconds and held the pole rigid in the moss—at least until the thaw came. At the end of June miles of telephone poles all collapsed at the same time, disrupting all communication.

While we worked on firewood logging we were in a heavily forested area and we did not know the exact location of our camp, only its number. We became aware that we were in the vicinity of other mysterious camps, very heavily guarded, situated some way from the Abez-Kotlas winter motor road. One day in April we heard distant shots. Next day we saw several military planes flying to and fro and heard machine-gunning for long periods. Rumour had it that the mysterious camps were those holding the Russians taken prisoner during the Finnish war in 1939. When these prisoners were liberated by the Russian troops they were promptly arrested and sent to the Pechora *lagers* and kept in isolation with their liberating colleagues acting as guards. Apparently the prisoners had revolted, overpowered the guards and were marching towards the base camp when the planes strafed them.

There were numerous discussions among the *zeks* about the possibility of escaping from the camps to the west and hopefully to freedom in Finland or Norway. Of the three or four attempts that did take place in the spring of 1941 from the camps where I was held none was successful. Two or three days later the escapees would be brought back by the local *komye*—inhabitants who were paid several roubles per head. They found it most rewarding to track such escapees. The most daring escape, according to the stories circulating among the *zeks*, was one undertaken by two Russians who decided to go east across the Urals and then south along the River Ob instead of attempting the shorter route to the West. They collected supplies for the journey—stone dried slices of bread, flour, fat and sugar—and then invited two other *zeks* to join them. All four managed to break out and they were over the worst of the Ural crossings when one of the invited *zeks* disappeared. By this stage food supplies were virtually exhausted. Then one of the Russians who had first planned the escape told the others that he had trapped a wild animal and had it all ready cooked in the pot. The meat from the animal lasted them a couple of days when the *zek* who had been invited to join the escape attempt at the last minute suddenly realized he was eating meat from a human bone. He knew that he would be next on the menu, so at the first opportunity, he escaped and sought the nearest NKVD post along the Ob river. His two companions were later apprehended.

The weather in the north is freakish, even in the spring. The first of May is celebrated in Russia as a national holiday and even the *katorga zeks* were promised a day off. This was one of the very few days free from work. But before noon we heard sounds of agitation coming from the NKVD barrack. All the *zeks* were ordered to report to the gate, where we were issued with spades and pickaxes. Lorries arrived and we were told that we were needed to dig out a snowbound convoy of lorries due from Kotlas. We were driven for two hours along the winter road until we came to a large snow drift in one of the open areas which the road crossed. We were told to dig as fast as possible with relays of diggers changing every few minutes to maintain a high tempo. After some hundred yards we finally broke through to the trucks on the other side of the snowdrift, thirty or forty of them in the convoy. The first priority was to get to the cabs, but all we found were frozen bodies, even though the men had been well protected in padded clothing. Most of the *zeks* were only interested in finding anything edible in the pockets of the cabs' occupants. Small chunks of ham or salted bacon were especially favoured. After ransacking the pockets of the bodies, the *zeks* continued to clear the snow around the trucks and we were then taken back to camp.

Surviving in a camp along the Abez-Kotlas railway line depended on the enterprise of each individual *zek*. If you could secure any sort of container, in which to receive soup or gruel, you were assured of having a minimum of hot sustenance. If you failed to find a container you had no option but to use your hands. Next in importance to a container was a piece of wire. That meant that the container, which was usually a tin salvaged from the guards' food supplies, could be hung over a fire. It could then be used to melt the snow and prepare *kipiatok*—hot water for drinking. A wooden spoon was very useful but any stick could be used to push the gruel into your mouth from a container. A piece of string was also invaluable for tying loose ends of sleeves and leggings. Every *zek* developed a hoarding instinct and the one who had the appropriate thing for the moment, was the one who survived. I never discarded anything that could prove useful, but at the same time we had to guard against accumulating too much.

My luxurious life of a *stakhanovite* hero finished around mid June when the snow started to melt and logging was no longer the top priority. Our logging group was disbanded and I was assigned to a variety of different jobs that lasted a few days at a time. The first one was a direct consequence of the thaw. We had to hunt for the bodies of *zeks* that had been buried in the snow during the worst of the winter. This was a gruesome task, picking up the gradually decomposing bodies and digging new graves for them in the nearest elevated site above the flood water. After wading for nearly a whole day in the freezing water pools well above the knees and dealing with the corpses

I did not feel like eating my evening meal of rotting potato. What made matters worse was there were no means of drying my wet boots and trousers in the six hours before the next day's work. I often wondered how my work was evaluated—what was the norm?

I was next assigned to a group that was re-routing the old winter truck road around the numerous ravines that had been filled with the enormous snow drifts during the winter. We then had to make cuttings through the hillocks and embankments in the low lying areas and ravines to support the rail line. We had to penetrate permafrost several feet thick below the surface, occasional pools of quicksand and petrified trunks of ancient forest. The work was desperately arduous. But strangely, I found some comfort in thinking of how slave labour had been used to build the Egyptian pyramids some six thousand years before. During this time in the second half of July the sun was above the horizon for nearly twenty-four hours a day and we were forced to work eighteen hour shifts. I remember a rare moment in the routine of endless work and I lay down for about half an hour among the vegetation. I was astonished by the spectacular colours of the flowering plants. Only a couple of days previously these had been frozen below the snow. It was impossible to believe that such an abundance of life could spring up so fast in the frozen north.

Unfortunately, the sudden blooming of plants and flowers was accompanied by an equally sudden explosion of mosquito and black fly infestation. Within a couple of days it was impossible to go out in the open without covering every inch of skin. We swathed our hands and faces completely and wore a fine mesh netting over our eyes. We were issued with the netting but even with this protection, life was miserable as the black flies could penetrate the netting.

According to the camp gossip, an investigative commission arrived from Vorkula, following a shooting in the neighbouring camp. The death rate in the last months of 1940 and the first three months of 1941 was so high that the camps only had a fraction of the manpower left to work on the construction plans. The result was that the railway line was well behind schedule. In a bid to meet target plans there was a shake-up of NKVD management for the whole lager district along the Pechora as far as Vorkuta. The food improved slightly but only for a very short period. The camps were fenced off and watch towers were constructed every few hundred yards. The hours of work were noticeably lengthened. Many more camps were set up and some new *zeks* started to appear. The first contingents came from the Vorkuta coal mines followed in July by those from the camps on the Kola peninsula, which were being evacuated before the expected German occupation.

CHAPTER ELEVEN
The Nazi Invasion of Russia

THE new influx of *zeks* gave me my first opportunity to discover what had been happening in the outside world. Life in the camps was confined to a day by day struggle for survival. We had no news of the war, let alone what was happening to our families or our country. It was from these newcomers that I learned that Germany had invaded Russia on June 22, 1941. Some Poles I had met during my time in Nikolaev and Przemyśl prison, were among those who arrived from the Vorkuta mines. As I was in a roving brigade of workers assigned to a variety of jobs, I had unrivalled chances to meet many of these people and talk to them, often working alongside them during the eighteen hour shifts.

A few had professed communist ideas in prison and what I could not comprehend was that these avowed communists had learned nothing from their experiences so far. They considered that the camps and extermination of *zeks* were perfectly acceptable for the good of ideals expressed by Lenin and implemented by his successor Jozef Stalin. Excesses were the faults of subordinates, and the preferential treatment meted out to the select few in power was just. There was no way to stem their communist learned propaganda, mouthed by rote without any reflection on real life around them. They were not going to be confused by facts.

Another group, mostly young peasants from the Moldavian part of Romania, occupied by Russia in 1940 when the Baltic countries of Latvia, Lithuania and Estonia had been incorporated into the USSR, also fell for the promises of communist propaganda spouted by the NKVD *politruks* in the camps. They were told to work one hundred and twenty per cent of the norm for the glory of communism—and they did until it killed them within a few weeks. The food provided for the *zeks* did not replenish half of the energy expended, you could not work hard and survive. I could never understand what mesmerised people when they heard the communist slogans. The uneducated peasants usually had enough commonsense to tell the truth from fiction. But it was astonishing to see the aspiring or professed communists, whatever their nationality, being brainwashed by the rhetoric and slogans, without the slightest heed to reality.

When the news of the German attack on Russia on June 22, 1941 reached the northern camps in the Kotlas-Vorkuta region, the NKVD immediately segregated all the Poles from the rest of the *zeks* in a barbed wire enclosure within a base camp. The multi-national work brigades were disbanded and new units were formed. These were restricted to Poles, who were assigned the heaviest work supervised by an increased number of guards. The Russians' great fear was that as they had conspired with the Germans against Poland in 1939, the Poles would now side with the Germans against the Russians. They could not understand the Polish determination to be independent of both Russia and Germany.

The long, exhausting hours of digging soon started to take its toll—more and more Poles fell sick with diarrhoea and scurvy. But this was not enough to be excused from work, the pressure to complete the railway construction was too great. After more than a week of constant diarrhoea I collapsed while digging and was finally sent to the hospital, two or three kilometres away. I vaguely remember dragging myself what seemed an interminable distance, and then being sent to a *bania*—bath, where I lost consciousness. When I recovered, I found myself lying on an inclined plank covered with a sheet. At the lower end of the plank, there was a bucket to catch the blood dripping from my intestines. I was told by the occupant of the next bunk that I had been unconscious for eleven days. At one point I had been taken out to be buried. However I had moved my hand when the first spadeful of earth hit me and a compassionate digger had pulled me out and brought me back to the hospital.

My neighbour also told me that in order to survive I must not drink or eat anything, so that my intestines would have a chance to heal. The medical orderly told me that I had scurvy of the intestines. The only treatment was intravenous injections of some white fluid—milk substitute I believe—to help the ravaged intestines heal. For the next few days—I don't know how long it was—maybe ten or fifteen days, I underwent a constant battle of will not to drink. I had the most terrible thirst which made the skin on my lips peel and my mouth and tongue felt desert dry. But my determination was reinforced when I saw that those who were suffering in the same way and had succumbed to the temptation to drink, were dead a day or two later. Fighting the desire to drink, I tried to recall the past and found to my horror that I had difficulty in listing the names of my brothers or remembering the names of places in Poland where I had spent summer holidays or the names of friends in Kraków.

After several days the blood stopped dripping and I started feeling better and I knew I would pull through. Only then did I allow myself to moisten my lips with water. I still did not drink for another day or two. As I was lying on the plank I remember looking up at the sunlit opening in the wall which served as a window. As I held up my forearm and fingers to the light I could see the perfect outline of bones and veins through my transparent skin, but no sign of any muscles. By this stage I had started to take some fruit juice and a limited quantity of cream of wheat, and I was beginning to feel much better. Then one day a group of three people appeared. They were NKVD accompanied by a *vrach*—medical orderly who turned out to be Wasyli Nikoforowich. They passed by all the bunks, listing the names of some of the patients. After they left I asked one of the patients whose name had been put on the list what it was all about. He said that all the Poles who were not too sick, were scheduled for release from the camps to the join the Polish Army being formed near Kuybyshev.

This was the first time I had heard of the agreement that had been made between General Wladyslaw Sikorski, the head of the Polish Government in exile in England, and Stalin. This allowed all Poles, who had been taken prisoner of war in 1939, and those civilians who had been transported to Kazakhstan and the neighbouring republics from the eastern parts of Poland occupied by the Russians in 1939, to join an army under Polish command to fight the Germans.

For a day or two I lay on my plank and contemplated the situation. If I was left behind while the others were released, I knew the hopelessness of my position would kill me. Even if I could recover physically in a few weeks, there would be no possibility of getting south to Kuybyshev as the rivers would be frozen and the track for the proposed railway had not even been levelled. From mid-October until mid-June the northern regions of the Komi republic were virtually cut off. I knew that psychologically my chances of surviving another winter in the north, with all my fellow Poles having left were nil. I decided I must get out at all costs. The following morning I tried to get up and walk to the administrative office, adjoining the hall but I found that I was unable to walk. I could only crawl very slowly. I finally reached Wasyli Nikoforowich's office, though it took some time for Wasyli to recognize me. But after some preliminaries, the old rapport that had existed between us when we were logging was re-established.

I asked Wasyli about the evacuation of Poles and when he confirmed what my neighbour had told me, I asked him to put my name on the list. Wasyli said: "But you are dying". I replied: "I will die if I don't get put on that list. Once I become free, I'll survive. If you don't put my name on that list I won't be able to get out for months and I won't survive." Wasyli said: "You are too sick to be put on that list. It's for those who are fit enough to travel long distances and become soldiers." I discovered that the date for release was the following day. But I still argued vehemently, saying it would be more trouble for Wasyli if I died in the camp because it would mean more paper work for him. "I've told you before that I will not stay in Russia for more than three years, and now nearly two years have gone already," I said. Wasyli replied: "Go to hell!"

But he did put me on the list and the next day, September 2, all the Poles who had been listed were taken out from the hospital. I couldn't walk without assistance. I had to be helped out and once outside I immediately collapsed. While we waited outside the hospital an NKVD officer divided us into two groups without guards. One group had to walk to the river and board a barge, the other group which included me were to be transported by lorry to the barge. Wasyli came out from the hospital to say a final goodbye to me. He pushed some tobacco and a small bag of lump sugar into my hand. He had tears in his eyes when we talked of my firm belief that I would not spend three years in the north.

There were only Poles on the barge but I was astonished to hear the familiar voice of Kazik Markocki, my friend from Grodzisko. He was hardly recognizable in his padded clothing and beard. He immediately took care of me and nursed me during the few days we spent on the barge en route for the Kozhva camp where the Poles were going to be pardoned and officially released from *lagers*. Kazik had spent his time as a *zek* in camps in the Kola peninsula near Murmansk, and arrived in the Pechora district towards the end of July.

Thanks to Kazik's care on the barge and for a few days in the camp before he was released, I gradually began to recover and started to move around a bit. But I was still very weak and could scarcely eat. The camp at Kozhva had the requisite NKVD authorities empowered to release Poles from the labour camps and there was a Russian military commission enlisting volunteers for the army. Many of the Poles were sent first to the commission and some were intimidated into joining the Red Army. They were promised their release from the camp only when they signed the volunteer enlistment. Those who refused were sent back to the camp to think it over. It was probably here that my illiteracy cover proved the greatest disservice to me. I was sent back to the camp seven times because the educated officers of the commission could not understand why they could not persuade an illiterate soldier from the Polish Army to join the glorious Russian troops. After their eighth attempt the exasperated members of the commission sent me across to the committee issuing the official release papers. It was September 6, 1941. I was forced to listen to a lecture about the magnanimity of the Russian authorities in releasing me from a well deserved sentence that still had twenty-four years to run. But then I signed my last X on the papers, closing my file. I was given a small piece of paper, the *boumazhka* that was my identity document and a ticket to travel on railways to the place where the Polish Army was to be formed.

Their last words were a warning. I was told to guard the *boumazhka* most carefully, without it I would be re-imprisoned and never see freedom or find the Polish Army. The last instruction, given at the gate of the camp was to go along the path to the nearest railway line several kilometres away, where a train of cattle trucks was waiting to take us to Kotlas. The distance to the railway proved to be much further than we had been told. I started walking in the late afternoon and then had to rest. I walked again and then rested. I was so weak I finally ended up crawling. Most Poles had been released earlier and they had stopped at various points en route and lit fires to warm themselves during the night while they slept. I didn't dare sleep because I knew I would be unable to make up the lost time because of my slow progress. What I feared most was getting left behind, so I rested for short periods at the fires, walked, crawled and then rested again. I kept going through the night and at last, in the morning, I caught sight of the railway line in a clearing. I made one last effort and as soon as I reached the line I climbed into a cattle truck. A few minutes later the train started on its journey to Kotlas. I have no idea how many kilometres I walked during that endless night but I was only too thankful that I had reached the train in time.

Many weeks later we heard that when the other *zeks* in the camps appreciated the significance of the *boumazkha* issued to Poles, escapes by Russians from the northern camps became more frequent. It became common practice to waylay Poles who had been released and then steal their *boumazkhas*. When I was in Nikolaev, I had heard that one of my professors from the Akademia Górnicza, Professor Adam Skapski, a physical chemist specializing in corrosion, was in a Russian prison in the Ukraine. He had been deported to work on corrosion problems in one of their institutes but when he refused he was sentenced and sent to one of the camps along the Kotlas-Vorkuta line. When the Sikorski-Stalin agreement was signed at the end of July 1941, the release of Professor Skapski was sought by the Polish officials from London on a top priority basis. Skapski was given his *boumazhka*, and turned out of the camp. He was told to go to the railway for transport to Kotlas, like all the other Poles in Kozhva. But before Skapski could get very far, a guard from the camp called to him that the commandant of the camp wanted to see him. Skapski returned to the guard room at the gate and was told to surrender his *boumazhka* before he could enter the camp and see the commandant. He was assured that this was only a formality, the *boumazhka* would be given back to him when he returned to the gate. Once inside, the guard that had called him disappeared. The commandant had never wanted to see him. When Skapski returned to the guard room at the gate, the guard laughed in his face when he asked for the return of his *boumazhka*. The Polish authorities in London were told that Skapski had received his release papers, a copy of his signature on the release form was available for inspection. But they were informed that Skapski had disappeared once he'd left the camp. Several weeks later when Skapski was back working on the railway line, a train with released Poles passed by. He shouted a message to one of the Poles, asking him to tell the authorities that he was still held prisoner. As soon as the Polish authorities in London discovered his whereabouts, they were able to extract him, sending on some pretext a special liaison officer accompanied by a high ranking NKVD man to the camp. In the barrack the Polish officer "accidentally" recognized Skapski, who was flown to England.

This incident emphasized to me that the numerous double-crossings perpetuated under Stalin from 1939 onwards on Poland did not cease with the agreement which General Sikorski signed with him in 1941.

CHAPTER TWELVE

Release

O NCE the train started on its way south-west towards Kotlas, I was able to relax among my compatriots. The sliding door of the truck was left open in contrast to all previous journeys in Russia and the only sign of guards or NKVD was three or four uniformed men, who were piloting the train occupying one of the front trucks. At every major station they had to argue and negotiate to have the train forwarded to the next station, so we could advance to our final destination. They arranged infrequent meals for us at communal feeding places which were large enough for more than a thousand people. They did not bother individual passengers and we felt freer than before. But we were constantly reminded how elusive this freedom was by the unending series of watch towers which were located near every single settlement or group of houses until we reached Kotlas, some 1,000 kilometres further on. Each one of these towers along the railway line was manned by guards and they were convincing evidence that the density of slave workers building it must have been close to one *zek* used for every metre of the length of railway. That would mean some one and a half to two million *zeks* were used as slave labour along the Kotlas-Vorkuta stretch alone.

During an enforced delay at Kotlas, we were relatively free to wander. Kotlas was the first Russian city that I saw as a free man. Most of the houses were one storey high and built of wood. The only brick buildings were the NKVD headquarters, a huge rectangular three storey building and a similar, but smaller building which housed the district communist party. The streets were unpaved, there were wooden walkways along both sides of some streets, raised above the level of the dirt roadways which were covered by enormous puddles of mud. There was hardly any traffic on the streets, and very few shops. The only shops that existed had placards and slogans splashed all over the windows advertising goods for sale. But they had scarcely anything to sell, except when they received a special delivery. Then

queues formed immediately and within a short time everything was
sold out. Peace was restored until the next delivery a week or so later.
The bakery was the only place that was continuously busy. Queues
would form at least two hours before the anticipated time that bread
was ready.

For two days we wandered about the streets, waiting for the
announcement to return to the train to continue our journey. Any
news in the camps was spread by word of mouth—and with surprising
speed. The next afternoon we found out that a barge carrying wine
had arrived on the river bank. Everyone started converging towards
the barge—the inhabitants of Kotlas, off duty soldiers and Poles. You
didn't need to ask the way to find it. When our group reached the
street leading towards the bank by the barge, we found an enormous
queue already formed and growing rapidly. We only had three bottles
between the six of us. So we separated into three pairs, each successive
pair occupying a position in the queue, some twenty or thirty places
behind the preceding pair. When the first pair received three bottles of
wine, these were promptly emptied, each man drinking half a bottle,
and passed to the pair next in line. Meanwhile the pair that had
completed the purchase took a new position at the end of the queue.
Late in the evening after one and a half or two bottles per man had
been consumed, the last three full bottles were saved for later.

We waited in the queue for a total of five or six hours and so we all
had plenty of opportunity to talk to the locals, who surprisingly
formed a majority in the queue, despite the number of Poles on the
streets. Most of the inhabitants were ex-*zeks* who had been allocated
to live in Kotlas for a set number of years when they had been released
from camp. Some had worked on the Kotlas-Vorkuta railway
construction or in the coal mines in Vorkuta district. But most of those
that I spoke with were from the constructions already completed,
mostly canals and dams. Their life as free workers was a constant
struggle for survival, a far cry from the happy and prosperous living
proclaimed on the ubiquitous placards.

When we enquired about places to eat one of the locals told us there
were none. He offered to sell us some eggs and accommodation for the
night. Our group of six went to a dingy place in one of the houses in
the neighbourhood, with chickens scampering all over the place, and
had some scrambled eggs prepared for us. The meal was completed by
finishing the remaining bottles of wine. On the way we heard the news
that the train would depart next morning at 5am. Finishing the wine
proved disastrous for my companions. They became totally inebriated
and in the morning were unable to wake up. I don't know why I
should have been the least affected, but it fell to me to shepherd them

Place names marked □ indicate areas where Polish prisoners and deportees were concentrated. Total estimated at between 1,500,000 and 1,600,000.

△ The main Polish HQ, first at Buzuluk and later at Yangi-Yui. It was moved when it became clear that the winter climate at Busuluk was killing the emaciated Poles who were arriving there with no suitable clothing or accommodation.

~ Reporting centres where Polish units were located.

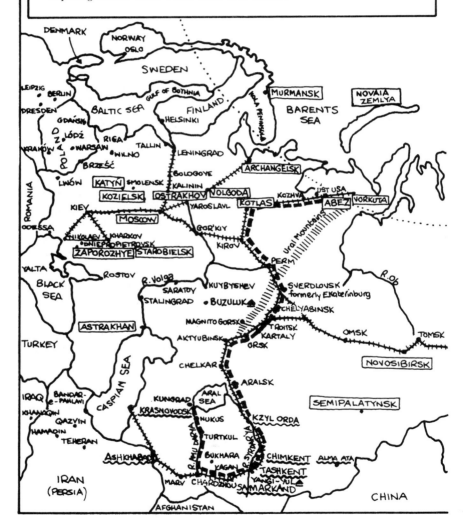

Journey from Abez to Kungrad.

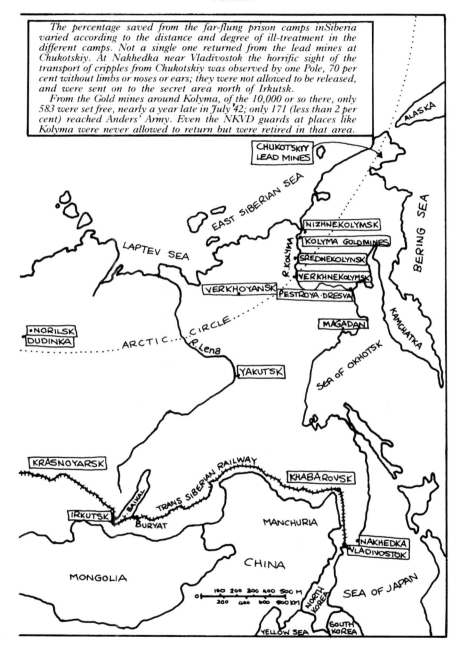

The percentage saved from the far-flung prison camps in Siberia varied according to the distance and degree of ill-treatment in the different camps. Not a single one returned from the lead mines at Chukotskiy. At Nakhedka near Vladivostok the horrific sight of the transport of cripples from Chukotskiy was observed by one Pole, 70 per cent without limbs or noses or ears; they were not allowed to be released, and were sent on to the secret area north of Irkutsk.

From the Gold mines around Kolyma, of the 10,000 or so there, only 583 were set free, nearly a year late in July '42; only 171 (less than 2 per cent) reached Anders' Army. Even the NKVD guards at places like Kolyma were never allowed to return but were retired in that area.

ALASKA

CHUKOTSKIY LEAD MINES

EAST SIBERIAN SEA

BERING SEA

LAPTEV SEA

NIZHNEKOLYMSK

KOLYMA GOLDMINES

R. KOLYMA

SREDNEKOLYNSK

VERKHNEKOLYMSK

VERKHOYANSK

PESTROYA DRESVA

KAMCHATKA

MAGADAN

•NORILSK

DUDINKA

ARCTIC CIRCLE

R. Lena

YAKUTSK

SEA OF OKHOTSK

KRASNOYARSK

TRANS SIBERIAN RAILWAY

KHABAROVSK

IRKUTSK

BAIKAL

BURYAT

MANCHURIA

NAKHEDKA

VLADIVOSTOK

CHINA

MONGOLIA

100 200 300 400 500 M
0 200 400 600 800 KM

SEA OF JAPAN

NORTH KOREA

YELLOW SEA

SOUTH KOREA

to the train, though I was still very weak and barely able to walk.

The train was composed of the same cattle trucks that came in from Kozvha, even the piloting NKVD crew was the same. There was no checking names or tickets. Anybody speaking Polish could board the train. The journey from Kozhva which had started on September 17 1941 continued after a two day delay in Kotlas for nearly three months in the same train, until it finally reached Chardzhou on the banks of the Amu Darya river. The journey from Kotlas took us first to Kirov, Perm, and across the Ural mountains to Sverdlovsk, where there was another delay of two days or so. At first the countryside was fairly well forested but gradually became more industrialized, particularly near Sverdlovsk. The watch towers became less frequent, though the former *zeks* could not mistake their presence.

When there was a hold-up we never knew how long we would be delayed. On the morning of our second day waiting in the siding at Sverdlovsk, my group told me it was my turn to go in search of bread. The city is on the eastern fringe of the Ural mountains, formerly called Ekaterinburg and was where the last of the Tsars, Nicholas II and his family perished after imprisonment at the hands of the Bolsheviks in 1918. Sverdlosk was a much bigger town than Kotlas, but I could tell the way to the bakery just by following the pedestrians heading in the same direction. The queue that I joined around seven or eight in the morning was already about half a kilometre long. When they started selling the bread, the queue moved forward for about twenty minutes; but the bread had been sold out before I had advanced more than a third of the length of the queue. By then it was already midday, the next baking was at 3pm. When this was ready and the sale started, a convoy of lorries arrived from the NKVD and they took the whole batch of bread. The people in the queue were told to wait for the next baking around 9pm.

When the sale of the first baking was completed, my section of the queue reached a position alongside a bookshop window. This was the only shop that I had seen which had its goods for sale actually displayed in the windows, rather than pictures of them. For more than three hours I looked at the books and then looked at the length of the queue. I came to the conclusion, confirmed by my neighbours, that the chances of any of us getting any bread that day were nil. As the closing time of 5pm was approaching I decided on impulse to go in and I bought several books. One was on Russian history, one on the geography of countries belonging to Russia, an introductory text to learn English, and one on arithmetic.

Since my illness I had discovered that I had completely forgotten all that I had ever known of arithmetic, even the simplest calculations were beyond me. I hoped the arithmetic book would enable me to recover some of my lost skill. But, in fact, I have never regained the standard in Calculus that Stryj had helped me to acquire. The books were very cheap and I even had a few kopeks change from the money I had been given to buy the bread. I was delighted with my purchase for I had not seen a book for nearly two years. The fact that the books were in Russian, and I hadn't a clue how to read the Cyrillic characters in which they were written, didn't bother me at all. My companions were much less impressed with my purchase, and promptly sent me back to get something—anything—to eat, and quickly.

As I was walking back along the railway siding I passed a group of Poles engaged in an animated discussion. One of the voices sounded very familiar, so I circled round the group and saw a man swathed in quilted clothing and bearded, but with a prominent Adam's apple visible. I hesitantly called to him: "Wojtek?" The other turned round and we recognized each other. It was indeed Wojtek Szklany from Grodzisko, the seminarian. After a few minutes of hurried questions and explanations, Wojtek suggested that I joined his group in another cattle truck as they were well supplied with food. They even had some milk to spare. I told him my story of the books and Wojtek managed to obtain some bread and milk from his group's supplies to pacify my companions. Eventually I joined Wojtek's group, taking the books with me. There I found one man, Edek Rynkiewicz, who not only welcomed the books but offered to teach me the Cyrillic alphabet.

If the truth be known, I was never to be entrusted with money by my new companions. At most, I accompanied the person who was looking after the money during excursions to buy food. The books proved to be a boon in the new surroundings. Edek Rynkiewicz came from the Prypet district of eastern Poland, the same area where the 1986 Chernobyl nuclear power station explosion took place. He was an officer in the Polish Army, and had been a district secretary of the local municipal government. He spoke and wrote Russian fluently and for several days he read the two books on history and geography to anybody who wanted to listen.

The book on arithmetic and the introductory text to learn English were entirely mine; nobody else took any interest in them. We had heated discussions about the books. The history text contained numerous errors and misrepresentations regarding the past relations with Poland, and these were disputed by all those who remembered their history learned in Poland. Even the geography text was full of propaganda—if it were not for Lenin and Stalin, the earth would not exist and the sun would certainly not shine. Stalin was referred to in

those days as "our sunshine". For the first time in as long as I could
remember, I felt mentally and intellectually stimulated.

From Sverdlovsk we travelled to Chelyabinsk, Troitsk, Kartalay
and to Orsk. It must have been somewhere between Kartalay and
Orsk that the train stopped in a siding by an open field. There was no
nearby settlement, except for a village on the horizon some three or
four kilometres away. After about three hours of waiting, Edek and I
were detailed to go to the village in search of some food for our group.
A few other individuals also made their way across the open fields
towards the village. We kept separate from each other so as not to
search for food among the same huts. When we were well past the
midway point between the train and the village a prolonged whistle
announced the train's departure. Edek and I had no hope of getting
back to catch the train, so we continued on our way to the village. As it
was off the beaten track, it had been spared from itinerant visitors, so
Edek and I were welcomed most warmly. We were not only offered
food in exchange for clothing—rather than money, but we were
invited to a meal. Thanks to Edek's knowledge of Russian, we could
talk to the locals and once they knew we were ex-*zeks* they were happy
to tell us about their lives. They grew their food on a small plot, an
area no more than the thirty feet by eight feet which each farmer was
allocated for private cultivation. The land that had been owned by
their father before the revolution, had been collectivized and he had
been taken away as an exploiter of labour. The family were obliged to
work twelve to fifteen hours a day on a collective farm and could only
tend their small plot when they returned from work. They were not
allowed to keep a pig or a cow. The most they were permitted were a
few chickens or ducks. The village community was run by communist
party appointees. They appeared to revel in their power and there was
no form of appeal to any other authority. Before collectivization the
yield from the land had been plentiful but now nobody cared about
proper cultivation methods. Yields were very poor and it was obvious
that there was no incentive to work. However, the privately owned
plots looked in top-class condition and were clearly thriving.

After spending several hours in conversation, Edek and I returned
to the railway siding hoping to catch another train so that we could
rejoin our companions. During the night a passenger train stopped on
the siding; with a number of other Poles who had been left behind we
climbed into the carriages. About a half an hour later a troop-carrying
train rushed past. The passenger train then moved on. Edek and I
made the first use of our *boumazhkas* showing them to the conductor
who found us in the corridor. He accepted these quite happily and
explained to us that our train from Magnitogorsk would have priority

over the Kotlas train, so that probably we would have to wait for it at
Orsk which was the next station. In the meantime, we stood in the
corridor watching the passengers in their compartment. When the
new day broke and the passengers started stirring, one of the civilian
families in the compartment started tucking into a whole roast
chicken. I had not seen such a feast for more than two years and I felt
as though I was dreaming. I could not believe that a civilized world,
where people travelled in comfort, sitting on seats and eating roast
chicken for breakfast, still existed. It goes without saying that these
well dressed passengers had nothing to do with us two ruffians, in the
so called classless society of the Soviet Union.

At Orsk we rejoined our companions in the Kotlas train, which was
then diverted to Aktyubinsk, Chelkar, Aralsk, Kzyl Orda, Chimkent,
and Tashkent. It was not until the train reached Aralsk that we
realized that we were not going to Buzuluk and Kuybyshev, which
was where the Polish Army was being formed and where the Polish
Embassy was located. The NKVD officers told us that the Buzuluk
centre was overcrowded and the incoming trains were being diverted
to the south on a short term basis. The next delay in the journey lasted
for two days and we stopped in Tashkent or Samarkand. We had the
strange experience of watching a film from the cattle truck. It was on
an open air screen set up in a park. It was a patriotic film showing the
heroic sacrifices made in defence of Mother Russia. The army was
portrayed as invincible, but it was no longer engaged in a
revolutionary struggle, but a sacred war being fought by the illustrious
descendants of soldiers who had fought against Napoleon. Previously
anything that had happened in Russia before the revolution had been
condemned wholesale.

Once the train passed Kzyl Orda, luscious water melons and other
varieties of fruit became readily available, and we gorged ourselves on
these for days until the stop at Chardzhou across the Amu Darya
river. We stopped for several days at Chardzhou before the next stages
of the journey were organized by the NKVD. A group of four,
including Wojtek and myself, went to Bukhara to have a look around.
My books on history and geography did prove useful, despite their
blatant propaganda as they gave us some information about the
country we were in. Bukhara is one of the oldest cities in Central Asia
and was an Islamic centre from the 8th century until it was destroyed
by Genghis Khan. It was later rebuilt as a city of mosques and
minarets. I was struck by the enormous contrast between the tall
imposing structures built in the past which despite neglect, were
magnificent and the mud brick shacks occupied by present day
inhabitants. In comparison to the streets of Kotlas or Sverdlovsk,

Bukhara was very crowded. Two distinct groups of Asiatic people predominated—Uzbeks with very colourful straps around their caps and midriffs and Turkmen in black *khalats* or long robes with enormous caracul hats lined with a band of long haired fur around the outside lower rim. There was also a sprinkling of European faces in typical nondescript black grey quilted clothing. The roadways were full of camels and donkeys loaded with enormous bundles of dry twigs, bales of freshly collected cotton or two people sitting on one small donkey. The bazaar had no bales of silk or jewellery or handicrafts, but only piles of melons, other fruits, vegetables, or used clothing.

We returned to Chardzhou by train from Kagan, as Bukhara is not on the railway line. When we got back we found lists were being drawn up to divide the whole trainload into small groups with the plan of putting us to work on individual collective farms along the Amu Darya river. It was emphasized that this was a temporary arrangement until the problems of feeding and accommodating the large number of Polish Army volunteers had been overcome. We were transferred to barges and taken down river for nearly two weeks, the various groups being disembarked at various points en route. My group included Wojtek Szklany, Edek Rynkiewicz, Marian Marks, a student of medicine who had completed three years at medical school, Olek Pędzimąz a 1939 graduate of high school in Kielce, Mundek Gross from Lwów and three others. The nine of us kept together for the next few months while we were shuffled from one collective farm to the next.

The feeding arrangements were left entirely to individual enterprise. The result was that every time the barge stopped to unload a group, hordes of hungry men rushed ashore in search of anything edible. At one stop my companions brought large quantities of residual oil-cake, left from pressing oil from seeds. It was used as cattle food. We ate them for days until becoming sick but at least our hunger was temporarily satisfied. At another stop late at night the shore raiders encountered a donkey. The creature was despatched in a moment and a fire was lit, using dry grass and rushes. Before the barges left the bank a semi-cooked hunk of meat was passed among the nine of us. Eventually our group disembarked at Kungrad.

It was impossible to get a picture of what was happening to other Polish ex-prisoners but it was clear that the Soviet authorities were taken by surprise by the numbers volunteering for the Polish Army being formed on Russian soil. In fact, attempts were made to limit the terms of the agreement, to exclude Jews, Ukrainian, Byelorussian and other minority groups with Polish citizenship . But still the numbers attempting to reach Buzuluk where the Polish Army was being formed in camps at Totskaya and Tatishtchev, were an embarrassment to the disorganized Soviet rail system, already under strain with the wartime demands upon it. Without consulting the Polish authorities, transports were secretly ordered to bypass Buzuluk, and travel onwards to Kazakhstan where they overflowed the Uzbek, Tadzhik, and Turkmen Republics. The Polish ex-prisoners which included my group, sent along the Amu Darya River to the marshy area of Nukus were those most adversely affected by this deception. Barges were pulled by tugs for several hundred miles, disembarked into desert, cut off from civilization, and the human cargo was left to fend for itself among the collective farms.

CHAPTER THIRTEEN
Collective Farms

AFTER disembarking at Kungrad we walked some miles to our allotted farm. We were taken there by an Uzbek who was one of the communist management officials. Accommodation was provided in one room of an unused school, and next day we were sent to pick cotton with the other workers of the collective. The norm for everybody was three large bags of cotton a day. Some of the local Uzbek women did manage to achieve the norm with great difficulty. They maintained a bent posture, used both hands to do the picking and had no breaks during the day. We did not take the job too seriously and collected less than a bag full of cotton each. After two or three days we were assigned to other jobs to stop us giving a bad example and destroying the discipline among the local workers.

We were then moved to another *kolkhoz* collective farm up river towards Nukus. We travelled on foot walking on the roads which ran along the top of dykes by the river. Those who were too weak to walk were allowed to hitch a lift in one of the several *arbas*. These were carts on two enormous wooden wheels six to eight feet in diameter, and drawn by donkeys or camels led by Uzbeks from the new *kolkhoz*. Our new task was the maintenance of irrigation canals and ditches. It was arduous work as there were no trees to provide any shade in the heat of the day, which was quite oppressive even though it was winter. While we were digging a channel in a flat plateau, we discovered some fish, two to three feet below the surface. The nearest water in the river was some two kilometres away so we assumed the field must have been flooded and then covered with wind blown sand. One of us scrounged a container and we collected about half a bucketful of fish. We went to the river to wash the mud away from the fish and as soon as the container was filled with water, some of the fish started swimming. We took them back to our lodgings and cooked them for supper. We were looking forward to our first nourishing meal for weeks. It proved to be a total disaster. We only cooked the fish that had revived in the water, but they smelt disgusting and the taste of mud was so strong that nobody could swallow even one mouthful.

We had to expend a lot of energy on the canal digging and the food we were given was nothing like enough. We tried to supplement it by searching for anything that was edible. There were some pheasants in the fields and they did not appear too frightened of people. For several days the nine of us tried to catch one. But we never managed to kill one. Once we found a stray dog. We hunted it and killed it and it produced a very tasty stew. That same afternoon a Polish Army liaison officer visited us. He told us that according to the agreement between Sikorski and Stalin, Polish Army volunteers should not be forced to work. We were apparently entitled to basic rations which he listed, and which the collective farms were obliged to provide. He said that in six to eight weeks we would finally be called up for military service. After hearing such good news, we invited the officer to share our meal, which he did only too willingly. Unfortunately after the meal, one of our group jokingly barked. When the officer realized what he had just eaten he promptly threw the whole meal up.

The next day a group of nine went to the collective farm office with a copy of the agreement about Poles not having to work and being issued with basic rations. They demanded it was instigated immediately. We were told to walk to another *kolkhoz* near Turtkul and that is where we spent the rest of the time until our call-up. We didn't see anything of the neighbouring towns of Kungrad, Nukus, or Turtkul, but we heard that the NKVD detachments were stationed there. We were again accommodated in a deserted school building. The school was on the edge of a settlement, among a grove of mulberry trees adjoining the expanse of desert sands—the Kyzylkum desert. Among the trees there were a couple of conical clay beehive type structures which were used for baking the flat unleavened bread wafers of the region.

Most of the schools in the district had been closed for the duration of the war. All the young men, including the teachers, had been called up, except for the communists in management positions on the collective farms. The farms and their settlements were spread along both sides of the Amu Darya river up to a distance of ten to fifteen kilometres from the river. All cultivable land was irrigated by programmed flooding from numerous canals and ditches criss-crossing the countryside. If the level of water in the canals was lower than the land to be irrigated, water was lifted by water wheels with containers attached to the rim, usually driven by donkeys. Our new *kolkhoz* cultivated a variety of vegetables, primarily the grain producing plant called locally *jigoura* which gave hundred fold yields from each grain sown. The grain of this plant was the staple food of the local population. It was used as flour for the flat bread or as groats.

The *kolkhoz* also had a herd of cows and a few donkeys used for pulling *arbas* or operating the irrigation water wheels. There was also an apiary and a piggery. A number of neighbouring farms, three to eight kilometres away, had flocks of sheep. During the night they were kept in large rectangular enclosures, surrounded by clay walls. These were about twelve feet high with a base three or four feet thick, narrowing to a rounded top of about nine or ten inches. The shepherds lived in one corner looking after the herds. Apparently, these enclosures had been built in pre-revolutionary days to protect the sheep from night prowlers such as tigers that must have lived in the rushes which covered large areas of the river banks and shallows.

When we arrived at the farm near Turtkul we demanded our right to basic food rations, regardless of work. We did not directly refuse to work but we only delegated a token force of two or three to help the local inhabitants. We said the others could not work on grounds of sickness or general debility. The basic food ration that we drew for the first five days lasted us exactly half a day. We consumed most of it for breakfast. It was imperative to find supplementary sources so we reconnoitred the whole district noting the sheep enclosures in the neighbouring farms, the piggery in our own farm, and the fields of vegetables ready for picking. During our first strategy session, we established the basic principles of our future operations. First, we would not attempt to deprive any under-privileged collective worker of private means, whether it was food, tools or wood for burning. Second, anything we would be forced to take in order to ensure our survival would be government owned, and third, if we were caught we would fight, to the death, rather than be imprisoned again.

The piggery was our first objective. Using the flour remaining from our ration we made a dough and mixed it with glass needles which had been picked out from a window pane that had been broken to provide sharp edged and pointed fragments. One of us then fed the mixture to a pig through the fence of the piggery early evening and next morning. Nothing seemed to happen to the pig. But on the third day one of the *kolkhoz* management officials, — there always seemed to be more functionaries than workers on the farm, — came to ask whether we, as non-Moslems would be willing to kill a sick pig. To our dismay it was not the fat pig we had chosen. It was a sickly, small specimen, reduced to skin and bones. Apparently all the Uzbeks in the *kolkhoz* were Moslems and although they were not allowed to practice their religion, and were forced against their will to look after the pigs, they were not prepared to kill them. We were only too grateful for the heaven-sent gift. We accepted it with alacrity and made preparations to deal with it immediately. Within an hour we were surrounded by a crowd of about twenty local inhabitants, including officials. They brought the pig and remained to watch the proceedings. We tied the pig to a mulberry tree, leaving about six feet of rope spare and fetched a washing basin to catch the blood. The plan was to knock out the pig with a blow to its head, using a short-handled axe, while another volunteer plunged a knife into its heart. I was positioned to collect the blood into the washing basin. When it was knocked on the head, the sick pig suddenly acquired the energy of a charging bull and scattered all three would-be executioners. He ran round like a mad thing, winding its rope around the tree until there was no more free rope left. By that time we had recovered ourselves and managed to kill the pig. Unfortunately as soon as the blood started gushing out into the basin, the pig fell over landing on the basin and spilling the blood all over me. The crowd enjoyed an entertainment they had never expected. We didn't bother to find out what the pig had died from, within an hour and a half it was cooked and most of it was devoured the same evening. One of our group suggested that as the local Moslems had such a strong taboo about pigs, we should hang some pig skin above the door. This would prevent anyone barging into our living quarters uninvited and snooping around. This indeed proved to be the case. It was a most welcome discovery and from then on we enjoyed complete privacy during our stay in the school.

One bonus was the school had a small library which had a few literary books among the mass of communist propaganda publications. Edek selected a few of the Russian stories by Anton Chekov and novels by Leo Tolstoy and Fyodor Dostoievsky and read these aloud for two or three hours every day to those who were interested. There was usually a hardcore group of three of us. I finally learnt the Cyrillic script in typescript, though I never perfected the written form. With Edek's help I occasionally read aloud too. But when it came to learning arithmetic and English, I was on my own. The text book for introductory English started with English words and pictures accompanied by the equivalent Russian word. The pronunciation of the English word was written in Russian, so the knowledge of the Cyrillic alphabet and the exact meaning of the Russian words was essential. The problem was that the *kolkhoz* had a strict timetable and reading could only be done in the evening by the light of a homemade oil lamp, using sheep fat and a twirl of raw cotton as a wick. This created dense smoke which progressively blackened and gradually obliterated the two pages at which the book was open. This process took just two evenings and so the contents of these pages had to be learned in that time. There was no need for a bookmarker to find how far I had got. My companions thought I was a fool for wasting my time on a foreign language, as there was never any thought that we would be sent anywhere but overland, westwards towards Poland.

We discovered that there were large numbers of Polish families living in the area. They had been transported by the Russians after their occupation of the eastern half of Poland in 1939. This was in line with Soviet policy to strip the country of all potential leaders. In Uzbekistan the transported Polish community were mostly from the professional classes, who had been dumped and provided with no means of supporting themselves. Wojtek Szklany found out that some of these people were ill. He asked Marian Marks, the medical student, if he could help. They teamed up and helped the community all they could. Marian even advised on childbirth and on several occasions he was called out at night to assist in deliveries in neighbouring collective farms. His unsolicited fees were given in the form of fruit or dried tobacco leaves. Marian didn't smoke but Wojtek took charge of tobacco.

Our accommodation must have served as the living quarters of the schoolteacher. The room was about ten by eighteen feet, with a stove made of clay bricks next to the door. Straw was spread on the floor right up to the far wall, which had a small window in it. This served as a communal bed for all nine of us. We brought one of the bench-desks from one of the neighbouring classrooms to serve as a table for cutting tobacco leaves and reading books. There was no other furniture. The room adjoined a corridor which gave access to several classrooms on both sides. The back door of this corridor opened straight on to the dunes of the desert. The front door led to the mulberry grove and on to the road leading to the collective farm settlements, two kilometres away.

The president or chief of the *kolkhoz* lived about half a kilometre from the settlement in a house of superior construction. There was a stable accommodating cows nearby. It took us less than two days to discover that a tribute was paid to the president every evening in the form of a bucket of milk left at his door. From then on it was never safe. The milk would either disappear entirely or mysteriously evaporate to half its original volume. At first we shared it among our own group, later we gave some to the children of the Polish families. When an urgent need arose, we would sneak out at night and milk the cows ourselves.

It soon became obvious that if we wanted to feed ourselves properly and also help families in the neighbouring collective farms, we had to organize our activities according to the phases of the moon and the weather. It was no good venturing into the neighbourhood during a full moon. With the absence of trees and the light coloured soil, anything that moved was visible for a great distance. When we were outside we had to maintain a strict silence and relied on touch and sign language. We left as little as possible to chance, making our plans several days ahead and reconnoitring our surroundings thoroughly. If an expedition had to be cancelled at short notice, two hunting parties would set off at the next opportunity—every chance had to be seized. The neighbouring dunes proved ideal cover, not only for killing sheep, but also for hiding incriminating evidence. It was vital that our lodgings were completely clean if they were searched. One frosty night I was in the party sent to the apiary to collect honeycombs. This was the ideal time to go as the bees were inactive. Two hives were cleared of all frames supporting the combs. I was the only one of the group who knew what to do as I had watched my father removing honeycomb frames from hives in order to spin out the honey. The frames with combs were packed tightly into sacks. These were buried in the sand dunes to be disposed of later. Our first priority was to deal with a sheep that had been killed the same night. The meat certainly had no chance to deteriorate, it lasted at most three days and any rejects, like skin, bones, intestines, were carefully buried deep in the outlying dunes.

The following day our routine rations were issued, an event which only happened every five days. A row broke out when six of us from our group were collecting the rations from the warehouse. We saw the farm officials helping themselves to whatever took their fancy—sugar cubes, carrots, or fruit—and consuming them on the spot. We followed suit and a fight broke out as we claimed we had the same rights as the officials. To protect ourselves we formed a circle, back to back, arming ourselves with bricks and sticks. We finally backed out of the premises but not before casualties were suffered on both sides. The president of the *kolkhoz* had his face scraped by a brick and I was hit on the head by my friend when his opponent ducked. By the time we got out of the store complex, the three other members of our group were running to our aid, armed with a knife and an axe. These last two items were the most telling argument. The officials backed off despite their superiority of numbers.

That evening we decided to sweeten our meal with honey. We brought the sacks from the dunes and removed the combs from the frames and began melting the honey out of the wax. While crunching on a piece of comb full of honey, I found out that one bee was still inside and it stung me in the mouth. My face started to swell and before I fell asleep that night my cheek, ear and surrounding part of the neck were all swollen. A few hours later we were awoken by a shout: "the NKVD is here." One of our group had gone out to relieve himself and had heard the sound of horses' hooves on the road. He then heard a command to surround the school and he dashed in to wake everyone up. Someone dumped a bag of flour on to the solidified wax in the iron pot, while another threw tobacco leaves on the embers underneath the pot to smother the smell of honey in the room. Then we all lay down, feigning sleep. The NKVD burst into the room and started to shout at us accusing us of stealing and wounding the president of the *kolkhoz*, who had come in with the NKVD. He pointed out those who had participated in the fight. Edek Rynkiewicz became really angry, and in fluent Russian, full of the obscene curses that the NKVD had used when addressing the *zeks*, threatened to report the officer to his superiors in Samarkand for failing to see that the Polish Army volunteers under his jurisdiction, were properly fed and housed, as prescribed by the agreements. The effect was astounding. Once the intruders were threatened with being reported to their superiors their whole attitude changed from intimidation to subservience. Edek was able to give further authenticity by quoting the authority order number, given to him by the Polish liaison officer, a few weeks previously. He went on to complain that the *kolkhoz* robbed us of the prescribed quantity of rations by underweighing. The NKVD officer then turned on the *kolkhoz* president and started berating him. Edek even used my swollen face to advantage, saying that dental services were not provided for the suffering volunteers. The flour heaped on top of the wax in the iron pot proved a godsend. When one of the intruders started to poke it with a bayonet, Edek accused him of contaminating our food. He immediately stepped back, leaving the honey undetected. It was certainly a lesson to all of us in how to turn a potential disaster to our advantage. After Edek had finished, the intruders actually apologized for the invasion and departed. We could hear the scolding being administered to the *kolkhoz* president from some distance away. After that visit our group was never bothered by farm officials or by the NKVD, despite stepping up our meat hunting activities.

I was responsible for the next expedition to find a sheep. The plan was to climb over the wall, wring a sheep's neck, tie it to the rope and then lift it back over the wall. When I was lowered into the enclosure, I couldn't see a thing. I could only hear the sheep bunching away from me and hitting a gate. I caught hold of one but it was so skinny and bony, I concluded that it was a goat. I moved further in among the animals and the sheep hit the gate again. The noise alerted the shepherds and I heard an urgent whisper from my companion on the top of the wall to get out quickly. By the time I got to the rope the shepherds realized they were being robbed. They came after me, but I was pulled up in the nick of time. My failure was excused by my night-blindness. But the following night we tried again. We took turns in leading expeditions in order of our position on the straw bed and this time the leader brought back two sheep, one for us and one for the families in the neighbourhood. In the period until March 10 we disposed of eight sheep.

On March 8 a relay runner brought us news that we were to depart by barges in two days' time. This hardly left us time to say goodbye to the families that were to stay behind. Wojtek, the seminarian, suggested that despite the unfavourable full moon we had no alternative but to rob the warehouse of our own *kolkhoz* that night, in order to leave some food for the families. He was put in charge and organized the whole expedition. All nine of us worked through the night in the light of the full moon. We broke through the hole in the mud wall into the warehouse and locked the nightwatchman in his cubicle. We then transported the sacks of flour and groats to the houses which were three to five kilometres away. With the increase in sheep stealing and other food robberies, NKVD horsemen had been assigned to patrol the *kolkhozes*. In the middle of the night they rode over to the warehouse to ask whether everything was all right. The nightwatchman, under the threat of a knife, was forced to assure the patrol that everything was normal and to send them away. The following day there was a lot of activity around the warehouse which we observed surreptitiously. But no NKVD or any official appeared at the school with accusations. The NKVD were obviously busy with arranging the transport barges and our group of nine spent the day giving most of our possessions—rags, axes, and containers—to the families who would be left behind. We knew we were under close NKVD scrutiny after the previous night's operation so we carried nothing with us when we walked to the river bank to board the barges.

We later learnt that the families of deported Poles that we helped were typical of the large number that were scattered throughout the USSR. Most tragic was the fate of the children. More than two thirds of them were orphaned, all were starved, and many were forcibly placed in children's homes by the NKVD for indoctrination and humiliation. Only about 7,000 of the several hundred thousand children were evacuated with the Polish Army of Anders to the Middle East.

CHAPTER FOURTEEN
Leaving Russia

IT was on March 10, 1942 that all the Poles from the surrounding *kolkhoz* farms around Nukus converged on to the barge tied at the bank of the Amu Darya. Two other barges were already filled with Poles collected from farms downriver. I was surprised to find some women and children accompanying the men volunteering for the army. They did not have separate toilet facilities or any sort of privacy.

The journey to Chardzhou by barge and subsequently train to Kermine, now Navoi, was exceptionally fast, ending on March 16, 1942. After disembarking from the cattle trucks we marched several miles to a rock strewn plateau among the hills, which had a distant view of the snow-covered Pamir mountains. Numerous tents of all shapes and sizes were set up in a huge field. We were told we would have to camp here temporarily until we were called before the Military Commission. Our group of nine spent two days scavenging the surrounding hills for food. In one of the canyons we found a large tortoise, which we managed to cook after collecting some twigs for fire. The nights were chilly, which we felt especially, as we had given most of our warmer clothing to Polish families. We only had shirts and thin pants as we had expected to be issued with uniforms on arrival. There was not even any wood to build a fire during the night.

On the third day we were called before the commission, which was a mixed Polish–Russian one, and the *boumazhkas*, which were issued at Kozhva on release from the camp were carefully checked by the Russian NKVD. The medical examination was also thorough, in marked contrast to the examination in Nikolaev before we were sent to labour camps. Of the nine in our group I was the only one rejected by the medical team, because of my eyesight. The others were allowed into the fenced-off area, but I was told to go back outside it. This was a crushing blow, completely unforeseen by me. I was desolated. After my struggles I felt completely abandoned—and I was in a very poor

Polish ex-prisoners at a Polish Army Recruiting Centre, 1942.
Polish Institute and Sikorski Museum

condition to cope. I had nothing but the thin pair of trousers and shirt I was wearing. I didn't even have a cup to get a drink of water from the nearby stream. I managed to catch a glimpse of my companions as they were led to a tent. They called to me to stay close by, and assured me that help would come.

I spent my first night outside walking or dragging myself from place to place to keep warm. In the day I could sleep under the sun. The following afternoon as I was circling the perimeter, hoping to catch sight of my companions, Wojtek appeared on the other side of the fence. He brought me some food which he threw over the top and gave me some encouraging news. Edek's knowledge of Russian had proved to be in demand by the mixed commission and he had been enrolled to act as their secretary. Edek sent a message saying as soon as he could he would destroy my rejection papers and find my *boumazhka*, which would facilitate my re-examination by the commission. In the evening I received a slip of paper sent by Edek. It had all the symbols that were used by the commission for testing eyesight. He instructed me to learn these by heart, and during the eyesight test I had to stand directly behind the examiner in line with the hand that he used to point at the symbol. Then I would be able to guess the symbol from its approximate position in relation to the size of the chart.

The following night was even colder and windier and I found it increasingly hard to keep walking and to stay warm. After a couple of hours a light snow started to fall, so I decided to try and find some shelter. Shuffling around, not seeing anything because of my night-blindness, I felt the ground starting to slope down. I followed the slope and as it felt a little more sheltered I lay down to rest. I fell asleep but during the night I was woken up a couple of times by the noise of a cart being driven just above where I was lying. It appeared to stop, I heard the sound of voices and then rumbling noises as though stones had been let loose down the slope. When the disturbances died down, I went back to sleep. Towards dawn I was again woken by the same sequence of noises. The rumbling continued until it stopped close by me. As I stretched out my hand, it touched a cold skin-like object. I explored further and discovered the hand of a body that had been dumped down the slope. I realized that I was in a large dugout which was being used as a common grave. I immediately scrambled up the slope, and was greeted by shouts of alarm. The cart drivers were frightened by my sudden, unexpected appearance from the grave. I later discoverved that this was indeed a common grave, where the victims of typhus, a disease which was rampant in the enclosed camp, were being buried. I had been lucky to escape before the daily disinfection treatment.

I spent another night on my own before my *boumazhka* was returned to me across the fence. A few hours later I was called before the commission again. Acting as instructed beforehand, with encouraging nods from Edek, the secretary, I was passed by the commission and after a shower, injections, and change of clothing— my rags were all burned—I was finally re-united with my group. My relief at being accepted into the Polish Army with my friends was enormous. Almost immediately we heard the rumour that the unit being formed in Kermine would soon be dispatched abroad to the Middle East. It had always been accepted that the agreement between the Polish authorities and the Soviet government, meant the Polish Army being formed on Russian soil would fight against the Germans on the eastern front alongside the Red Army. This new rumour seemed too good to be true to those of us who wanted nothing more than to leave a country where we had received such abominable treatment.

It was at this time that we began to learn about the Poles who had escaped in 1939-40 via Romania to Turkey and on to Lebanon which was then under French domination. They were formed into the

Polish troops receive battle dress uniform of the British Army.

Imperial War Museum

Carpathian Brigade under General Kopański, and were recognized as a constituent part of the Polish Army formed in France under General Sikorski. When France collapsed in June 1940, the remnant of the Polish Army on the continent was evacuated to England together with the British Expeditionary Force. The Carpathian Brigade rejected the French order to surrender and marched to Palestine to put themselves under the protection of the British who had jurisdiction there. The Brigade was employed by the British Army on a standby basis in the North African campaign against the Italian forces, who had by then entered the war on Germany's side. In September 1941 the Carpathian Brigade relieved the Australians in Tobruk, and were under German siege until the beginning of 1942. As a result of the fighting the brigade was seriously depleted, and the unit being formed

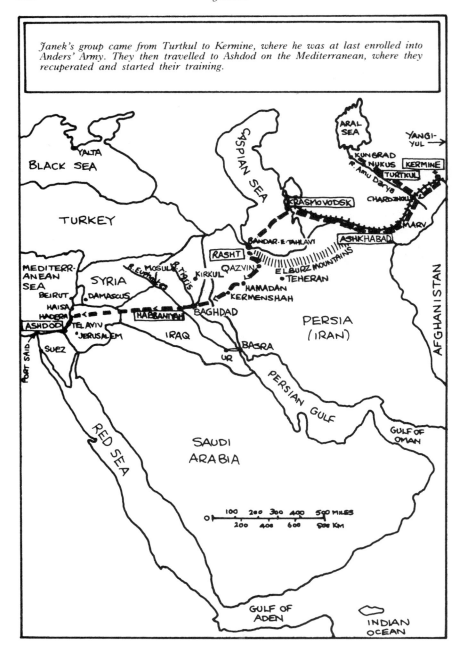

Janek's group came from Turtkul to Kermine, where he was at last enrolled into Anders' Army. They then travelled to Ashdod on the Mediterranean, where they recuperated and started their training.

Exodus from Russia, March 1942.

Polish transport from USSR, Pahlavi, 1942.   *Polish Institute and Sikorski Museum*

in Kermine was to act as its reinforcement, being the closest available Polish unit to the Middle East.

On March 26, just a few days after receiving temporary clothing in Kermine camp, we were issued with the battle dress uniform of the British Army. Three days later we were marched to the railway track where we boarded the familiar cattle trucks of the Soviet State Railway and started the journey via Chardzhou, Marv, Ashabad to Krasnovodsk on the Caspian Sea. For the first time we were under Polish command in our individual military groups but the NKVD were still piloting the train. Looking out from the train, the countryside looked desolate with isolated mud-hut settlements separated by long stretches of bare rocky or sandy areas. There were no trees or bushes in sight, it appeared to be an inhospitable desert. Unlike the northern areas that we had travelled through, there was no sign of concentration camps with their watch-tower trademark. But every station or settlement of any size in the vicinity of the railway had its NKVD contingent in evidence, with their characteristic markings on caps and uniforms.

When we arrived at Krasnovodsk, the whole trainload was

transferred to a waiting ship, under the watchful eyes of numerous NKVD personnel who made sure that no unauthorized man slipped by—only those whose names were called were allowed on board. English uniforms were checked, and any Russian money was collected before boarding. On the same day, April 2, Maundy Thursday, the ship steamed away across the Caspian Sea towards Persia. For three days and nights we spent the time lying around on deck with dry rations and water being issued daily. I could not help recalling how different this trip was from my journey on the Russian coal boat from Archangelsk to Nar'yan Mar. Now everything was peaceful with no storms and no sea-sickness—all accentuating the anticipated pleasure of the moment when we would finally leave Russia. For we were still on a Russian boat, sailing on a Russian sea.

We arrived at Bandar-e-Pahlavi early on Easter Day. After disembarking we marched a mile or so along the sandy beach before being told to set up camp for a few days. What struck me most at this moment of freedom was the amazing number and variety of birds in the area. In the far north, along the Pechora and Usa rivers we had seen no evidence of birds. Further south along the Amu Darya river we saw an occasional pheasant in isolated places, though in January and February we saw large flocks of crows and rooks flying very high up in the sky in a north-westerly direction, towards—presumably—battle zones. What instinct guided these birds? In Pahlavi there were several varieties of seagulls and numerous other colourful birds. As soon as we were settled in our camping zones the whole area was invaded by groups of boys and adults carrying large baskets filled with an unbelievable display of eggs of different sizes, colours, and spot markings. Bartering took place immediately and very soon the natives departed with empty baskets only to reappear an hour or so later with a fresh supply. Fires were lit using the available twigs and brushwood and we all started to gorge ourselves on scrambled eggs. We all began to suffer the consequences of delayed sea-sickness or perhaps over-indulgence to unaccustomed rich food, and the sanitary facilities were severely strained.

The British authorities in charge of this camp made a determined attempt to delouse the newcomers. Only when we had been checked over and found free of vermin were we allowed to pass, naked into an enclosed camp with tents, kitchens and all the paraphernalia of a normal military camp. The relief was tremendous. Unless you have been pestered by lice, as all of us imprisoned in Russia had been, you cannot appreciate the feeling of bliss when finally freed of them. Equally nobody can appreciate the true meaning of freedom until you lose your liberty and are then lucky enough to regain it.

PART III

CHAPTER FIFTEEN

The Fate of Poland

JANEK'S account of the previous two and a quarter years, written forty-five years later, is inevitably coloured by the style developed in a long career as a research scientist. The matter of fact way he describes appalling events, often with sardonic humour, the precision, and apparent detachment, typifies the scientific approach. The material reveals that Janek even then possessed the principal necessary attributes for a scientific career—intellectual curiosity, and a seemingly insatiable appetite for factual information, which he had been unable to satisfy during his time in Russia.

Until he purchased the text books in Sverdlovsk he had had to rely on conversations with fellow prisoners to provide him with new material to stimulate his restless mind. In the Middle East he found a whole new field awaiting his discovery—Biblical history, archaeology and hieroglyphics—all of which helped to distract him from the tedium of army life. But more importantly, he was at last in touch with people who could give him a coherent picture of what had been going on in the war during his time as a prisoner.

Soon after Janek was arrested early in 1940 the Russians started the large scale deportation of Polish civilians from the eastern territories under their control. The first of four enormous rail convoys left for Siberia, containing selected groups of Poles, deemed by the Soviets to be potential leader material. Two more convoys left in April and June. It is estimated that 1,200,000 citizens, mostly Poles, found themselves in the USSR beyond the Urals, most of whom were taken to Kazakhstan. This number was swollen by the soldiers like Janek who were taken prisoner for such 'crimes' as crossing demarcation lines set up by the partitioning powers. By September 1941 the total of deportees was in the region of 1,700,000, and about one third of these were children. The estimated death toll by March 1942 was 760,000.

Poland had a large Jewish population, the result of large scale immigration in previous centuries when the country had offered a safe refuge from various persecutions. Persecution of the Jews in Nazi occupied Poland began shortly after the arrival of the Gestapo units in 1939. On November 14, 1940 the Warsaw Ghetto gates were closed, which meant that no Jews were allowed outside its confines on pain of death. There were 400,000 in the small area by the beginning of 1942. Later similar ghettos were set up in other towns in eastern Poland after the Russian retreat in June 1941.

Those Poles who had managed to escape to the West to ally themselves with General Sikorski, Prime Minister of the Polish Government in exile and commander in chief, refused to surrender when France fell to the Nazis in June 1940. The Carpathian Brigade in Syria under General Stanislaw Kopański, formed from escapees via the Balkans, under French command, also refused the order to surrender in June 1940. They marched to Palestine and placed themselves under British command. After taking part in the North African campaign, notably at Tobruk, this unit was to merge with General Anders' army from Russia. At Dunkirk 17,000 Polish troops were evacuated to England, and a further 7,000 reached England by other routes. Many more were taken into German captivity; some escaped to neutral Switzerland and Spain.

The Polish liner Batory, was the last big ship to escape from Jean de Luz on June 22, 1940, with many refugees, including Poland's deputy Premier Mikolajczyk. The Polish troops who escaped capture by the Germans were the nucleus of a future army of 250,000. Polish airmen served with the RAF in the Battle of Britain July 10–October 31, 1940. A significant contribution was made during September 1940 when the German Enigma code was cracked with the help of pre-war Polish military intelligence aided by a group of brilliant young Polish mathematicians from the University of Poznań. They had broken the Enigma system as early as 1932 and were reading the German Enigma traffic until 1939. On the eve of the war, they passed on their knowledge to the French and British, and though France was defeated before they could make much use of this information, the Poles had passed on a torch to Britain which was to prove of inestimable value.

In July 1940 the deportations from eastern Poland to Kazakhstan and the Arctic Circle unexpectedly stopped, probably because the astonishing fall of France caused the Soviet Union to fear that Germany would turn eastwards. Convoys were not resumed for a year and the June 1941 convoy was the last. Later that month, much to Stalin's surprise, Hitler invaded Russia.

This dramatic change in the war produced a rapprochement between Soviet Russia and the Polish Government in London, which was instigated and encouraged by Britain. After negotiations in

London under British Foreign Minister Anthony Eden's chairmanship, on July 30 an agreement was signed by General Sikorski and Ivan Maisky, Soviet Ambassador to Britain, resuming diplomatic relations and granting an amnesty to all Polish citizens and soldiers in Russian captivity. The plan was to form a Polish Army on Russian soil to fight alongside the Red Army.

General Anders was nominated as Commander of this army and he was released from Lubianka Gaol in Moscow on August 4. A military agreement was signed on August 12 but it was not until two months after the Nazi invasion that the Soviets agreed to send enrolment commissions to the Prisoner of War camps scattered throughout the Soviet Empire to process those being released. The Soviet authorities insisted on classifying Polish citizens of Ukrainian, Byelorussian, Lithuanian and Jewish origin as Soviet subjects. Those who were able to avoid being classified in these categories were willingly accepted by Anders as Polish citizens.

But he was concerned by the lack of any news or information about 15,000 Polish officers, who he knew had been taken prisoner. At the end of September Professor Stanislaw Kot, the newly appointed Polish Ambassador to the USSR, met Andrei Vyshinsky, deputy Foreign Minister, to enquire about the missing Polish officers, none of whom had reported to Anders. A further meeting on October 6 produced no news, a note was sent on October 13 and in London Sikorski addressed enquiries to the Soviet Ambassador Bogomolov. A reply came a month later claiming that all Polish personnel had been set free. Stalin, still in Moscow, on November 14 received Kot in the presence of Soviet Foreign Minister Vyacheslav Molotov. Kot enquired specifically what had happened to the Polish officers from the Starobielsk, Kozielsk and Ostashkov camps, none of whom had turned up to join Anders' new army. Stalin said that the amnesty had no exceptions and picked up a phone to make an enquiry. After hearing the reply, he refused to speak about the officers during the rest of the meeting.

This unsatisfactory response prompted the Polish leadership to produce lists of those whom they knew had disappeared. These were produced at the meeting at the beginning of December between Stalin and Sikorski, at which Anders, a fluent Russian speaker, was also present, but still no answer was obtained. Stalin expressed bewilderment and even suggested that the missing officers had escaped to Manchuria. The mystery was not to be solved until April 1943, and then only partially, when the corpses from the Kozielsk camp were discovered at Katyń.

Stalin agreed to order the release of all Poles still held, increasing the Polish Army in Russia to 100,000, and the headquarters to be transferred to better climatic conditions in Central Asia. A declaration of Friendship and Mutual Assistance was signed on December 5 though Stalin refused to discuss the question of Polish post war frontiers. At the end of December orders came from Moscow for the new centre for the Polish Army to be set up at Yangi-Yul near Tashkent. At the same time Stalin secretly started organizing the Union of Polish Patriots at Saratov under the Polish communist Wanda Wasilewska who had accepted Soviet citizenship. She was a member of the Supreme Soviet Council and ranked as a colonel in the Red Army. This proved to be the forerunner of the Lublin Government.

Further evidence of conflict with the Soviet view of the agreement was becoming daily more apparent. The new army headquarters at Yangi-Yul were found to be bugged and when the Poles disconnected the microphones the NKVD offered to come in "to check the electrical installations". They were assured that there was no need. The Soviets also attempted to impose bureaucratic restrictions to limit the numbers joining Anders' army but the sheer numbers of Poles arriving made most of these impossible to implement. Nevertheless, the presence of Soviet representatives, particularly those who were medically qualified made it difficult for the Polish authorities to accept applicants as easily as they would have liked. Janek's experience was but one example of this, though it also showed how Polish initiative and co-operation could overcome obstacles.

In Poland the Home Army had grown to 300,000 under the command of General Stefan Grot-Rowecki. The Soviet authorities had no wish to see another powerful Polish Army owing allegiance to the London Government on their territory. General Georgi Zhukov, the NKVD liaison officer to General Anders was instructed to ask for the Polish 15th Division to be made ready for action on the eastern front. This was totally unrealistic in view of the pitiful physical condition of the Polish released prisoners, and General Anders refused the request saying firmly that his army was to fight when fit in full complement or not at all. He had no intention of allowing it to be destroyed piecemeal.

The reaction was quick. Moscow announced on March 10 that despite the recent agreement allowing a Polish Army of 100,000 to be formed, food rations would be cut on March 20 to cater for 26,000 men. There were then already 70,000 enlisted soldiers in addition to the Polish refugees and families that had to be fed and housed. Anders' response to this flagrant breach of the recent agreement was to fly to Moscow with his chief of staff, General Leopold Okulicki and meet Stalin on March 18. This courageous move towards a dictator, who was quite unused to any opposition from his Russian subordinates, resulted in Stalin suggesting that numbers in excess of 26,000 should be disbanded and sent as labourers to *kolkhoz* farms. This was categorically rejected by Anders who proposed that units without food rations should be sent to Persia where they could be supplied by Great Britain. A compromise was reached with the USSR supplying rations for 44,000 men, the rest being evacuated to Persia.

Anders was therefore obliged, at very short notice, to evacuate 40,000 soldiers and families, starting that same month, March. This explains the sudden makeshift arrangements to which Janek and his companions were subjected. Anders decided to retain the fittest and evacuate all the physically debilitated and unacclimatised, thereby improving their chances of survival. Significantly Janek and his companions found themselves in this second group and so escaped from Russia six months earlier than the main body of Anders' army. These were not evacuated until the following September when co-operation with the Soviet authorities had finally broken down. General Sikorski was anxious to maintain Polish military units in all fields, as there was no knowing at that time where Poland's ultimate deliverance would come from. It was logical to try to ensure that if deliverance came from the east, there would be a non-communist Polish military organization on hand to take over. It was also important to have a collecting centre in Russia for as long as possible so that Poles still straggling in from all the different and incredibly distant places, could be saved. But when Stalin finally realized that he would never have control of the Polish Army on his territory, he ordered it to go, knowing that he could then organize the remaining Poles into units under communist leadership. It was for this role that Zygmunt Berling was destined, after his desertion from Anders' army when it left Russia. The fate of the Poles left behind, believed to be about a million, was tragic. The Soviet authorities had classified them as Russian citizens who were not therefore entitled to be repatriated— their labour was needed by the USSR. Of the 115,000 that left with Anders in the two waves, 37,000 were civilians. Many were desperately ill and over six hundred died during the evacuation to Persia.

CHAPTER SIXTEEN

The Middle East

WITHIN a couple of days of arriving in the Middle East, Janek and his fellow soldiers were transported to Palestine. An extraordinary variety of different sorts of vehicles began to arrive at the camp gates, buses, trucks, and military lorries, and these started to be loaded on April 14 in what appeared to be a totally haphazard manner, with small groups departing at intervals. The apparent lack of co-ordination was explained by the terrain before them. From the Caspian Sea to the Persian Plateau, a range of the Elzburg (Reshteh-ye-Alborz) mountains had to be crossed. The only road was extremely narrow and made of gravel with just enough room for one way traffic. Passing places were few and far between at switch-back points on the zig-zag route over the mountain ranges. A long convoy would have made it impossible for any trucks to pass in the opposite direction in or out of Pahlavi.

The valleys between the mountain ranges appeared lush with vegetation and were under cultivation. The drivers, mostly natives, were very skilful manoeuvring their unwieldy vehicles along the narrow steep road but at two places along the route debris was visible in the deep ravines alongside the road, the result of previous mishaps. All the vehicles travelled independently, never in convoy, and without rest until a two-way road near Rasht. From there a tarmac highway leading to Teheran allowed them to reach their first stop-over at Qazvin, early in the afternoon.

They found themselves at a *chai-khana*—tea-house which was a sprawling single-storey dwelling situated in a huge fenced-off area. There was space for large numbers of people and animals and it was obviously much used by all travellers. Within the *chai-khana* there was a large hall with several wooden posts supporting the roof, a bare floor with a few turbaned patrons squatting on mats, sipping tea from bowls and smoking water-pipes—*hookas* of elaborate designs. In one area of the hall there were a few wooden tables—a concession to the modern traveller. As the Poles entered they were surveyed quizzically by the smoking patrons but there was no conversation, as there was no common language. Only when the driver entered the hall and explained the situation, did the uneasiness of the patrons subside. More buses and trucks arrived at the *chai-khana* for the night and all the Poles slept outside in the open.

Next day they continued their journey westward away from Teheran, towards Hamadan, Kermanshah (now Bakhtaran), and Baghdad. They soon realized that they were travelling along an ancient trade route for silk and spices—and they saw strings of loaded camels with attendants trotting on foot beside them.

Journeying westwards through the Zagros mountains they passed the famous Behistun Rock, a few miles before reaching the ancient city of Kermanshah now renamed Bakhtaran. The vehicles carrying the Poles then passed through Baghdad and crossed the Tigris river without a halt. Their route then took them across the Euphrates river at Al Falluyah to Habbaniyah, the site of an enormous military transit camp. They rested there two days and then were driven in military trucks on the last leg of their journey to Palestine, across the desert via Rutbah and along a disused oil pipeline to Hadera. Most of the way they stood in the back of the trucks holding handgrips. There was no visible road to follow in the desert most of the time, and a number of lorries frequently travelled abreast, forty yards apart, for long distances. Every two or three hours there was a short stop for the soldiers to stretch their legs and allow another driver to take over. Two longer stops were made for picnic meals. The journey to the Mediterranean from the transit camp at Habbaniyah took some sixteen to eighteen hours, though some trucks were delayed by breakdowns for much longer periods.

The Poles arrived at Hadera in the dark of the early morning of April 29, 1942, and a few days later they were moved from Hadera to Ashdod north of Gaza. After a week or so at the camp the whole group of Polish units in the Middle East was completely re-organized. Officers like Edek Rynkiewicz were assigned duties appropriate to their former training, those with secondary education who wanted to go to cadet-officers' school also left while the rest were organized into details, companies, and battalions. Janek and Wojtek decided to stay with the ordinary recruit group as privates, as neither of them had been impressed by the way certain officers had behaved back in September 1939. The first month or two was a time for recuperation, not only from the malnutrition that had affected all who had been in Russia, but also from the rigours of long and uncomfortable travel. All the soldiers were extremely thin, and still suffering from vitamin

Janek Leja pictured in Palestine, 1942.

deficiencies, particularly scurvy. They were encouraged to eat up to thirty oranges a day to counteract this and they soon came to hate the fruit. This rest period was also used to assess and train the newly enlisted soldiers so that they became fit and competent enough to be militarily useful. They had first hand experience at using their guns because the local Arabs frequently tried to rob them of arms and ammunition in dawn raids. It was a welcome change for Janek and his colleagues to be at the right end of a gun.

In August and the beginning of September their training became more strenuous and ended with general manoeuvres that took them over different terrains in Palestine. In turn, they were near Beersheba in the south, Rehovot near Jerusalem, the Dead Sea, Nablus, Tiberias by Lake Galilee, Haifa and back to Ashdod. Frequently they had to 'hide' in groves of citrus or vine plantations for hours on end, and it was not long before the exotic fruit and grapes lost any attraction. Following the manoeuvres, the soldiers were allowed on their first leave and Janek and Wojtek went on a sightseeing trip to Jerusalem, then Bethlehem, the Dead Sea and finally to Tel-Aviv.

Jerusalem is the holy city for three distinct religions: Jewish, Christian and Muslim and with few exceptions, nearly all of the major Christian groups are represented. Individual churches, chapels, monasteries and tombs are in the possession of different denominations as well as the holy places such as the Holy Sepulchre, revered as the site of Jesus' tomb.

Janek, a Roman Catholic by faith, was deeply disturbed by the apparent lack of reverence in the behaviour of monks and priests of various sects and the mercenary atmosphere surrounding the shrines. As Janek's experiences in Russia left him with a hate for queueing, his few days in Jerusalem had a similar effect on his attitude towards 'charitable' collectors. Tel-Aviv presented a complete contrast to Jerusalem and other Palestinian towns. A modern city with concrete high rise apartment blocks, it was inhabited by rich-looking Jews in European clothing. There was hardly an Arab in sight. Every other Jew appeared to have come from Poland, and they welcomed the soldiers with the "Poland" insignia on their uniforms. There was no difficulty getting around the city, speaking only Polish.

This was the first period of rest and relaxation that Janek and his fellow Poles had enjoyed since the outbreak of war, but in Poland the suffering continued unabated. The Nazis now controlled all of pre-war Poland and the Jewish ghettos set up in the Nazi occupied zone were now extended into the parts previously held by the Red Army. In Spring 1942 the starvation rations supplied to the ghettos were not killing the occupants fast enough for the Nazis. It was at this time that the first rumours of mass extermination of Jews from eastern provinces, taken to western Poland by the Germans, came to the ears of the Underground authorities. In the Lublin Ghetto deportation of Jews began in the summer of 1942 with 130,000 disappearing to Belzec concentration camp. In July 1942 liquidation of the Warsaw Ghetto began with 5,000 a day being deported. The Polish Underground learned on July 29 that transports from Warsaw were going to Treblinka for extermination.

General Grot-Rowecki, Commander of the Home Army, offered help in the form of arms and ammunition and urged co-ordination of attacks from the outside to be timed with Jewish resistance from within. This was rejected by the Jews because they still hoped that quiet behaviour would limit the deportations. Appeals to the Allies from the Jews were transmitted by the Polish Underground to London, together with daily reports on the situation in the Warsaw Ghetto. Tragically, the idea that mass extermination was being carried out was so incredible that it was not believed by the Allies and the BBC remained silent. On September 1, the daily quota was raised to 10,000. A small number of Jews escaped through subterranean passages and sewers and, many of these were given refuge by Polish families, who knew the risks they were incurring. The Warsaw Ghetto extermination campaign, by deportation and execution in concentration camps, was temporarily suspended on September 10 1942.

CHAPTER SEVENTEEN

Reunion

WHEN Janek and Wojtek returned from leave, all units were ordered to prepare for a move to Iraq. It soon became known that a number of Jews who had enlisted in the Polish Army in Russia, had failed to return from leave and had deserted. Marian Marks the medical student, was among them. A number of Zionist organizations with underground radical cells, such as the Haganah, Irgun, and Stern gangs, were preparing for an armed campaign at the end of the war to establish an independent Jewish state. These organizations recruited as many Jews as they could from the Polish Army, conveniently waiting until they had been trained in the use of weapons.

This was an unforeseen problem for General Anders with a total of three thousand Polish Jewish soldiers deserting, from the initial wave of four thousand who came out from Russia under his protection. Corporal Menahim Begin was one of those who arrived in Palestine as a member of General Anders' army. He chose to stay and fight the British, eventually becoming Prime Minister, despite, or perhaps because of his early involvement in terrorist activities against British forces. Anders had done his duty in enabling these Jews to escape from Soviet Russia. He made no attempt to pursue those who deserted—he had no place for unwilling volunteers in his army.

Jews in Nazi-occupied Poland were not the only ones to be persecuted. In November 1942 100,000 Poles were removed from two hundred and ninety-seven villages around Zamość. The town was renamed Himmlerstadt and repopulated with Germans from Romania and Bessarabia. The reaction of the Polish population and the Home Army was so intense that this scheme and similar ones were abandoned as resettled villages were burnt and the German settlers were driven out of their farms. Home Army partisan detachments made their headquarters in the surrounding forests and gradually came to control large areas. The Germans, who were limited to towns

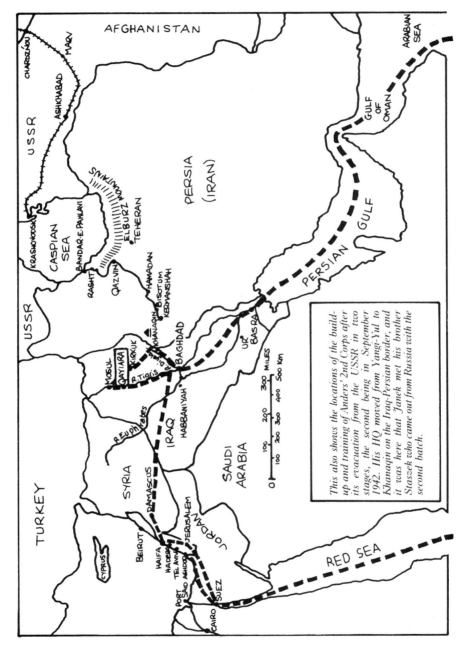

Journey from Suez back to the Middle East with the Carpathian Brigade from Tobruk.

General Sikorski, left and General Anders talking to Polish troops in the Middle East.
Imperial War Museum

and large centres, could only travel between them with strong cover. The German occupiers ruled by terror, executing from between ten to a hundred innocent Poles, chosen at random, for each German death. In contrast, the Home Army chose their targets with great care. Any Gestapo officer, who was responsible or signed posters for mass executions, was liable to be sentenced to death by the Polish Underground courts. Such a sentence was later caried out on Krueger, Chief of Police and S.S. Deputy of Governor Frank in Kraków on April 20, 1943 at 9.50am, and announced to the Polish public on posters.

News of these terrible events in Poland, was not reported in the West and the Polish units in Palestine, preparing to move back to Iraq, had no real idea what was happening to their friends and families at home. The first stage of their journey, which started on September 20, was by military trucks to transit camps near Port Suez, at the southern end of the Suez Canal. Here the Polish units in Palestine joined the Carpathian Brigade, who were recuperating after their recent involvement in the Libyan campaign. The joint force embarked on ships for the voyage to Basra and some pre-war friendships were renewed over the next few days. Janek met an old colleague from Akademia Górnicza in Kraków, Janek Figiel, who had been on the same courses with him for two years. Figiel had escaped to Hungary at the beginning of 1940 and then got to Syria, where he joined the Carpathian Brigade and participated in the defence of Tobruk as an artillery cadet-officer. He had just returned from a two-week leave visiting Egypt's pyramids and temples of the Old Kingdom and Janek with his insatiable appetite for information learned a great deal about Egyptian history. Before reaching Basra, some fifty miles inland from the river mouth, the ship moved slowly up the river alongside banks covered in lush greenery with magnificent-looking villas and palaces dotting the shores. After disembarking they spent a few days in a transit camp and then started north in a convoy towards Baghdad.

On July 7, 1942 following negotiations with General Anders, the Soviet Government agreed to the evacuation of the remaining Polish Army to the Middle East. It took a month to complete this final evacuation, from mid August to mid September. The Soviets also agreed to include the families of soldiers, who had been deported to Russia. Families gathered around the encampments but many were rejected if they had no evidence of soldier relatives. These regulations, rigorously imposed by the NKVD, were very often bypassed when single Poles 'adopted' strangers as their family. Yet there were many families left behind as the NKVD insisted that only those named on the rolls could embark on the ships at Krasnovodsk. Equally tragic was the case of those soldiers who were too ill to be evacuated. Many feigned good health in order to escape, knowing that to be left behind would mean a return to labour camps or death. These determined individuals were supported and propped up by their colleagues at the parade before entrainment.

The Soviets also excluded soldiers and families with Polish citizenship, but not Polish nationality from the evacuation. This meant Polish Jews. Anders insisted on the right to include all Polish citizens, irrespective of their racial origin, but he could not prevent the Soviet authorities from imposing more stringent conditions on relatives of Jewish soldiers. Many families of Polish Jews pleaded to be evacuated. When they were informed of the prohibitive regulations, they appealed to the NKVD, only to be told that it was the Polish military authorities who had refused their passage. This was one example of how the Soviets spread rumours that the Polish military authorities were anti-Semitic.

The last transports left Russia from the exit port of Krasnovodsk in mid September 1942 with General Klemens Rudnicki supervising the final arrangements. A Liquidation Committee was left behind under

Wanda Wasilewska, left, with Colonel Zygmunt Berling.
Polish Institute and Sikorski Museum

General Bohusz-Szyszko to supervise the evacuation of any Polish stragglers but he was only able to function until October when the Russians forbade any further enlistment in Anders' army. Lieutenant Colonel Zygmunt Berling bade farewell to Rudnicki who left with the last transport, and assured him that he would be linking up the Anders' army in Persia. He took a car and all the documents from Krasnovodsk and deserted to join the well-established Union of Polish Patriots, which was led by the communist Wanda Wasilewska. From then onwards all Poles left in the USSR, estimated at over a million, were sent to this organization.

It was not until October 17 when Janek and his companions learned that this main group of the Polish Army, formed in Russia under General Anders, had been evacuated from Soviet territory and was encamped on the approaches to Khanaqin in Iraq; this was just a few miles away from their camp site. When Janek met soldiers from the new camp, they told him there was another Leja at their camp. Wojtek Szklany and Janek applied for a day's leave to visit the Khanaqin camp. When they reached the site on October 25 they realized their search was virtually hopeless. Over 100,000 people had been evacuated from Russia and they were confronted by a sea of tents, arranged in a grid pattern stretching for miles. There were no lists to consult and they had no idea where to begin looking. The only possible method was to start a systematic enquiry at each tent along the innumerable avenues. Wojtek took one side of an avenue, Janek the other, and poking their heads into each tent they asked "any Leja here?" After three hours, on a day of blistering heat they were both exhausted. They decided that they would give up when they reached the end of the row of tents. Just then Wojtek was hailed from the tent he was approaching. Janek, who was some distance away on the other side of the rows of tents, recognized his brother Staszek calling to Wojtek. Before Janek was able to reach them, he heard Staszek saying that he had received the note that Janek had thrown from the train passing through Lwów on his way to Nikolaev in March 1940. He therefore knew that Janek, Kazik and Wojtek had been taken to Russia and he had subsequently heard that Janek had died in the concentration camp. He had been convinced of Janek's death because he had talked to the prisoner who had taken his brother's body to the morgue in the Abez Penal Colony. The prisoner had left before Janek was found to be alive and Staszek believed he would never see his brother again. He did not recognize the approaching figure and it was only when Janek spoke to him that he realized his brother had returned from the dead.

Staszek and Janek had last met in October 1939 in Lwów, both having recently escaped from the Russians. At this stage, the NKVD only worked at nights, gathering deportees, so Staszek and his wife Basia evaded the first deportations by lodging with friends and spending the nights in classrooms in the university. They were finally caught on June 29, 1940 and were put on a cattle train to be transported to a remote settlement north of Sverdlovsk. The journey, undertaken in terrible conditions, took six weeks. A week before they reached their destination, Basia gave birth to their first child, a daughter. They eventually arrived at Serov, some two hundred kilometres north of Sverdlovsk and were taken by cart to a settlement called Tesma, where they remained for over a year. Staszek was employed on hut construction and hay cutting, earning just enough to keep the three of them alive. In order to survive the 'free' workers on the construction site used similar techniques to those employed by *zeks* in the concentration camps. As soon as one hut was completed and passed by the *diesiatnik*—evaluator the workers building the next one would surreptitiously rob the newly finished hut of doors and fittings so that they could achieve the construction norm.

Following the announcement of the "amnesty" for Poles in August

Staszek Leja with his son Janusz, Palestine 1945.

1941, Staszek was issued papers allowing his family to travel to Yangi-Yul. It was so overcrowded there they were transported to Turkestan, a town north of Tashkent and placed in a nearby *kolkhoz,* Staszek was employed in digging an irrigation canal, while Basia looked after their two children—another had been born at Tesma. In the spring of 1942 Staszek went on his own to enlist in Anders' Polish Army at Chokpar, north of Alma Ata, but immediately fell ill with typhus. At this time, Janek was being evacuated to Persia with the first wave to leave the USSR. During the summer, the rumour spread that all the Polish Army was to be evacuated to Persia; Staszek, by now convalescent, returned to the Turkestan *kolkhoz* to fetch his family. They then joined a military transport for Persia at Kermine, where a few months earlier Janek had been enrolled into the Polish Army. They reached Pahlavi on August 15, 1942. Basia and the children were sent to Teheran and Staszek went with the army to Khanaqin.

In the winter of 1942/3, the two children died during a typhus epidemic in a Teheran hospital. Basia, tragically childless, joined the Women's Auxiliary Unit, where she worked as a truck driver and later as an educational officer. When the army moved from Iraq to Palestine, Staszek and Basia were briefly reunited, teaching in the same school for Polish children, established by the army in Palestine. When the Second Corps under General Anders moved to Italy, Staszek was assigned to a signals unit, and participated in the whole Italian campaign—Monte Cassino, Ancona, Bologna. Janusz, their third child, was born in Palestine on the day that Staszek took part in the assault on Monte Cassino, May 14, 1944. It was not until eight months later that Staszek was given leave to visit Palestine and see Basia and his new son.

CHAPTER EIGHTEEN

Military Training

JANEK and his friend Wojtek were officially incorporated into the Carpathian Brigade with their units from Kermine, and they left the camp on the shores of the Diyala River on November 23. They travelled in lorries through Kirkuk to Mosul and then south to Qayiara, some fifty miles down the river Tigris from Mosul. The various units encamped in the vicinity of Qayiara, spread for several miles on the right bank of the Tigris, along the road from Mosul to Baghdad, among the hills and valleys. Figiel, Janek's friend from his student days, was with an artillery detachment encamped along a small stream—*wadi*, a tributary of the Tigris in a wide valley. Wojtek's and Janek's battalion of the 3rd Carpathian Brigade occupied the bare slopes of the hills overlooking the *wadi*. It was some two kilometres away as the crow flies, but five or six kilometres by the gravel road that made a detour in order to cross the *wadi* over a bridge and then join the tarmac road to Mosul.

The military routine of camp life was soon established. Units trained either on foot among the hills or were taken in lorries further afield into the desert to the foothills of the Kurdistan mountains in the north and north-west. For those training locally, the early evenings were devoted to recreation sporting contests, football and volleyball. Then following the daily roll-call of individual units, there was an hour of loudspeaker announcements, news and music which blared over the camps from the hills. If training took a unit further afield they either roughed it in the desert or returned exhausted, often too late to hear the announcements. The music following the news always ended with Ave Maria, sung at dusk. This song, echoing among the hills as night was falling, was deeply moving evoking memories of the soldiers' past life and their families in Poland. It is something Janek has never forgotten.

The soldiers of the Polish Army saw their departure from Russian territory as a great deliverance. They had escaped from, in the words

Janek Figiel, left and Janek Leja, Qayiara 1943.

Wojtek Szklany.

of American Alexander Dolgun, a prisoner under Stalin, "a state that wanted their slave labour and had created an elaborate machinery for the creation of guilt where no guilt existed". British Premier Winston Churchill had been pressing for Polish reinforcements for the Middle East; and Stalin had eventually decided that this foreign army on his territory was more trouble than it was worth. Only Sikorski was disappointed. He had hoped that a Polish Army on Russian soil would act as a refuge for the missing Poles still in the USSR and would also be able to help liberate Poland from the east. In December 1942 he flew to the USA, and met US President Franklyn Roosevelt for the last time. He pressed him to support an invasion of Europe through the Balkans, a last attempt to ensure that Poland would be liberated by Anglo-American forces before the arrival of the Red Army. It was not to be. The Casablanca conference a month later in January 1943 confirmed that the ultimate blow against Hitler in western Europe would be from England across the Channel, with an earlier campaign against Sicily and Italy before then. No attack through the Balkans was envisaged, which meant the end of Polish hopes for deliverance by non-communist units loyal to the Polish Government in London.

January 1943 marked a turning point in the war with a disaster for Germany; the Army under Field Marshal Von Paulus surrendered at Stalingrad. From the very moment that the Soviet advance was started after victory at Stalingrad, difficulties arose between Poland and Soviet Russia. Moscow claimed all people resident on Polish territory that had been occupied by the Red Army in 1939 were Russian citizens. In February 1943 the Russians began forming Polish detachments within the framework of the Red Army. In March the Union of Polish Patriots under Wanda Wasilewska was announced. It immediately began broadcasting from Russia, launching slanderous attacks on the Polish Government in London and accusing the Home Army of remaining passive when action was called for against the German occupying forces.

On February 26 the Polish Ambassador from London Tadeusz Romer, met Stalin for three hours and told him of the aims of the Underground Home Army. The main plan was to sabotage all railway lines that ran from Germany to Russia through Polish territory. This was the route for 85 per cent of the German Army's equipment and food. The Polish Government was ready to implement this any time after March 1, provided they could co-ordinate with the Red Army to assure maximum success and justify the inevitable losses. Stalin rejected the offer and evaded Romer's questions about possible dates for the operation. In fact, the operation was eventually carried out in April 1944 when it was considered to be of maximum benefit to the approaching Red Army. The Soviet authorities were not prepared to accept help from sources they had no control over. Instead Stalin's propaganda apparatus appealed for immediate but unorganized spontaneous uprisings from the Polish population, despite the known consequences such as hostage taking and reprisals on the civilian population. The situation was all the more tragic when the highly organized Home Army, with a strength of 300,000, capable of specialized sabotage was being virtually ignored.

In the Middle East a special effort was made in the Carpathian Brigade to train as many soldiers as possible to drive military vehicles. Janek failed in this training in the early stages when he got a lorry stuck crosswise under a bridge below the military railway line, blocking the traffic on the main highway for a considerable length of time. He did manage to pass a motorcycle test and became a dispatch rider for liaison with other camps. He was assigned a two-cylinder motorcycle, Idiana mark, a beautiful machine. Unfortunately this job did not last long either.

On January 2, 1943 Wojtek left the camp to continue his studies for the priesthood at a seminary in Beirut, Janek felt isolated without him, they had been together since their reunion at Sverdlovsk in 1941. After Wojtek left, Janek started visiting Janek Figiel in the nearby camp when he had completed his duties as a dispatch rider. One evening he over-stayed his time and looking towards the camp on the opposite slope of the hills he suddenly realized that his battalion was assembling for the evening roll-call. Grabbing his motorcycle he revved it up and took off at high speed. He took a short cut across the desert heading in a straight line towards his camp, completely forgetting the existence of the *wadi*. When it loomed ahead, Janek was confronted by a gap of thirty-five feet with a drop of six feet gradually rising towards the other side.

Yanking the bike up with all his might, Janek tried to jump the bike across the *wadi* but his front wheel caught the opposite escarpment six inches too short—catapulting him and the bike on to the shore. As he was tumbling and sliding on top of the sand and gravel he willed the bike not to crash on top of him or to explode. He landed a couple of feet away from the bike and although very shaken he was unhurt. He tried to remount but the handlebar was crooked, the front wheel was stuck and the foot pedals were missing—the bike was useless. Janek sat down and waited for help from his companions, who had had a perfect view of his acrobatics. Eventually they came over to rescue him.

For the next three days he lay in bed, with all his muscles aching and black bruises appearing on his chest with a perfect imprint of the bike's handlebar. When he recovered he was told that his dispatch riding days were over and he had forfeited his leave for the next three months. Whenever the others had time off or were sent on recreational trips, he would remain on duty. This last penalty he found particularly hard when others were taken to tour Ashur and Nineveh.

Towards the end of March 1943 it was announced that volunteers were needed for the Polish Air Force and Parachute Brigade, both based in England. Janek applied immediately and though rejected for the Air Force because of poor eyesight, he was accepted for the Parachute Brigade.

He was one of six hundred volunteers for both the Polish Air Force and the Parachute Brigade who left the Mosul area on April 3, 1943, travelling by truck through Baghdad and Damascus to Port Suez, which they reached on April 10. A few days after their arrival in a transit camp, they heard the first news of Katyń.

CHAPTER NINETEEN

The Katyń Massacre

ON April 13, 1943, the German radio announced the discovery of ten thousand Polish officers' corpses at Katyń forest, in the region of Smolensk. Two days later General Anders urged the Polish Government in London to ask the Soviets for an official explanation. It was now nearly two years since he had first made enquiries about the missing officers. On the same day Radio Moscow claimed that the massacre had been committed by the Germans when they occupied the area in 1941. The Commander of the Underground Home Army in Warsaw, General Grot-Rowecki confirmed the next day that the Polish officers' corpses had been found as described in the German communiqué, though the numbers had been exaggerated. This information came from Poles who had been taken to Katyń and who estimated the number of corpses as over four thousand.

The Polish Government, aware of Germany's intention of sowing dissension among the Allies, knew that this disturbing evidence required independent investigation. In a statement issued in London on April 15, General Marian Kukiel, Minister of Defence said they deplored the German attempt to use this tragedy to excuse their own crimes. The Nazis could scarcely assume a position of moral superiority at the very moment they were carrying out the final extermination of the Warsaw Ghetto.

The situation of Polish Jews in Nazi-occupied Poland was calamitous, even though the Warsaw Ghetto extermination campaign by deportation and execution in concentration camps had been temporarily suspended on September 10, 1942; those still alive in October decided on active resistance, and contacted the Home Army for help in December.

On January 9, 1943 Heinrich Himmler head of the Gestapo visited the Warsaw Ghetto and ordered its destruction. Nine days later the Germans resumed the extermination programme, eighty thousand Jews were then in the Ghetto. The Jewish Militant Organization advocated that fighting for survival should replace the previous policy of accepting passively what was imposed by force. There was another option, the Nazis indicated they would accept ransoms for those willing to work for them. But the Ghetto inhabitants had just heard the fearful news of what had happened to the last group to be deported. A number who had escaped, brought back eye witness accounts. They recounted how Polish Jews had been ordered to dig pits and were then mowed down by machine-gun fire. The next group had to spread quicklime over the corpses before becoming the next victims. This process continued until no Jews were left. From then on there was no thought of accepting any bribes or ransoms. On April 19, less than a week after the Nazis expressed their cynical horror at the corpses discovered at Katyń, the Gestapo were scheduled to supervise the final liquidation of the Warsaw Ghetto. In fact, a spontaneous uprising from the starving but desperate inhabitants delayed the Nazi plan until mid May. They had scarcely any ammunition or weapons but resisted with the utmost courage until at last the Germans had killed every last Jew. Only then did they take possession of the empty Ghetto, where every house had been destroyed. Similar events in other Polish towns had resulted in extermination of Jews in Lwów and the eastern villages. By 1943 the Ghettos had disappeared.

It was against this background that the Polish authorities invited the International Red Cross to send a delegation to investigate the Katyń corpses. The Red Cross said that they could only do so if all parties involved agreed. The Soviets refused. Churchill appealed to Sikorski asking him not to magnify the affair, causing dissension within the Allied camp. At that time there was real fear of a separate German-Soviet peace. But Sikorski, responsible to so many Polish families anxious for news, could not ignore the need for clarification. The Polish Red Cross, who had investigated at the request of the Polish Underground authorities, discovered that all the evidence pointed to the crime having been committed in the spring of 1940 before Germany had occupied the area. The Soviet version, broadcast by Moscow Radio, was that the corpses were those of Polish prisoners of war who had been employed on building work in 1941 and had then been captured by the Germans. This explanation had not been offered during the ten months in 1941 when the Polish authorities had been making enquiries about the missing prisoners—and the evidence was heavily weighted against them. The method of execution was typically Russian, a bullet in the back of the head, and all documents found on the corpses were dated before the spring of 1940. The age of the trees planted over the graves provided further proof, which was fuelled by the memory of the evasive answers given by Stalin and his

The mass grave at Katyń.　　　　　　　　*Polish Institute and Sikorski Museum*

The International Forensic Medical Commission examine one of the corpses.
                    Polish Institute and Sikorski Museum

Archdeacan Jasiniki and representatives of the Red Cross say final prayers over the Katyń graves. *Polish Institute and Sikorski Museum.*

subordinates in 1941 when questioned about the missing officers.

It might have been expected that the Russians, if innocent, would have welcomed an independent investigation. The Soviet response was to condemn the Polish Government for approaching the International Red Cross and they used this as a pretext for breaking off diplomatic relations on April 25. All the while, they stressed their desire for a "strong and independent Poland" after the war. The Poles knew that this phrase would be interpreted by the USSR in its own way; Moscow had already started a campaign of defaming the London Poles, suggesting that some government members should be replaced.

Ivan Maisky, Soviet Ambassador to Great Britain, who had negotiated the 1941 agreement with Sikorski, then intimated that Professor Kot, Polish Ambassador to the Soviet Union, and others holding anti-Soviet views should be replaced. Sikorski, with a rare touch of humour, replied that this might be possible if Soviet Foreign Minister Molotov was in turn replaced by somebody less anti-Polish. Sikorski and his colleagues remembered Molotov's infamous declaration in 1939 after the fourth partition. "After one quick blow, first from the German, and next from the Red Army, nothing remained of the mis-shapen monster created by the Treaty of Versailles".

The full story of Katyń did not emerge until after the war. The 250,000 Polish prisoners taken by the Red Army in 1939 were separated into officers and other ranks. The September 28 amendment to the secret protocol of the 1939 Nazi-Soviet Pact, agreed between Molotov and Ribbentrop, specified that the Germans would return to the Soviets all Ukrainians and White Russians rounded up in their zone. In exchange, the Russians offered to send all Polish officers in their hands. Germany knew that under the terms of the Hague Convention it could not force Polish officers to work and so refused to accept them. The Nazis did in fact use other Poles, and indeed inhabitants from many other nations under their control, as slave labour in their factories.

In an account published in 1948 by Stanislaw Mikolajczyk, who took over from Sikorski as Prime Minister, he said that Stalin, who like Hitler delegated very little, was consulted as to what should be done with these Polish officers. Stalin, apparently wrote the single word: "Liquidate". This could be interpreted in several ways, either disperse the officers to other prisons or deport them to Siberia. The Red Army referred the matter to the NKVD who chose the literal meaning. In the autumn of 1940, Colonel Berling a Polish prisoner in Russia co-operating with his captors, asked if he could speak to the Polish officers in the camps at Ostashkov and Starobielsk in the hope of gaining recruits. Lavrenti Beria, the NKVD chief replied, in the presence of Merkulov, his deputy and future successor, "unfortunately these men are no longer available. A great mistake was made". Long after the Nazi-sponsored investigation of Katyń, the Soviets sent their own commission, when they had recovered the area in their counter offensive. Its members were all Soviet citizens—not even their Lublin puppets were permitted to investigate the graves. Berling, though spoke on the site after it was reoccupied, criticizing the London Government for having appealed to the International Red Cross.

When Professor Kot asked Stalin about the Polish officers on November 14, 1941, Stalin remembered his order. He did not know it had been carried out and therefore made the telephone call. When a staff officer told him what had happened Stalin was silent and changed the subject refusing to discuss the matter further. There is no doubt that he knew the Polish officers were dead when a month later he was questioned by Sikorski and Anders and pretended concern for their welfare.

The officers massacred at Katyń were from the five thousand in a special camp at Kozielsk near Smolensk. No trace has ever been discovered of the four thousand Polish officers imprisoned in the camp at Starobielsk near Kharkov, nor of the six-and-a-half thousand at Ostashkov near Kalinin. These two camps had been "wound up" in April 1940, and no letters were received from these inmates or the Katyń officers after that date. According to historian Louis FitzGibbon the inmates from Ostashkov were sent to Viazma by train and killed at Bologoye, two hundred miles west of Yaroslavl. Those from Starobielsk were sent to Kharkov and shot at Dergachi, nearby. None were seen again, but reports circulated shortly afterwards that Polish officers had been locked inside barges which were then sunk in the White Sea. The officers' bodies discovered at Katyń had been shot between April and early June 1940.

In June 1945 in a communist dominated Poland with new boundaries, Mikolajczyk, newly returned, was approached by General Prosecutor Sawicki with the idea of staging a hearing to acquit the Russians of the Katyń murders. The documents were by then in the hands of the West. When Sawicki and the Minister of Justice Swiatkowski went to Moscow to outline their plan for a hearing, they were told to drop the matter and return to Warsaw. Katyń appeared in the indictment against the Nazi war leaders at Nuremberg, but there was no mention of it when the sentences were pronounced. Not until 1988 forty-five years after the discovery of the corpses in 1943 was it suggested that the Russians might be prepared to admit their responsibility for the Katyń massacre. This 'unsolved' atrocity had poisoned the Russians relationship with Poles throughout the world and even with their puppet government in Warsaw. The name of Katyń was shouted by protestors in Poland at every opportunity and the issue became a focal point for all those fighting Soviet control. The Soviets, trying to defuse the situation, wanted to dig up the piece of pavement in Warsaw treated as a shrine to the memory of Katyń. Edward Gierek in power in the seventies dissuaded them, he said the Poles would only choose another site.

With the break of diplomatic relations in 1943 between the London Government and Soviet Russia, the Polish Ambassador left Russia on May 5. Three days later the Soviet Government gave its approval to the formation of a Polish infantry division on their soil under the command of Colonel Zygmunt Berling, who had deserted from General Anders' army. This was cynically named after Tadeusz Kościuszko, the Polish hero famous for his defence of his country's independence against Russian imperialism. It was formed under communist leadership and was the only refuge for those Poles still in Russia who had been unable to reach the collecting centres for General Anders' army, which had left for Persia by September 1942. Berling was promoted to the rank of General by Stalin.

CHAPTER TWENTY

Journey to England

O N May 1, 1943, about three weeks after their arrival at Port Suez, Janek's group embarked on the Île de France, by then a British troop carrier. Normally equipped as a luxury liner for nine hundred passengers, it had been converted to transport about twelve thousand troops, of whom about two thousand were Poles— one thousand four hundred or so from the Khanaquin area. The rest were a mixture of Indian, New Zealand and South African regiments. Indian troops predominated and Janek was surprised to find that separate washing and lavatory facilities were provided for their use on board ship as well as in the transit camp. In order to make more room aboard after the ship was requisitioned following evacuation of Singapore, most of the luxurious furniture, fittings and library had been thrown overboard. Even so, there was little free space. Passageways were narrow and all the decks, halls, and cabins were filled at night with sleeping soldiers, tightly packed in rows. The space above was also filled with rows of hammocks slung between beams, added to the ship's structure. During the day all hammocks and beams were removed, all kits, mostly duffle bags, were stowed away against the walls and the whole floor space was freed for gymnastic exercise, twice daily and instruction periods in small groups. Meals were taken in three shifts in dining halls where most of the tables and chairs had been removed, leaving only a few for the staff and crew. Soldiers ate standing at long narrow benches of mid-chest height, and as they filed out after the meal they washed the dishes at rows of taps outside the mess hall.

Apart from gymnastics and instruction, there were tours of duty assigned to the soldiers on a rotating basis as deck watchman, lookouts for U-boats, cleaners or porters for supplying kitchens. For the first time Janek was able to try out his English learnt from the Russian textbook. The first day after embarkation he was sent with a group of Poles to deliver food supplies to the kitchens from the stores in the bowels of the ship. As the only one of them who knew even a smattering of English, he became an unofficial interpreter for the Poles assigned to act as porters. This position was made semi-official by the third officer in charge of stores and kitchens, Johnny de Millman. He asked Janek to accompany all groups of Poles assigned to kitchen duties and the two became good friends during this voyage. Janek's task was to repeat the instructions for various jobs in Polish. Before long he was given a permanent pass by arrangement with an English speaking Polish officer, so that he could improve his English in Johnny de Millman's cabin in the evenings. During these sessions which usually lasted two hours or so, Janek enjoyed a drink of whisky and practised his English with Johnny and his friends. Janek's participation in conversation was limited by his lack of vocabulary and he often wondered if his answers to questions made sense. He heard about Johnny's time in the Merchant Marine in the years before the war and also the war experiences of his friends, who provided vital supplies to England. Johnny had been torpedoed twice. Each time he had been rescued after a few days at sea and was back in service as soon as he recovered from his wounds. He described his family, aristocratically connected, scattered all over the world, with uncles and cousins in the Far East, Australia and South America, and an aunt in Durban, which they were then approaching.

While the Île de France was making its way down the eastern side of Africa, the Allies, who had landed inAlgeria and Tunisia the previous November were driving the last remaining Axis forces out of North Africa. On May 12, 1943, the Germans under Rommel, trapped between the American forces to the West and the British Desert Army, capitulated, thus laying open the way for a landing on the Continent of Europe.

Leaving Port Suez, the Île de France steamed without escort along the Red Sea and through the Indian Ocean reaching Durban on May 16. When the ship was docking, soldiers lined the railings to listen to songs sung by a lady dressed in white, alone on the quay, welcoming the troopship. Apparently she did this throughout the war to all troopships docking en route at Durban. During the three days there, Johnny took Janek ashore to visit his aunt, he was probably the only private among all the troops to be allowed ashore. It was during this trip that Janek bought a wrist watch to replace the one bartered for bread with a Russian soldier in 1939.

Later, in 1944, when Janek was in London, Johnny invited him to a family gathering in one of London's expensive hotels. Janek felt embarrassed to be clumping around in private's hobnailed boots over the carpets and marble staircases, and in battledress amidst the ladies in glittering dresses and jewels and the naval and army uniforms of high ranking officers. The English lessons in Johnny's cabin had not prepared Janek for this sort of occasion and his overall memory of the evening was one of misery and dismal failure.

From Durban the ship continued towards Cape Town. As they were rounding the Cape of Good Hope they saw a distant ship blown sky-high, clearly outlined against the red sky and setting sun. The alarm horns immediately blared all over the ship, which suddenly accelerated with maximum power from all engines. As she veered sharply to the left, the distant delayed boom of the explosion was heard. All soldiers took up their positions at "action stations" and for the next two hours or so remained on full alert. Meanwhile the ship zig-zagged at high speed towards darkness in the south. Next day routine drills, with detailed instructions for each unit in case of a torpedo attack, were introduced as well as survival techniques on rafts. For Poles, all instructions had to be translated word for word—taking twice as long as for the other troops. Next day Janek was taken ill. When he was recovering he looked through the porthole in the sick bay and was surprised to see snow falling. This continued for several days—the ship had taken a course far into the southern regions towards the Antarctic to avoid U-boat attack.

When Janek was fit enough to rejoin his unit on the deck, the weather was warm again. Soon the ship was moored in the bay outside Rio de Janeiro, with the Sugar Loaf and its huge statue resembling a cross, clearly visible from the deck. Nobody was allowed ashore, provisions were brought to the ship by boats of all types and sizes; loading took two or three days working round the clock. When they left Rio de Janeiro, the daily routine on board included frequent alarm practices, with anti-U-boat and anti-aircraft guns. During these practice alarms, those employed as porters or kitchen helps continued with their chores, but they were not allowed to use the lifts. If they were below deck when the alarm sounded it was impossible to know whether it was practice or genuine. Johnny advised Janek to tell his friends that they should watch the rats to know whether the torpedo danger was imminent. There were some magnificent specimens of rats, particularly around the heavy wire netting enclosure for frozen meat carcases buried in ice. Some of them, the size of rabbits, lined the massive beams and girders of the ship structure, watching the porters working. Johnny said that on both occasions when he was torpedoed, the rats left the ships about half an hour before the torpedo struck. Nobody had paid much attention to it the first time but when the same thing happened again, Johnny became convinced that rats' behaviour should be watched; he trusted their intuition.

Janek had one stroke of good fortune when he and Johnny discovered there were a few books still in existence from the ship's magnificent library. They had been packed in a couple of boxes when the fittings were being stripped and had somehow escaped being thrown overboard. Janek discovered several leather-bound gold-imprinted books in Polish, a real treasure trove of classic literature. He chose twelve volumes and in order to move them, he emptied his duffle bag of most of its contents, throwing these overboard at night and packed it with the books instead. His duffle bag proved to be enormously heavy when it had to be carried later on from the ship to the train and from camp to camp. When they settled in camp, Janek's companions were keen to borrow the books. But they returned them faithfully before any move—so that it was always Janek who had to carry the library. The next port of call after Rio was Freetown in Sierra Leone, West Africa, where they arrived on June 11. Re-provisioned as at Rio, the ship steamed towards New York, but was then diverted towards Iceland, zig-zagging in uneven but rapid moves, always unescorted and relying on speed to avoid U-boat attack. As she approached the British Isles she was provided with protective air-cover from a flying boat, and later from several planes flying in shifts. She docked safely on June 30 at Greenock.

Within a month the Polish cause suffered a severe double blow. On June 30, 1943 General Grot-Rowecki, Commander of the Home Army for the previous three years, was arrested by the Gestapo. He was taken to Berlin before the Underground movement had any chance to free him. Relatively unknown in the West, he was a prominent figure in occupied Poland, known universally by his pseudonym Grot. It was only discovered after the war that he had been executed on Himmler's order during the first week of the Warsaw uprising in August 1944. Attempts to free Grot-Rowecki by exchanging him for German generals captured by the British were rejected by the Nazis. They offered to exchange him for Rudolf Hess, Hitler's deputy, who was then in Britain, but this was not acceptable to the British Government. On July 4, 1943 tragedy struck again when General Sikorski, the Polish Prime Minister and Commander-in-Chief, was killed in a plane crash just after take-off from Gibraltar. The German occupiers in Warsaw, gloatingly broadcast the news of his death by loudspeakers to weeping crowds. There were rumours of sabotage, eagerly spread by the German propaganda machine, but no evidence was ever found to substantiate this. It appeared his death was a total accident, possibly caused in part by the plane being too heavily loaded for safe take-off from the short Gibraltar runway. General Tadeusz Bór-Komorowski was appointed Commander of the Home

Army to replace Grot-Rowecki in Warsaw. In London two men were needed to replace Sikorski; on July 8 General Kazimierz Sosnkowski, the former aide of Pilsudski, was appointed Commander-in-Chief and Stanislaw Mikolajczyk, leader of the Peasant Party in London, became Prime Minister on July 14. Unfortunately these two were at loggerheads politically and personally; neither had the influence nor experience of Sikorski on the world stage.

After Janek's group of Poles disembarked at Greenock, they travelled east by train through Glasgow to a camp at Auchicarroch. Two weeks later, with Janek's library promptly returned to his duffle bag—they moved to Elie in the county of Fife, where a few days later they heard of the death of General Sikorski. Parachute training now started in earnest. The various stages of this training requiring specific equipment, were divided between different camps, so they moved successively from Elie to Largo, then to Leslie. Towards the end of September they were given a three-day leave, which Janek spent in Edinburgh, sightseeing and browsing in bookshops. The additional books bought there, required the purchase of a small suitcase. The next day after his leave, this was discovered underneath his bunk by an inspection officer. Janek was reprimanded and told to remove it. He concealed the suitcase full of books on the roof of an outhouse, where it was less likely to be seen—a Polish private with English books under his bunk—it was practically a criminal offence in the army!

During training Janek became friendly with a young man of about his own age, who he understood came from the north-eastern part of Poland adjoining Byelorussia. He was very bright and athletic, but kept very much to himself. When he returned from his leave, spent in London, he confided to Janek that he was not a Pole at all but an Estonian university student of economics, son of the Estonian Ambassador to the USA. During his leave he had contacted the Estonian authorities in London who had promised to extricate him from the Polish Army. During the next few evenings the Estonian, whose name Janek never knew as he used a different name in the army, told Janek his story. When Russia incorporated Estonia together with Latvia and Lithuania after the Finnish war in 1939–40, he was arrested as a son of a government official. He spent months in prisons, mostly in Moscow, undergoing interrogation. One of the techniques used by the NKVD to force a confession, was to pronounce a sentence of execution and then fire with blank cartridges. When he passed out with the shock, he was brought round and interrogated immediately. During transport to a concentration camp he escaped and decided to travel away from European Russia towards China. He met a group of Poles trying to join Anders' Polish Army and decided to try his luck with them. He learnt enough Polish to become enlisted as a volunteer from the Byelorussian minority on his Russian-Polish. It was not until he reached England, that he could get in touch with his own Estonian people in London. He knew German and English perfectly, but never disclosed this to anybody in the Middle East, or during the journey to Scotland. In about two weeks his papers arrived and he showed Janek his Estonian passport. On the day Janek and his unit boarded the train for Ringway near Manchester, the young Estonian left as a civilian for London.

The Allied invasion of Sicily on July 10, 1943 provoked a crisis in the Italian government. On July 25, Italian dictator Mussolini was arrested and Marshal Badoglio took over the Italian Government. By August 17 Sicily had been liberated by the Allied forces. Soon afterwards at the Quebec conference between Churchill and Roosevelt, the future military policy of the war was discussed. Churchill was eager to attack Europe. "On its soft underbelly through the Balkans, the quickest way to central Europe", as he expressed it. However, the Americans, suspicious of Britain as an imperial power, were antagonistic to any plan that might result in perpetuating Britain's favourable trading position and imperialism. They foresaw themselves dividing Europe with the "non-imperialist" USSR into two spheres of influence, ironically along the line of the future Iron Curtain. They insisted on the main assault being through Northern France, which effectively ended any hope of Poland being liberated by non-communist forces. The campaign to liberate Italy was strictly limited in its objective, with the Allied Armies—US, British and Polish forces—forbidden to advance beyond the Po valley. On September 3, the fourth anniversary of Great Britain's declaration of war, the Allies landed in Calabria on the southern tip of Italy. Five days later Badoglio's Italian Government surrendered, but German forces immediately occupied the country and continued a stubborn military resistance.

The last stage of parachute training was carried out at Ringway, near Manchester where instruction was also given to personnel being parachuted into Poland. These included couriers like Jan Nowak, who needed to get back quickly to report to officials of the Underground state or volunteers such as Colonel Leopold Okulicki who had served with General Anders but had volunteered to return to duty with the Polish Underground Home Army.

Janek's training in 1943 involved two preliminary jumps from the gondola of a balloon tethered at about 500–700 feet above the ground, and five jumps from planes, including one at night. The weather was the deciding factor as to when the jumps could be made. If it was too windy the jumps had to be postponed, so that sometimes half a crew made a jump, while the rest were delayed for a day or more. There were some casualties suffered on landing, and more rarely due to parachutes not opening during descent. After the war Janek read that a five to six per cent casualty rate that year was average, but his "stick", the group of ten jumping together, was successful in completing all their jumps, with only minor mishaps. Janek suffered a slipped shoulder on one landing which was painful but he did not need to go to hospital.

Nearly a year later, the courier Jan Nowak suffered a severe fracture to a shoulder in March 1944 during training at Ringway. This made it impossible for him to return to Poland by parachute, where he was due to carry messages from the London Government to General Bór-Komorowski. He eventually returned by Air-Bridge, the occasional flight to underground-controlled airfields in occupied Poland. His flight was scheduled for July 1944 with the task of bringing back to England the parts of a V2 rocket that the Underground Army had captured intact and dismantled, ready for inspection by British intelligence.

Janek completed his parachute training in mid October 1943 and returned to his unit in Scotland where he and his colleagues were issued with the swooping eagle emblem of the Polish Parachutists. A few days after qualifying as a parachutist, Janek was told that his application to continue his studies, started six years before in Poland had been approved, and he was transferred to London.

On October 23, 1943 Janek arrived in London and after a night in a military hostel near Waterloo station he went to report to Professor Stanislaw Pluzànski, who organized the continuation of studies for the former technical university students. Accustomed to camp routine, Janek was up at 5am and caught the first underground train for Chelsea. Before 7am he knocked on the door of Professor Pluzànski's flat and after a lengthy delay a sleepy voice answered through the closed door. When Janek explained his business, the door opened and an elderly man in pyjamas told him to report to the office at Imperial College, Exhibition Road, to register at 9am. When Janek had completed the formalities for registration, Professor Pluzànski phoned Professor C. W. Dannatt, the acting head of the Royal School of Mines and told Janek to attend for an interview with him.

It was not until this interview that Janek realized how quickly the few months spent among Poles in Scotland had wiped out the effect of the English lessons in Johnny's cabin on the Île de France. When Professor Dannatt asked him what scheme of studies he had pursued in Poland, Janek replied that skiing in Poland was excellent, particularly around Zakopane. It was only the puzzled expression on Dannatt's face that made Janek realize that he had completely misunderstood the question. Despite this confusion Dannatt allowed Janek to attend classes and laboratories for the third year metallurgy course as an unregistered external student, until after the Christmas recess, when the situation would be reviewed.

For the first week or two Janek found classes completely bewildering. He could not understand what the lecturers were talking about or what he was supposed to do with the equipment, particularly in the electrical engineering laboratories. Having found a bed-and-breakfast room near the college, Janek bought books to rectify his electrical engineering deficiences. The result was that he had scarcely any money left from his £20 private's allowance to live on. For the next two months he lived on a diet of bread and herrings. At the end of the term just before Christmas, he took his first written exam in electrical engineering. Although he had never been able to carry out the experimental assignments in the laboratory, two months of hard work with English books enabled him to pass the written exam, mostly calculations, with a second class mark. This not only surprised his fellow students but was also quite unexpected by Professor Dannatt. As a result Professor Dannatt allowed Janek to continue with other courses as a Royal School of Mines student, which would enable him to acquire higher qualifications.

CHAPTER TWENTY-ONE

Teheran and Operation Burza

WHEN Germany invaded Russia, Churchill had declared that any enemy of Germany was an ally of Britian—no matter what their previous relations might have been. America's later entry into the war set up the Big Three—Britain, USSR and USA, led by Churchill, Stalin and Roosevelt—to decide on the progress of the war and the peace that was to follow.

In the autumn of 1943, Germany increased the pressure on Poles who had remained in their country and Himmler, head of the Gestapo, sent SS Major-General Kutschera to destroy the increasingly effective Polish resistance movement. During October, one hundred and seventy-seven civilians were publicly shot in Warsaw and there was similar repression in Kraków, Radom, Kielce, Przemyśl, and Rozwadow. Chance pedestrians would be rounded up, their names were posted and their release was promised if the families would disclose names and whereabouts of Underground members. General Bór-Komorowski decided that Kutschera should be tried by an Underground court; he was found guilty, and sentenced to death. Mass murders ceased after similar selective action against named Gestapo personnel. During the first six months of 1944, seven hundred and sixty-nine members of the Gestapo were sentenced and later executed by these courts. When informed of their sentence, many made desperate attempts to have themselves posted away from Poland. The care with which the Underground authorities chose their targets contrasted sharply with the indiscriminate killing of Germans by the few Soviet inspired partisans of communist sympathies who were operating on Polish soil. Their behaviour became a source of conflict as the Underground had learnt that indiscriminate activity was counter-productive and resulted in more hostages being taken from the local population. This division indicated the differences, even at this point, between the Home Army who looked to an independent Poland, and those elements who were ready to turn to Russia.

Even so, the Polish Government was anxious to repair the breach with the USSR. The Red Army's advance towards Poland made it essential that some form of liaison be established, so that the Home Army could co-operate in action against the German forces and hasten liberation. The Home Army were also anxious to be seen to be actively involved in Poland freeing herself, by her own efforts. It was now apparent that with Russia allied against Germany, the three big powers, the USA, Great Britain and the USSR, considered themselves competent to take decisions, not only on the progress of the war, but also on the future of Europe.

The British Foreign Minister, Anthony Eden, was shortly due to go to Moscow, to plan a summit conference at Teheran. Mikolajczyk, Polish Prime Minister in exile, met Eden on October 5 prior to this journey to ask him to help re-establish relations with the USSR. Eden said there was no hope of this unless the Polish Government was prepared to discuss post-war frontiers. Mikolajczyk pointed out that the recently signed Atlantic Charter, setting out the war aims and the peace hopes of the allies, expressly forbade any change of frontier without the population concerned being consulted. Mikolajczyk refused to let him negotiate away Poland's pre-war boundaries, which had been established by international agreement. Eden put this to his opposite number in Moscow, Molotov, who said that Russia was no longer interested in a London Government which included Commander in Chief General Sosnkowski and other members of whom they disapproved. He accused the Home Army of passivity and of directing action against Soviet partisans, a false accusation to be repeated by Stalin two months later to Churchill and Roosevelt at Teheran.

Polish forces were eager to take an active part in all the theatres of war. In Persia, General Anders' Polish Army, which Janek had now left, was ready for action. In November two and a half divisions were prepared for action in Italy. The 3rd Carpathian division left Persia on December 15 and was followed by other units during the next few months. The majority of the Second Corps was in Italy by February, though the last units did not reach there until mid April 1944. Some of this force was in action as early as February 2, 1944 on the eastern sector of the Italian front from the Adriatic Sea south of Ortona along the line of the River Sangro. The Polish units' lack of reserves, normally considered essential for operational fitness, caused concern to the British and American military authorities. Anders made light of this difficulty. He was confident that reinforcements would come from Poles taken by force to serve in the German Army, who would take the first opportunity to escape. He also thought they would be joined by volunteers flocking from the occupied and liberated territories, once it became known that there were Polish units fighting in the area. This concept, novel to the British and American military authorities, proved to be an accurate forecast. In fact, more volunteers came forward than could be easily accommodated.

Diplomatic battles were proving more difficult. On November 22, before the Teheran conference had been held, Mikolajczyk again met Eden and requested a meeting with Churchill. This was turned down because it was feared that Stalin might regard such a meeting as provocative, and use it as an excuse to back out from going to Teheran, which was his first scheduled sortie outside Soviet territory. It was becoming clear that the allies who now denounced the pre-war policy of appeasing Hitler, were prepared to accept a line of deferential appeasement towards Stalin. Amidst unusually strict security, he attended the conference at Teheran just across the USSR border, which opened on November 28, 1943. Polish post-war boundaries were not only discussed, but decisions were taken, in secret, on which the Polish Government in London were neither consulted nor informed. Once again, as so often before, Poland's interests were sacrificed to Russia.

Stalin had two aims—to create a buffer zone so that Soviet territory could never again be invaded, as it had been by Hitler, and to reclaim the territory that had once been ruled by Russia. Stalin was set to recreate the empire of the Tsars. He was determined to have the Curzon Line—a name it was more astute to use in place of the almost identical Molotov-Ribbentrop line—as the frontier. This followed the line of the River Bug. It took its name from Lord Curzon, who at the 1920 Versailles Peace Conference had proposed it as an armistice line, when the Bolshevik Army was on the point of capturing Warsaw. It was believed to represent the minimum ceding of territory that would persuade the new Soviet regime to suspend their assault on Western Europe. It had no more moral or legal validity as a frontier than the indefensible one imposed on Czechoslovakia in 1938 at Munich, and the motive in suggesting it in 1920 had been as discreditable. Pilsudski's unexpected miraculous victory at the Battle of the Vistula eliminated the need for such appeasement; the frontier agreed at the Treaty of Riga in 1921 was accepted by those concerned. Stalin however, could not resist the opportunity in 1939 of regaining the territory the USSR had so nearly won nineteen years before. With Nazi connivance he had seized so much of pre-war Poland's eastern provinces that it was easy for him then to be generous with another country's territory. He agreed that Poland, which would be subservient to him, should be compensated by a roughly equivalent

An historic picture of the Big Three: Stalin, Roosevelt and Churchill at Teheran in 1943.
Hulton Picture Company

area from Germany, east of the Oder. The Teheran conference ended on December 1; a communiqué notable for vagueness and brevity was not issued until five days afterwards. It later became apparent that the Teheran conference sealed Poland's post-war fate, though it was not until another summit conference at Yalta over a year later that most Poles were made aware of their betrayal.

Churchill was taken ill after the Teheran conference and was unable to meet Mikolajczyk until January 20, 1944. Churchill's words to Poland in 1940 had stirred the enslaved nation: "This war will be long and hard, but the end is sure. The end will reward all toil, all disappointment, all suffering, in those who faithfully serve the cause of European and world freedom." But now his reassurance that post-war Poland would be free from the Curzon Line to the Oder worried Mikolajczyk. He repeated that he was not empowered to agree to frontier changes and would have to consult his Government and the Underground. The Poles were united in resisting the loss of their eastern provinces, particularly the traditional Polish centres of Lwów and Wilno. The proposed award of part of Germany was no adequate recompense, nor could they see why so blatant a breach of the Atlantic Charter was to be imposed on them alone of all the Allied nations. There was less unity with regard to the possibility of improving relations with the USSR which appeared determined on enmity. The British Foreign Office dismissed these differences as the usual problem of squabbling Poles, and seemed unprepared to make allowances for the genuine difference of opinion represented by the different political parties in the Polish Government, the sort of difference that was regarded as perfectly normal in a British Parliament.

Ignorant of the Teheran decisions, the Polish Government in London and the Underground decided upon a new campaign, Operation *Burza*—Tempest. Units of the Home Army under General Bór-Komorowski were to rise selectively as the Red Army approached and as the German armies retreated, the Home Army would co-operate in Poland's liberation, acting as hosts to the Soviet forces. It was not clear how far the Red Army would go in accepting the Home Army as a partner, and prospects for co-operation with the USSR became even bleaker when on January 1, 1944, Boleslaw Bierut—a communist agent of the Comintern and loyal Stalinist—was clandestinely returned to Nazi-occupied Warsaw from Moscow. He announced that a new Polish Government was to be formed on the same day that a communist controlled Polish Committee of National Liberation was unveiled in Moscow. This was an alarming development, for it showed the Russians were not prepared to accept a government of Polish choosing, either underground or in exile. Two days later the Red Army crossed the pre-war eastern border of Poland.

In the West, General Anders flew to Italy to take command of the Polish 2nd Corps on February 6 and later that month a bombing attack preceded the Allied forces assault on Monte Cassino, which was soon to figure prominently in Polish military history.

In Great Britain Mikolajczyk replied to Churchill on February 15 that his Government could not agree to the dictatorial demand for the Curzon Line as its frontier. He was willing to consider a temporary demarcation line east of Lwów and Wilno for administration of the liberated territories. Churchill said that there could be no restoration of Polish-Soviet relations unless these demands were conceded.

Mikolajczyk replied that he was not empowered to surrender half of Poland. Churchill passed on the message to Stalin who rejected the Polish argument. A week later Churchill made a statement in the House of Commons revealing for the first time what had been discussed at Teheran—the plan to move Poland bodily to the West. Churchill maintained that Great Britain had guaranteed Poland's integrity and freedom but not its particular frontiers, particularly those in the east which had not been settled at Versailles. There were immediate protests from Poles everywhere. Romer, the Polish Foreign Minister, protested to the Foreign Office and the Underground Parliament—Council of National Unity unanimously rejected the Curzon Line proposals and Stalin's demand that Generals Sosnkowski and Kukiel should be dismissed.

In April, despite the ever-worsening political situation, Operation *Burza* began to operate in eastern Poland. The fate of the towns, Kowel and Wlodzimierz Wolynski in Polish Volhynia, were typical examples of early successful co-operation between the Home Army and the Red Army on the ground. When the political commissars arrived on the scene, however, this early comradeship was followed by arrests of Underground officers who were shot or imprisoned. Other ranks were conscripted into Berling's units or deported to camps in the USSR. A new systematic wave of extermination of the Polish nation started when the Red Army re-entered pre-war Polish territory in 1944. *Burza* became a synonym for betrayal.

The Home Army offered another campaign—Operation Jula, which had been suggested to Stalin over a year before—an offer he ignored—now it was put into operation on April 6. The Home Army blew up the bridge over the River Wislok on the Przeworsk-Rozwadow sector and paralysed all German rail traffic for a period of forty-eight hours as an example of what concerted action against the Germans could achieve. No co-operation from Soviet forces resulted, and doubtless the Soviet authorities were not best pleased to realize the strength of the partisan troops, but a message of thanks was received from Lord Selborne, the British Minister of Economic Warfare.

May 1944 became a famous date in Polish military history when the renewed battle for Monte Cassino began. The assault on this strongly defended point, which had resisted attacks from many units of the Allied Armies, was now entrusted to the Poles. On May 17, Monte Cassino fell to the Polish forces. The Home Army in Poland, at bay with difficulties of non co-operation from the advancing Red Army, was much encouraged by news of their comrades' success in Italy. Three days later the Home Army had a spectacular but private success of their own, when they captured intact one of the new experimental V2 Rockets which had landed on the bank of the River Bug; with the help of the local Underground they hid it successfully from the searching German forces. It was dismantled, examined and photographed, and the information transmitted to London.

On May 21, General Okulicki parachuted into Poland to rejoin the Home Army. He had been a prisoner of the Russians after the 1939 campaign, became Chief of Staff to Anders when released in 1941 under the "amnesty", and later volunteered to return to the hazardous life of an officer in the Home Army, knowing the risks he ran. Less than a year afterwards, in tragic circumstances, he was again a prisoner of the Russians.

June that year marked an important stage in World War II. On June 6—D Day—Europe was invaded by the Allied Armies. Two days earlier Rome had been liberated after the road towards it had been cleared by the capture of Monte Cassino. Mikolajczyk had broadcast an appeal to the Polish Underground in France to rise with the Maquis. On the political front, Mikolajczyk visited the USA and met Roosevelt who boasted that he had come to a better understanding with Stalin than Churchill had at Teheran. Evidence for his power to influence the Russian dictator was somewhat belied by the fact that Stalin refused Roosevelt's request for him to receive Mikolajczyk. Roosevelt, at this meeting, assured Mikolajczyk of his support but omitted to tell him that he had already agreed with Stalin at Teheran on the Curzon Line for Poland's eastern frontier. Stalin subsequently sent an invitation to Mikolajczyk for the first week in August but almost certainly only because it then suited him. During discussions on the possibility of Poland receiving territory from Germany after the war, Oskar Lange, an American Pole, later to be Ambassador to the USA from the Polish Provisional Government, quoted Stalin's reply to a question about the possibility of Germany taking revenge in parts of their country awarded to Poland: "Germans from there must be expelled—we will find room for three million in Siberia". A chilling threat, to be taken seriously from one who had unequalled experience in deporting whole populations.

The naivety of the United States in its dealings with the USSR at this time was typified by the visit of Vice-President Wallace in 1944, when he was taken to see one of the notorious gold-mining camps at Kolyma. Adam Galinski, a prisoner under Stalin at Vorkuta and later Kolyma, has described how the Kolyma camp was prepared for the visit of the US Vice-President. Guard towers were taken down, barbed wire was removed and the prisoners taken away, and replaced by security men. Wallace wrote "The Kolyma miners are big husky men who came out to the Far East from European Russia—the spirit and meaning of life in Siberia today is certainly not to be compared to that of the old exile days."

The Polish 2nd Corps continued their advance up Italy taking Ancona on July 17. Three days later came news of an attempt on Hitler's life. The following day in Warsaw, Bór-Komorowski and Jan Jankowski, the Polish Deputy Premier, supported by General Okulicki, made a fateful decision. They determined to deploy the Home Army for a once and for all rising in Warsaw, so that the city would be free and independent as the rest of the country was liberated from the Germans. The plan was approved by the leaders of the Polish Government in London, who instructed that those on the spot must decide the actual timing of the rising.

The Red Army had just captured Lublin; and on July 23 the communist sponsored committee of unknown Poles arrived there to assume power. Operation *Burza* had so far failed, as all the Home Army units that had come out of hiding had been arrested by the Russian forces. Instead of revealing their allies, the Russians appeared to consider that Operation *Burza* had conveniently uncovered those Poles most capable of leadership, whom it would be best to remove before they could assume control in the face of the Russian advance.

Nevertheless, it was hoped that a successful rising in Warsaw would encourage military co-operation and that those in charge of the Red Army would not be so foolish as to spurn the opportunity of liberating the Polish capital, when bridgeheads over the Vistula had been secured by the Home Army.

CHAPTER TWENTY-TWO

The Warsaw Rising

BEFORE the agreed date arrived, the Home Army performed another invaluable service to Britain and the Allies.

The courier Jan Nowak, arrived in Warsaw from London by Air Bridge, the least often used form of communication with occupied Poland, with instructions for Bór-Komorowski. Flying in a Dakota from Brindisi on July 25, he landed at a secret airfield in Poland under Home Army control. The plane had the important secret task of taking back to London the parts of the new V2 rocket, captured two months earlier by the Home Army. On take-off the weight of the cargo caused the plane wheels to sink into the soft ground at the first attempt. Locals managed to find enough material to enable the wheels to turn for a successful take-off just before German troops arrived. Passengers on the return flight included the veteran Socialist leader Tomasz Arciszewski, who was shortly to succeed Mikolajczyk as Premier in London.

Only a few days later on July 28 a Moscow communiqué reported that Russian Commander Marshal Konstantin Rokossovsky's troops were approaching Warsaw. Next day, at 8.15pm Kościuszko Radio Station in Moscow urged the Poles in Warsaw to rise. On July 31 the order was given by Bór-Komorowski. Too late for it to be countermanded, he learnt that an unexpected German counter-attack had begun with Panzer reinforcements. The rising began on August 1 at 5pm. The people of Warsaw were ready to fling themselves into this last thrust to rid themselves of the German occupation. On the same day on the Western front the 1st Polish armoured division became involved in France on the Falaise sector. They fought there for the next few weeks with the plight of Warsaw constantly in their thoughts.

Mikolajczyk, with Romer, his Foreign Minister, and Professor Stanislaw Grabski, Speaker of the Parliament in Exile, flew to Moscow, at Stalin's invitation and arrived there on July 30, knowing that the rising was imminent. He trusted the timing was after all

*Polish Government in exile, Premier Stanislaw Mikolajczyk, second left, seated next
to Foreign Minister Tadeusz Romer.*   Hulton Picture Company

favourable and that if the Poles could offer Stalin a Warsaw free of
Germans, they might be given in exchange co-operation over the
choice of Polish leaders and over the post-war frontiers. Yet before he
even set foot in Moscow, Mikolajczyk was becoming painfully aware
that these hopes were doomed to disappointment. At stops in Cairo
and Teheran, en route for Moscow, he was told that the Lublin Poles
had secretly agreed with Stalin that the administration of liberated
territories would be in the hands of the Red Army, Home Army
members would be surrendered to them and deported to Russia and
the Curzon Line would be accepted by them. When Mikolajczyk
heard of this treachery, he was tempted to turn back. But he
continued his journey when Churchill and Roosevelt sent him copies
of wires urging Stalin to change his attitude to the London
Government. Mikolajczyk and his colleagues met a bleak reception.
Molotov ignored the messages from London and Washington and
insisted that Mikolajczyk must meet the Lublin Poles before seeing
Stalin.

When Mikolajczyk met Stalin on August 3 he had news that the
Home Army had seized control of a large part of Warsaw. He could

reasonably have expected that this splendid news would have given him a trump card in his negotiations. But Stalin accused the Home Army of not wanting to fight the Germans and he even denied that any rising was taking place. Mikolajczyk received no support from the Lublin Poles who also claimed that Polish communist Boleslaw Bierut in Warsaw had reported no fighting. In fact, it turned out that he had not been there. Wanda Wasilewska was no help either when she said the Curzon Line was "most just for Poland".

The people of Warsaw had no doubts that the rising was taking place. They were locked in struggle with the occupying German troops and their hostilities were tearing the city apart. The Home Army had planned a sudden surprise attack which would win them control of the city for several days, giving time for the Red Army to swing in with reinforcements and equipment. At no time did the Home Army believe it had arms and ammunition for more than a few days' combat. At first all went well, in accordance with the news Mikolajczyk heard in Moscow. The German forces were driven out and once more after five years the people of Warsaw breathed the heady air of freedom. It was a magic time. Then the impetus slowed down.

The Germans inflicted a defeat—the first in months—on the Soviet forces outside the city so that the Red Army fell back for a brief moment unable to help the city. Then, instead of immediately re-forming and preventing the German Army from returning to Warsaw, the Red Army waited and watched. They did absolutely nothing, directing no fire against the German Army, sending no planes against its gathering strength and making no attempt to send arms and munitions into the city which had begun the rising with supplies to last no more than a week. As they waited, they were able to watch the German forces systematically destroy Warsaw.

On August 12 Churchill appealed to Stalin to help the Warsaw fighters. Stalin's response was to send a message to Mikolajczyk that the Warsaw action was a thoughtless adventure and he refused to take any responsibility for it. Two days later Churchill and Roosevelt sent a joint appeal to Stalin for the help that only he was in a position to give. Again a curt refusal came two days later. On August 20 there was yet a further request from the Western Allies, with no response. Not until September 12—Day 43—did Stalin allow some American bombers to land at Soviet airfields after dropping supplies for Warsaw.

It was only gradually that the significance of the tragic events unfolding in Warsaw gained publicity in the West. A pamphlet published in London on August 25, *Warsaw—A Warning, Zygmunt*

Litynski, described the tardiness and brevity with which the news was published in the British Press, which devoted its limited space to news from other fronts. The contrast with Paris, which had been liberated on August 24 by the Americans, was most marked. The Parisians had risen and were immediately assisted by forces near at hand. Bór-Komorowski contrasted this with his situation in Warsaw, where the Russians were at hand but immobile on the opposite bank of the Vistula. He had little ammunition and had not expected his supplies to last for more than a week to ten days. Relying on capturing enemy material and supplies being dropped by air could only briefly prolong the Warsaw resistance.

On September 8 the first V2 bombs fell on London; the authorities had been forewarned of their limited capability from the material sent by the Polish Underground. Three days later Bór-Komorowski appealed yet again to Rokossovsky for supplies and co-ordination with the Home Army. Churchill and Roosevelt also sent yet another joint message to Stalin urging help for the Warsaw garrison. The RAF, including Polish crews made valiant attempts to drop supplies from Italy, but there was no practical way of doing this effectively while the use of Soviet airfields for refuelling was, astonishingly, denied the Allies despite repeated appeals. It was not until September 12, four days after the latest joint appeal from Roosevelt and Churchill, that America's Flying Fortresses were granted grudging permission to land on Russian airfields after dropping supplies. It was another six days before the weather was suitable and the supplies were ready, by which time Warsaw's forces were doomed. Morale was raised in Warsaw when the planes appeared but most of the dropped supplies failed to reach the defenders in the reduced area held by the Home Army.

In Western Europe the ill-fated Arnhem operation had begun on September 17 with units from the Polish Parachute Brigade taking part. Four days later the main body of Polish Parachutists under General Sosabowski were in action at Arnhem, knowing that Warsaw was dying for lack of help. On September 25 the forces north of the Rhine at Arnhem had to retreat south with the failure of this operation.

On the Vistula on September 22 Berling's unit with the Red Army made a sortie towards the Warsaw garrison, without artillery cover. Berling was removed from command and sent to Russia for "further training". He later returned as Head of the Scientific Institute for the Army. The Germans made use of their own air power to reduce the city to ruins, then sent in tanks and artillery dividing the city into sections and destroying them one by one. The Poles crawled underground and crept through the sewers to another district, to fight once more.

Hoping every day that help would come, Bór-Komorowski's forces held out for an astonishing sixty-three days. When help did arrive it was too little and too late. An appeal for the Parachute Brigade had to be turned down on logistical grounds. The RAF would not contemplate an action that would have involved towing slow defenceless gliders across German occupied Europe without fighter protection. Bór-Komorowski's request for the Parachute Brigade was certainly unrealistic, so it has been used as evidence that he was impractical and therefore culpable for the failure of the rising. Such an assessment takes no account of his desperate situation—his forces were making extraordinary sacrifices and facing certain destruction, only able to move from one part of Warsaw to another via the sewers. He could reasonably have supposed that it would have been possible to launch the Parachute Brigade from the Soviet held airfields nearby. On September 10—Day 41—the Germans began a final clearing-up operation. Systematically all civilians, men, women and children, were rounded up and shot. Hospitals were burned, with doctors, nurses and patients still inside. All remaining buildings were levelled, so that no settlement could ever exist there again. The few surviving troops were marched away as prisoners. Some kind of resistance went on until October 2—Day 63—and then all resistance was at an end.

The Warsaw Rising was perhaps the most desperate attempt by the people of Poland to put their passionate desire for independence and their patriotism, above everything. Much has been written on the rising and with the benefit of hindsight some writers criticised those who took the decision that was followed by such tragedy. It is now fashionable to assume that someone must always be held to blame for any terrible event, but it is as likely that the tragedy was unavoidable. Those who were in Warsaw just before the rising have described an atmosphere of suppressed excitement and determination on the part of the population, which made a rising inevitable. The leaders on the spot believed they had no option but to commit the Home Army to support the population. Criticism of the timing and lack of liaison with the Russians should be addressed to those who controlled the Red Army and who made such liaison impossible. No regret for the decision to rise was ever expressed afterwards by survivors who took part.

Yet the failure of the rising, whatever its cause, fatally weakened the Poles' negotiating position in relation to Stalin. The autumn of 1944 saw every advantage lost. On August 7 Bierut reappeared in Moscow and offered Mikolajczyk the position of Prime Minister in a new

The market was the scene of the heaviest fighting. The telephone exchange can be seen in flames.
Hulton Picture Company

Warsaw is reduced to ruins. *Hulton Picture Company*

government, if he lent his support to Bierut's bid to be President. Mikolajczyk, already Premier of the legally constituted government, met Stalin again on August 9. Instead of holding the trump card, the Army rising in Warsaw, he found himself in the position of a supplicant, seeking help for the now beleaguered Home Army. However he was able to hand Stalin a message from a member of the Red Army, a Colonel Konstanty Kalugin who was in Warsaw and attempting to co-operate with the Home Army. This contained an appeal for help which Stalin ignored, along with all other evidence that did not suit him. Edward Osóbka-Morawski, one of the Lublin Poles, even suggested that Bór-Komorowski was not really in Warsaw. Next day Mikolajczyk left Moscow.

Mikolajczyk's Government, having failed to secure military help for the fighters in Warsaw, submitted a new plan on August 30 supported by the Underground. This was for a future Polish administration, consisting of representatives from the four main parties and the Lublin group. Britain and America accepted in principle. There was no answer from Russia who passed it on to the Lublin group who had no intention of sharing power with rivals, even had the Kremlin permitted it. Disagreements between Mikolajczyk and Sosnkowski

October 3, 1944. The survivors leave Warsaw.   *Hulton Picture Company*

came to a head in September and on the last day of the month, the Commander-in-Chief was dismissed. On October 2, lack of food, water and ammunition in Warsaw was causing the resistance to collapse; Bór-Komorowski learnt as he surrendered that he had been appointed Commander-in-Chief. One of his last acts was with his deputy Jankowski to send four couriers to London to report on the Warsaw Rising. Nowak was the only one to succeed in reaching London. Bór-Komorowski appointed General Okulicki as his own successor and he took over as new Commander of the Home Army. Unknown to the Gestapo, he slipped out of the ruins of Warsaw and remained underground to reorganize the shattered Home Army.

As Bór-Komorowski, together with the survivors of the Home Army garrison became prisoners of war—a status granted them because the Western Allies had proclaimed them to be part of the Allied Forces—he recognized that his appointment as Commander-in-Chief was a tribute to the Warsaw defenders. The last radio message from Warsaw said: "We were treated worse than Hitler's satellites, worse than Italy, Romania, Finland." Moscow Radio's comment as the resistance was finally crushed was dismissive: "Traitors! They surrendered to the Germans."

The Warsaw Rising was a tragedy, not only in its outcome, with the civilian population deported, the deaths of so many Poles and the later razing of Warsaw on Hitler's orders. It was also a defeat for the Home Army and it marked the end of the London Polish Government in Exile's influence on events in Poland. After this, Stalin met no further opposition of any note to his plans.

A German historian Hans von Krannhals later wrote: "Here and nowhere else the 'Cold War' between East and West commenced."

CHAPTER TWENTY-THREE

The Underground Leaders Betrayed

JANEK was joined in London by another former student from Akademia Górnicza, an army lieutenant called Staszek Wróbel. They collaborated in their studies and lived in the same digs. As an officer, Staszek had a much higher allowance and he also had a much better knowledge of English than Janek, as he had been in Scotland for over three years. They both successfully passed their exams in June 1944, taken while flying bombs were exploding nearby, and Professor Dannatt suggested they applied to London University for a Bachelor of Science degree at the same time as the Associateship of the Royal School of Mines (ARSM). So in January 1945 they both took the final university exam which comprised practical and theoretical assignments. It was an incredibly tough test and the work took twelve hours a day for five days and was supervised by outside examiners from other colleges of London University. Both passed this final exam with very high marks and Janek was awarded half of the Glorney Scholarship towards a Ph.D. Throughout his studies at the Royal School of Mines Janek had to apply every three months for an extension of his leave. When he graduated with a B.Sc. and applied to continue for a Ph.D. the army authorities balked at the suggestion and ordered Janek back to camp. Fortunately, Professor Pluzànski and his colleagues were able to have this order countermanded and Janek was allowed to remain in London on condition that he also studied to complete the requirements for the Polish Degree—Dipl. Ing. For the next two years he and Staszek Wróbel remained in London, living and working together, until they completed the Polish Degree in the early part of 1947. The changing political and military situation during these years materially affected decisions that Janek and his fellow Poles subsequently made about returning to their homeland.

Those in Western Europe, and certainly in Britain, were largely oblivious of the fact that, as their hopes rose with the approach of victory, so simultaneously Polish hopes began to decline. It became progressively clearer to the Poles that there was to be no victory for their country, but only submission to Stalin and his puppets. This was vividly demonstrated by an incident in 1945 when a Polish officer, goaded by the newsreel commentary eulogizing the Red Army "liberating" Warsaw, strode out of an English cinema, shouting "This is no liberation, only another form of occupation". For the young English lady whom he was escorting, obliged to follow with their coats, it was a memorable if embarrassing lesson of different perceptions. Exiled Poles rarely displayed such lack of restraint to their hosts; usually their natural well-mannered politeness hid the suffering and misfortunes that all had endured. They all realized how fortunate they were to have survived and reached freedom, compared with the fate of the great majority of their colleagues who had either perished in Russia, or worse still, had been left behind in slave labour camps.

An inevitable consequence of the collapse of the Warsaw Rising at the beginning of October 1944 was the waning influence of Poland's London Government. There was also a marked change of attitude from the Lublin Poles towards the Home Army. After army officers had been eliminated they hoped it might prove a ripe recruiting ground. They soon discovered that the rank and file were also irredeemably anti-communist, as was the Polish population. From October onwards, opposition to the Home Army in Poland was orchestrated by Bierut and Wladislaw Gomulka from the part of the country then controlled by the Soviet Union. On October 13, less than two weeks after the collapse of the Warsaw Rising, Mikolajczyk was summoned to Moscow for a meeting with Churchill, Eden, Averell Harriman, observer for the US, Stalin and Molotov. Ostensibly this was to discuss the plan proposed by the London Poles on August 30 for a Provisional Government which would include the Lublin group as well as the four main parties represented in the London Government. Because Mikolajczyk and his colleagues refused to accept the Curzon Line, no agreement was reached. Molotov then revealed to a shocked Mikolajczyk that this had been already decided as the future frontier by the Big Three at Teheran a year before, where Poland had not been represented. Churchill confirmed the arrangement, and suggested an agreement to a temporary frontier, only to be vetoed by Stalin; the frontier had been fixed.

At a private meeting immediately afterwards, Churchill and Mikolajczyk had a heated exchange during which the Polish Premier asked permission to parachute into Poland: "It's better to die fighting for independence than to be hanged later by the Russians in full view

of your Ambassador," he said. He reluctantly agreed to recommend
the Curzon Line to his colleagues with the loss of Wilno, but only if
Lwów and the areas containing potash and oil deposits could be
retained. Churchill passed this suggestion on to Stalin and proposed
Mikolajczyk as leader of a new Provisional Government. Stalin
rejected both propositions.

On October 27 Churchill told the House of Commons that he still
hoped Mikolajczyk could return to lead a new Government in Poland.
By now, Mikolajczyk's position as Premier was no longer tenable, his
Cabinet in London considered he had already given away too much.
On November 24 Mikolajczyk, in a minority, resigned as Premier and
was succeeded by Tomasz Arciszewski, the Socialist leader. He had
spent five years in occupied Warsaw before being flown out by
Operation Bridge, with the V2 parts, the previous July.

The Polish Government in London had often requested that a
British military mission should be sent to report on the activities of the
Home Army, both to counter slanderous Russian propaganda and to
emphasize the need for arms supplies which other underground
organizations in Western Europe had been receiving. To avoid
offending Stalin, this had been repeatedly shelved. The Warsaw
Rising, with its clear evidence of Soviet hostility to the Home Army,
clinched the decision to send a mission, but only when it was too late
to be of any use. On December 26 three British Officers parachuted
into Poland to make contact. It was not until January 3, 1945, that the
British Military Mission, sent so belatedly, succeeded in linking up
with General Okulicki, as the Polish Underground State lay in ruins.
The Home Army was ordered to disband shortly afterwards, when, on
January 19, General Okulicki decided that as the German Army was
now retreating from Polish territory, there was no longer any reason
for it to exist. This was a last attempt to prevent Home Army
personnel being deported to Siberia by the Russian occupiers.

On the last day of 1944, the Lublin Committee had been instructed
by the Kremlin to proclaim itself the Provisional Government of
Liberated Democratic Poland and on January 5, 1945 was recognized
by Russia. President Edward Beneš of Czechoslovakia, on January 31
was the first of the Allied Governments in exile to dissociate itself
from its fellow governments in exile and recognize the Lublin
Government. It was to do the Czechs no good in the end; subservient
behaviour then was not enough to protect them against takeover in the
future.

As though to accentuate the tragedy being enacted in Poland, the
Germans acting on Hitler's orders began systematically to raze
Warsaw as the Red Army prepared to advance again. The last great

Soviet offensive was launched unexpectedly early on January 12 with winter still hampering normal military activity. Stalin was determined to ensure physical occupation of Poland before the Yalta conference, because even though he had been pledged control, he did not trust the Allies to fulfil their promises. The Russians, accompanied by Berling's units entered the empty ruins of Warsaw on January 17. All the surviving population had been deported and they found a desolate wilderness. Poland's capital, which could have been captured from the Germans in September 1944 and its population spared death or suffering, endured the greatest destruction of any capital city during the whole war.

On January 19 the Germans retreated from Kraków, the only city of any size to escape major war damage, the same day that General Okulicki issued his order disbanding the Home Army. It was not until February 9 that the London Government confirmed this order; but many units remained in existence hoping to resist sovietisation of Poland. The Russian advance was now swift and almost unopposed. By January 23 Red Army units had reached the Oder and Poland was in their grasp.

Next day, Jan Nowak met Mikolajczyk, now in opposition to discuss hopes for rallying the Polish nation around the former Premier in Warsaw. His hopes for assistance from the Western Allies proved in the end to be unfounded and his efforts to salvage something from the Teheran decisions, so soon to be endorsed at Yalta, were also to end in failure.

The Yalta conference from February 4–11, was seen as a major tragedy for Poland. Roosevelt was now mortally ill and with only two months to live he appeared a very different figure from the one seen at Teheran, little more than a year before. Decisions made by Roosevelt, Stalin and Churchill at Yalta had already been agreed in principle at Teheran. The USSR's 1940 annexation of the Baltic states, Estonia, Latvia and Lithuania were meekly ratified and a free hand was conceded to the Soviets in eastern Europe. It was agreed that a Provisional Government should be set up in Poland, with representatives to be selected by the foreign ministers of the Big Three powers, to be followed by "supervised free and unfettered elections". Few Poles had any illusions about how these elections would be conducted or what the results would be. The Yalta decisions were published immediately, unlike those of Teheran, and there was bitter reaction from Poles everywhere. The strongest protests came from the Polish 2nd Corps in Italy, the great majority of whom came from eastern Poland which was now to be handed to Russia. Their homeland had been surrendered to the USSR, and they felt there was nothing left to fight for. Anders, deeply concerned about the morale of his men, consulted with Allied commanders about withdrawing the 2nd Corps from the front line; loyalty to the military needs of the Allies precluded this.

On February 20 Anders flew to London. He met Churchill the next day, who defended the Yalta decisions. On February 24 Anders talked to Mikolajczyk who was now a private citizen and pleaded with him not to go to Poland and join the Lublin Poles. He warned Mikolajczyk that they were traitors and he could well end up in his old cell in the Lubianka Prison. Mikolajczyk disregarded these warnings. He was adamant, some would say obstinate in believing that the only hope for saving any Polish independence was to go and try and win an election there. Anders, who had observed communist organized elections on Polish territory in October 1939 when he was in prison, predicted correctly that any elections would be rigged.

On March 5 forty-four countries were invited to San Francisco for the inaugural meeting of the United Nations. Poland, for whose defence Great Britain and France had entered the war, was not invited. Next day, in Poland, invitations were sent from the Russians to Okulicki, Jankowski and other underground leaders to meet General Semen Ivanov, commander of the 1st Byelorussian front. The meeting was to take place in "liberated" Poland and there were guarantees of personal safety. They were to be considered for inclusion in the Provisional Government in Poland, but Okulicki, deeply suspicious of the Russian invitation, was under orders from Anders to stay in hiding. On March 25 the Council of National Unity—the Underground Parliament in Poland—faced with the fait accompli of Yalta, agreed that Okulicki should meet General Ivanov, the Russian commander. They clung to the hope that the Allies would ensure that the promised elections would be democratic and the communists would be defeated. Despite his suspicions, Okulicki, with Jankoswki, and Kazimierz Pużak speaker of the Underground Parliament came out of hiding to meet Ivanov. On March 28 a further thirteen Underground leaders also emerged to join the meeting, having received the same guarantees of safety.

All sixteen Underground leaders disappeared. There was some consternation in the West, particularly in Polish circles, but the excitement of the approaching end of the war in Europe soon relegated this news to the back pages. Three days later, on March 31, the NKVD arrested Wincenty Witos, the veteran former Peasant Party leader, who was also on the list for possible inclusion in the Provisional Government. He was taken to Brest-Litovsk but was soon released in very poor health. Even then, when the outlook for Polish hopes was so bleak, the Polish Government in London made a last unsuccessful attempt to discuss frontiers with Stalin.

On April 6 Anders flew back to Italy to lead the last battle of the 2nd Corps. Three days later the Spring offensive opened on the Italian front with the British 8th Army attacking. Polish forces under General Klemens Rudnicki liberated Bologna on April 21. A week later the Germans in Italy surrendered and on April 30, Hitler committed suicide in a bunker in Berlin. In the midst of these dramas, Roosevelt was succeeded by Harry S. Truman.

On the Western front the Polish 1st Armoured division advanced from Breda to Wilmshaven and accepted the German capitulation there. At Niederlangen they liberated a camp of their fellow countrymen, soldiers of the Home Army who had fought in the Warsaw Rising. Haren on the river Ems was handed over to Polish units, and existed as a small exclusively Polish enclave for two years in defeated Germany, a haven for Polish refugees. During this time it was renamed Maczków after the local Polish commander.

On May 3 Eden was told by Molotov in San Francisco, that the sixteen Polish Underground leaders, missing since March 28, had been arrested and awaited trial in Moscow. Eden was particularly disturbed because the Allies had provided the names of the Underground leaders in good faith as persons suitable to participate in the Provisional Government. He refused to continue further negotiations on the Polish question.

On May 7 peace was proclaimed in Europe. But once again, as in 1918, fighting was to continue in Poland for another two years. At the end of the First World War the Poles had been fighting to secure their eastern boundaries from Bolshevik attack and there had been a sense of exultation which permeated the newly independent nation. In 1945 the situation was entirely different. The fighting had degenerated to a civil war between guerilla forces who had refused to disband when the Home Army had been stood down, and the communist controlled security forces seeking to establish power. It was merely a prelude to eventual submission to the new unknown imposed leaders from Russia and the loss of Poland's pre-war independence. To add to the confusion and misery in post-war Poland, all remaining Poles who had escaped earlier deportations by the Soviet authorities in 1940 and 1941 from the eastern provinces, were transported from their homes to the so-called recovered territories. These had been arbitrarily awarded to Poland from Germany, and became the focal point of further large-scale deportations.

The Yalta decision to set up a Provisional Government presupposed preliminary discussions about who was to be invited to take part. The disappearance and arrest of the Underground leaders was an ominous portent. Before the foreign ministers of the Yalta Big Three had decided or even discussed which Poles should be invited to participate, Stalin had already signed a treaty of friendship with Bierut, who had no authority to act on behalf of Poland. After Roosevelt's death, Truman, new to this problem, sent his representative Harry Hopkins to Moscow to break the deadlock that had arisen because of Russian determination to exclude Mikolajczyk. Hopkins submitted to Russian pressure that the Lublin Poles should dominate the Provisional Government and failed to get any assurance about the sixteen arrested leaders. But Mikolajczyk was seen by Lublin as an inescapable choice if recognition were to be granted by the Western powers.

Mikolajczyk received his invitation to go to Moscow on June 12. His decision to attend was prompted by two meetings with Churchill, who argued that though it was now clear that Russia intended to rule Poland by force, the absence of support in Poland for the Lublin group gave grounds for hope. He said that with properly conducted elections, Mikolajczyk should achieve power. The British and Americans would never accept the result of the forthcoming show trial of the sixteen, and he urged Mikolajczyk to "go for the sake of Poland; they need you". Mikolajczyk seeing Poland now as a nation without boundaries, believed it essential that an independent voice, separate from the subservient Lublinites, should be heard on Poland's behalf at the forthcoming Potsdam conference.

On June 16 he flew to Moscow where the Provisional Government was to be formed. Next day Mikolajczyk met the Lublin Poles, but both his proposals and the almost identical ones brought by the acting Peasant leader in Poland, Dr Wladyslaw Kiernik, were rejected during the next days by Bierut and Osóbka-Morawski. As though to emphasize the pressures being put on the "negotiators", the show trial of the sixteen Underground leaders opened in Moscow on June 21. After eleven weeks of brutal NKVD interrogation, General Okulicki, suffering from sleep deprivation and desperate ill-health, retained sufficient strength to castigate the trial publicly. He was sentenced to ten years imprisonment and Jankowski was given an eight-year sentence. Both were to die in Russian captivity.

Mikolajczyk pleaded with Bierut to ask Stalin to release the sixteen Underground leaders after they had been sentenced. Bierut's chilling reply was that it would make Stalin angry. "Besides we don't need these people in Poland now," he said. When Mikolajczyk made a final plea via Molotov, he was told that Stalin was too busy to see him. Mikolajczyk returned to Warsaw with his new colleagues on June 27 and stood on Polish soil for the first time since leaving Poland in 1939. It seemed he was the only one to be aware of how the Poles had been humiliated in agreeing to the Russian-imposed Government at the very moment when their compatriots were being taken away to serve sentences imposed at the show trial. When they arrived at Okecie airport outside Warsaw, a large crowd had gathered to greet the curious mixture of strangers and old friends who were to govern them until elections could be held. Bierut told Mikolajczyk to address the crowd as *obywatale*—citizens, an older revolutionary greeting than "comrades". Mikolajczyk chose the more Christian "My sisters and brothers", before promising to try and restore a free, sovereign and independent Polish republic. Shortly after his arrival he called on the ailing leader of the Peasant Party, Wincenty Witos, whom he was distressed to see, had never recovered from those few traumatic days in the hands of the NKVD. The ensuing story of repression and terror against Mikolajczyk's Peasant Party and all other non-communist groups was observed helplessly by Janek and his fellow exiles in London.

At the end of June the Underground Political organization, loyal to the London Government, was formally disbanded. Five days later Poles in Russia were given until November 1 to file applications for repatriation. At the same time Great Britain recognized the Warsaw Provisional Government and withdrew recognition from the London Government. This created an anomalous situation for the Polish Army, mainly in Great Britain but also with sizeable detachments in Italy, Germany and the Middle East whose members were still bound by oaths of loyalty to the legitimate President in London.

Bierut and Mikolajczyk were among Polish representatives at the Potsdam conference. Great Britain was represented at the later stages by Prime Minister Clement Attlee and Foreign Secretary Ernest Bevin after Churchill had been defeated at the general election in July. Bierut obeyed Kremlin orders to alienate the Western governments by accepting Poland's client status to the USSR and in mid-August leading Poles in the Provisional Government were summoned to Moscow to discuss frontiers and reparations. Molotov revealed that Osóbka-Morawski had signed away Lwów, land in the north near Konigsberg and Chyrow before the Warsaw Rising. Molotov had then made a rare concession to route Polish shipping from Elbing to the Gulf of Danzig. Mikolajczyk has described the extraordinary scene that followed when Stalin angrily retracted the concession and forced Bierut and Osóbka-Morawski to renew the original agreement. He shouted at Molotov that he would have no foreigners spying on his naval base at Konigsberg. The Poles were dismissed like vassals and accepted their return to Warsaw, with servile mumblings from Bierut and Osóbka-Morawski.

Immediately after the Potsdam conference, the war in the Far East unexpectedly came to a climactic end with the dropping of atomic bombs on Hiroshima and Nagasaki. VJ day was celebrated in Western Europe, again as on VE day without the Poles being able to participate. A year later, when the Victory Parade was held in London on June 8 1946, only twenty-five Polish airmen were invited to take part. They declined because the Polish Navy and Army had been excluded.

On August 20, 1945 Bevin speaking in the House of Commons, had urged Poles in the West to go back to assume responsibility in rebuilding the new Poland. At this time Mikolajczyk's Peasant Party was larger than all the pro-communist bloc parties put together. It was strong enough to refuse to merge with a communist inspired Peasant Party. Amidst the growing climate of terror and repression, Wladyslaw Kojder, a member of the executive committee of the Peasant Party, was murdered and at the end of October the veteran leader Witos, died. Mikolajczyk was in Quebec at this time negotiating for aid. In Poland the industrial assets which had not been destroyed in the war, had been seized by Russia. Very often, whole factories were dismantled and taken back there. The situation in Poland deteriorated rapidly and on December 5 Boleslaw Scibiorek, secretary of the Peasant Party, was murdered in Lódź by Security Police. The Peasant Party rejected the proposal for an "electoral bloc"—the communist device for elections from a single list—and the violence against individual members increased from this time.

The communists knew they now had little hope of winning an election so they decided to hold a Referendum. This was designed as a convenient way of postponing the election and as an unavoidable trap for Mikolajczyk. Questions were chosen which were hardly in dispute, and in fact the entire Referendum was fought on Mikolajczyk's tactical campaign to retain the Senate. In Kraków the volume of his support was demonstrated when eighty-four per cent voted in his favour. This result was published in a freak error by the communist authorities and Kraków was thereafter branded as a reactionary city which had to be punished. The official result, now known to have been reversed, was not declared until ten days afterwards, when the communists claimed sixty-eight per cent against the Senate and only thirty-two per cent in favour.

In the mounting terror, there was a pogrom in which Jews at Kielce were murdered by army units in July. At the end of August Stalin decided the election could not be delayed any longer and the communist and socialist leaders were summoned to Moscow to receive instructions. Stalin wanted the real results to be sent to him "I want to see how influential you really are", he said. He could not have any real expectation that the Poles would welcome communism. He had himself likened its imposition in Poland to fitting a saddle on a cow.

On October 7 the Peasant Party announced it would fight the election independently of the Government Bloc and on October 10 Mikolajczyk sent a memorandum to Stalin describing the reign of terror and recalling Yalta, Potsdam, and Moscow's pledges for free elections. Predictably, he received no answer. In December he sent the same memo to the United States and Great Britain. On January 19 1947, Poland finally had its communist rigged elections. The Peasant Party local organization had been broken, dispersed and paralysed. Nevertheless, Peasant Party surveys estimated that the result was sixty-eight per cent for the Peasant Party and twenty-seven per cent for the "Bloc". The official result was again reversed to ten per cent for the Peasant Party and eighty per cent for the Bloc. Stalin was told privately that the true result showed seventy-four per cent of the population had supported Mikolajczyk's Peasant Party. On February 5 Bierut became President and next day Józef Cyrankiewicz became Premier of the "new" Government, retaining this position through all the twists and changes for a generation, until 1972. Mikolajczyk, under increasing pressure, was denounced as a traitor, a foreign spy and organizer of the criminal Underground. Under threat of death, Mikolajczyk fled to the West on October 20, with the help of the USA and Britain.

Between March 1946 and May, the decision was taken to disband the Polish Army on British and Italian soil and all troops were transferred to England. A Polish Resettlement Corps was set up to absorb those who did not wish to go back to Poland and who were unable to find jobs or emigrate to other countries. The Polish Army in Italy numbered some 112,000 at the end of 1945 and 14,200 applied for repatriation. Over half of these applications were from men who had joined after the end of hostilities. There were only three hundred and ten who wanted to return from the thousands who had come out of Russia and been with General Anders throughout his campaign. It is impossible to establish the numbers of those who were imprisoned, deported, released and forcibly detained after the 1941 "amnesty" and the repatriation agreements of 1945 and 1957, nor the numbers who perished in prisons, *lagers* or from hunger. According to some sources there were 6,150,000 Poles in the USSR after the Russian occupation of eastern Poland in 1939. 260,000 took part in the People's Army or the Red Army and 2,000,000 seemed to be missing after the war. The number resettled to the West, in parts of Germany awarded to Poland after the war, were between 1·239–1·553 million and those imprisoned and sent to labour camps were between 539,000–800,000. Those repatriated from the USSR numbered between 1·666 and 2·213 million, leaving 1·4 to 3 million unaccounted for. Official Soviet statistics for 1959 showed 1·38 million Poles in the USSR and 1·15 million in 1979; the reason for the decline is forcible assimilation due to a change in assigned nationality.

Thousands of refugees flocked to the Corps from Poland, Germany and France in 1946. Attlee and Bevin were keen to see as many as possible go back to Poland, but Great Britain was alone in recognizing a moral obligation to these soldiers, and was prepared to make provision for all who would not risk returning to Poland. All hope of going back to a free Poland had by now ended. The majority of Anders' army had come from the eastern provinces, so they were unable to return to a homeland which had now become part of the USSR. Those who wished nevertheless to rejoin families in Poland were faced with additional difficulties because any Poles living in these areas who had avoided previous deportations, had now been transported into the new territories awarded Poland from Germany.

By early 1947, Janek was completing his degree studies, while the Polish Army was being demobilized. The time had now come for all Poles to face the critical decision whether to return to Poland under the communist imposed government or to remain in exile. Pleas were made to Poles to return, because their votes were needed in the Polish elections, but most were only too aware that their votes would count for nothing.

Janek was theoretically able to return—his old home at Grodzisko was still in Poland, though now much closer to the Russian frontier. As a parachutist, he would certainly have been under suspicion, but he was far more concerned by the recent events in Poland; the Katyń Massacre, the Warsaw Rising, the arrest, trial and imprisonment of the sixteen Underground leaders, the fake Referendum, and the false elections, made it impossible for him to contemplate a life under communist rule. He was now engaged to be married to Mary Mountford, whom he had met in Birmingham at the end of 1943 and he was convinced that his new life must be lived in exile.

CHAPTER TWENTY-FOUR

Forty Years On

URING the post-war years, Janek lost touch with many of those who had shared his experiences in the USSR, but he knows the story of some of his fellow survivors.

In 1946 Janek Figiel joined him at the Royal School of Mines, to attend the same courses and laboratory work in analytical chemistry of ores and alloys that Janek had finished a year earlier. After a few weeks Professor Yeoman, who was in charge of the course, came to Janek and said: "Leja, will you be good enough to explain to your friend Figiel that he might have been directing the fire of combined artillery forces at Monte Cassino in 1944—but here at the school he is not in charge. I am". It seems that Figiel had been ordering the technicians about and taking over control of the lab. He had been awarded the Virtuti Militari Cross, the highest award, for his action at Monte Cassino. He graduated in 1948 and after months of hesitation decided to return to Poland in 1949. He was employed in construction of an aluminium plant near Kraków and was often in contact with Janek's family. In the mid sixties he was sent to Nigeria where he taught in a metallurgical school in Lagos and worked in the tin industry for eight or nine years until he died of a heart attack in 1972.

After marrying in April 1947, Janek secured a job with a South African company, and to begin with he had to do some research in London within the Royal School of Mines laboratories. So Janek and Mary spent the first two years of their married life in London. Their first daughter Magdalena Aniela was born in Birmingham in March 1948. A number of Janek's Polish friends including Staszek Wróbel, also married English girls about this time. It is interesting to note that all these marriages have stood the test of time. Staszek Wróbel and Janek worked in the same laboratory within the Royal School of Mines and were married on the same day. The two couples rented a large house in London that soon accommodated four Polish families, including Janek's brother, Staszek and family who had moved to London. After Janek and Mary left for South West Africa in May

Janek's marriage to Mary Mountford, Kings Heath, Birmingham 1947.

1949, Staszek taught at Diddington Camp near Cambridge until 1952 when he left with his family for the USA.

Wojtek Szklany was ordained to the priesthood in 1944/5 in Beirut and was then sent to northern Rhodesia to minister to camps of Polish families and invalids evacuated from Russia with the Polish Army. After a few months in Rome, he came to England in 1948 and visited Janek and his brother Staszek before going to the USA where he was assigned to a parish in Fall River, Massachusetts. Janek met him one afternoon when attending a conference in Boston in 1967. He looked ill, and the following year when he was visiting his family near Grodzisko, he died from stomach cancer.

Kazik Markocki was in the artillery throughout the Italian campaign. After the war he spent some time in France. He married a French girl and emigrated to Canada where he worked in Hamilton in a steel mill, becoming a foreman on the electric refining furnaces. Janek saw him briefly in 1966 and believes he is still working there.

Edek Rynkiewicz worked in Windsor after demobilization, where Mary and Janek visited him in the autumn of 1947. He later married and moved to an office job in London. He died during the Polio epidemic in 1956.

In 1948 Adas Skrzynski and Janek, who had last seen each other at Archangelsk, were reunited in London. Janek's brother Staszek had been in the same unit as Adas during the war in Italy. He later moved to the USA and got an engineering job in Detroit. Janek kept in touch with him by letters and through Staszek until Adas became paralysed after a stroke in 1971 and died a year later of heart failure.

If Janek had any reservations about his decision to start a new life abroad, they disappeared as news from friends who had returned to Poland, filtered back. Mikolajczyk's Peasant Party, deprived of electoral victory in January 1947 by fraud, was soon suppressed. The Government installed in February had no genuine mandate or popular support. Josef Cyrankiewicz replaced Osóbka-Morawski and presided over the changeover to a one-party state. Before Mikolajczyk was forced to flee in October, Stalin had forced an impoverished Poland to reject Marshall Aid from the USA. Cominform policy to collectivize the agricultural land was opposed by Gomulka who had witnessed its disastrous impact on the Ukraine peasantry in the thirties. The example of Tito's recent successful defiance of Stalin, made it imperative for those ruling Poland to curb disobedience by an independently minded Gomulka. Even his position as First Secretary, a dominant role in communist states, was not enough to protect him from dismissal in September 1948. He disappeared from view and was eventually arrested in 1951. Bierut stepped into his powerful position, also retaining the ceremonial duties of the Presidency. From 1948 he operated a rigid Stalinist regime, though dismissed colleagues like Gomulka were not subjected to the show trials and executions inflicted on dissidents in neighbouring Bulgaria, Czechoslovakia and Hungary. Collectivization was imposed after Gomulka's fall. Fortunately for Poland this was introduced only slowly and inefficiently, enough to cause food shortages but not starvation.

When Janek left for South West Africa, Staszek Wróbel remained in London and registered for a Ph.D. while working for the two consultant-lecturers. He later opened his own consultancy and back-room manufacture of flotation reagents, which successfully competed with the largest firms on a world scale. The reagents produced by Wróbel's Float-Ore Ltd, were used in Europe, particularly Italy and Yugoslavia, also in Canada and even in the USA. Towards the end of the seventies the firm was sold, but it was too late for Staszek Wróbel to enjoy a well deserved retirement. He suffered a mild stroke resulting in partial paralysis, which within a year led to his death in 1979.

During the three years Janek spent in Africa, his family grew with the birth of a daughter Catherine in 1949 and his first son Marek born

Janek and Mary with their three eldest children.

in 1951. Censorship prevented any normal correspondence with his family in Poland. Just as he was unable to tell them about his wartime experiences, neither were they allowed to describe conditions at home. It was therefore not until 1956, when the regime was slightly relaxed, that Janek heard what had happened to his uncle. Stryj had been arrested by the Gestapo in November 1939 and taken to the notorious concentration camp at Oranienburg near Sachsenhausen. Stryj, then in his fifties, managed to hold out against terrible deprivations until he was released in March 1940—following intervention from the King of neutral Sweden. He returned to Grodzisko where he lived with Stryjenka, growing vegetables and working on his book on Calculus, which was published in 1947. After the war, Stryj resumed his position at the University of Kraków. He lived until he was 94 years old and attributed his longevity to the fact that he had often been hungry. The pro-Stalin adulation reached heights of absurdity unbelievable in the West. Statues appeared everywhere; Katowice was renamed Stalinogród. Textbooks contained extravagant slogans about Stalin's friendship for Poland. *Stakhanovite* workers were held up as examples for Poland's employees. Conformism in dress, thought and expression was encouraged.

Between the two wars, Poland's population had been two-thirds Catholic. The result of new boundaries, the deportation of minorities,

Stryj pictured in 1960 at the 50th Anniversary of the orchestra he founded.

the horrific Nazi extermination of Jews, meant that Poland became ninety-six per cent Catholic. It was absurd for an anti-religious regime to be imposed on such a nation. The Catholic Church, tolerated by Gomulka, was now openly attacked and in 1949–1950 all Church property was confiscated. In fact, persecution was to give the Church an authority and influence greater than it had ever previously enjoyed. This was enhanced by the country's respect for such impressive Cardinals as Prince Adam Stefan Sapieha, Archbishop of Kraków, Augustyn Hlond, Archbishop of Gniezno, and Stefan Wysyński who succeeded him as Archbishop of Gniezno and Primate of Poland. The imprisonment of Cardinal Wysyński in 1953 only increased his popularity. The Church's influence was later to be intensified with the election of a successor Archbishop of Kraków as the first Polish Pope.

In 1952 Janek and his family returned to England. Flotation had become his chief interest and he accepted a job with Professor J. H. Schulman in Cambridge with research as his main aim. However, the only available scholarship fund of £600 a year was inadequate for his growing family which had increased with the birth of Clare in 1954. A seemingly inevitable move to a more remunerative job in industry was postponed when a financially rewarding trip to Rhodesia was speedily arranged by Dr Schulman, together with a long- term consultancy in Avonmouth.

Stalinism in Poland should have ended with the dictator's death in March 1953, but Bierut persisted with policies that failed to bring prosperity. It was only gradually that a thaw began. Colonel Jożef Swiatlo, a chief of the UB, the Polish equivalent to the NKVD defected to Munich and broadcast scandalous stories of how the UB had preserved their powers. This led to the release of Gomulka in 1954. Collectivization of the land was largely abandoned except for the large estates in former German territories. In the USSR, following Stalin's death, the NKVD chief Lavrenti Beria, who had personally supervised the release of General Anders from the Lubianka in 1941, was summarily executed. He then became a non-person and was assigned to the Soviet "memory hole". A fine example of this post-Stalin technique, was the circular sent to those privileged to possess the third edition of The Great Soviet Encyclopaedia, instructing them to replace—"with scissors and glue"—the page containing the biographical note on Beria, by a new page with an entry on the Bering Straits.

In February 1956, Bierut was in Moscow where he heard Soviet leader Nikita Krushchev denounce Stalin. He died, reportedly of a heart attack. After the unrest associated with the June riots in Poznań, and strikes at Radom, Gomulka emerged from internal exile as the obvious candidate to replace the discredited former leaders. He had escaped the fate of the other pre-war leaders of the Polish Communist Party who were purged and executed by Stalin, by the good luck of having been in a Polish gaol at the time. He would certainly have been "tried" and executed after his fall in 1948 had he been in any of the neighbouring Soviet satellites. Whether Poland was as fortunate is a hypothetical question; instead of the temporary liberalization and eventual return of tyranny over which Gomulka presided, the likely alternative, favoured by Moscow, would have been Rokossovsky's accession. Masquerading as the Polish Minister of Defence, Rokossovsky was known to all Poles as the Soviet Marshal who had waited on the east bank of the Vistula on Stalin's orders during the Warsaw Rising while the Germans did Stalin's work for him and destroyed the Home Army, and Warsaw itself.

Many Poles have also wondered how things might have turned out had Sikorski not been killed in the air crash at Gibraltar in 1943. Occupying the dual position of Prime Minister and Commander-in-Chief, there could then have been no split between them, as there was between Mikolajczyk and Sosnkowski. Sikorski's prestige might have been able to prevent some of the anti-Polish decisions taken at Teheran and there would not have been divided counsel at the time of the Warsaw Rising. Sikorski's military experience and prestige could well have had incalculable effects upon Rokossovsky's passivity when Warsaw rose against the German occupiers.

In October 1956, Gomulka was able to dissuade Krushchev from imposing a military solution when he flew into Warsaw unannounced, as he was to do the next month in similar circumstances in Hungary. Gomulka claimed his old post of First Secretary, and as a convinced Leninist and Marxist, he believed that the agreement he made which allowed the Church independence, the peasants to be partially free to farm in their old way, and a pretence of some independent political parties, was necessary, until communism was strong enough to impose a more orthodox form of socialism. Then, so the theory ran, religious belief would wither away and the peasants would be eager to amalgamate voluntarily for the good of all. It was not to be; the individualism of the peasants grew and any unification that developed was to emerge as Rural Solidarity, almost as though a transformed Peasant Party had reappeared. Religious belief also showed no sign of disappearing. Gomulka was to rule for the next fourteen years. At first some degree of liberalism improved conditions for Poles in their own land, but gradually it was realized that the reforms were cosmetic and temporary.

Janek's job at Cambridge ended in 1956 when Professor Schulman, accepted a chair at the Columbia University, New York, in preference to taxation problems in Britain, following a large inheritance from his father. He offered Janek a job there, but Canada seemed a more attractive option. Edmonton was the only university to answer his enquiry for opportunities to do research involving flotation and with their four children they left Cambridge for Edmonton and Janek worked at the University for eight years. Here his last two children were born, another daughter Gabrielle in 1959 and a second son John Josef in 1960. In 1965 he was offered a better position at the University of British Columbia in Vancouver and became Professor of Mineral Processing Engineering.

Shortly after he arrived in Edmonton he unwittingly revealed something of his past in the University cafeteria. He happened to say in the course of a sentence: "When I was in prisons I observed that . . ." and realized that all other conversation had stopped and his new colleagues were looking at him with surprise and incredulity. He had to explain his acquaintance with Russian and Polish prisons, and the fact that he was not a hardened criminal. He had the feeling that he had not entirely allayed suspicions about his past, and resolved to be more careful in future. It was not until Alexander Solzhenitsyn published his accounts of life in the Gulag some years later, that it came to be regarded as a mark of distinction to have been a prisoner under Stalin. Janek felt that if he had described favourable treatment from Russia towards Poland, acceptance would have been automatic without any need for verification, so great was the residual feeling that the Soviet Union, as an ally in the last war, had a presumptive right to be believed. Troublemaking detractors, however convincing their evidence, as for example about Katyń, were dealt with by simple denial, which was accepted automatically by Soviet apologists.

In July 1965, Janek attended the Gordon Research Conference, held annually in Meriden, New Hampshire. It is one of several week-long summer conferences organized by the American Chemical Society in selected residential colleges in New Hampshire. The attendance at each is limited to about a hundred scientists and the main purpose is an informal exchange of ideas. One of the foreign guests invited was Professor P. Rehbinder of Moscow University, well known for his work on metal surfaces; his book on embrittlement of solid metals by liquid ones had recently been translated into English. At an informal get-together in the entrance hall, Professor Rehbinder was talking loudly to a group of about twenty-five people with a Dr J. J. Bikerman translating very much more quietly. A group of Janek's colleagues standing on the periphery, from the National Research Laboratories of Ottawa were unable to hear the translation and asked Janek to interpret for them. When Professor Rehbinder noticed this second circle, he asked, in his booming voice, if Janek spoke Russian. On being told "a little", he asked where he had learnt the language. Janek replied equally loudly: "In your concentration camps—*lagers*". Rehbinder was taken aback and after a slight pause said: "There are no concentration camps in our country". Janek replied that though he did not know the present situation, at the time he had been deported during the war, the whole of northern Russia and western Siberia had been full of—*lagers* and that he had had personal experiences in a number of them. After a short delay, Rehbinder suggested that Janek should re-visit Russia to see for himself. Janek replied that he would if Rehbinder were to send an invitation which included a guarantee that Janek would leave Russia unimpeded. Except for the first reply: "a little", spoken in Russian, Janek's answers were in English, translated for Rehbinder by Bikerman. Rehbinder was very solicitous towards Janek during the rest of the conference, presenting him with lapel pins and postcards from Moscow. He was always accompanied by another Russian, supposedly a co-worker, who was dubbed by the conferees as Rehbinder's "shepherd". Despite the services of Bikerman as an interpreter, Rehbinder's "shepherd" never once participated in any discussion or gave any indication of knowing what topics were being discussed.

During the whole conference anything that Rehbinder said in Russian had to be translated by Bikerman for the benefit of others into English, and vice-versa—until the very last hour of the discussions. Then one of the participants began to criticize some aspect of Rehbinder's pre-war findings; an agitated Rehbinder, without waiting for Bikerman's translation, jumped to his feet and in perfect English began to deliver a rebuttal. The audience was stunned, and after a few sentences, began to applaud. Confused and sheepish, Rehbinder left the Assembly Hall. For whose benefit was the comedy of translation played? Around Christmas that year, and for several years afterwards, Janek received a card from Rehbinder with New Year's wishes—but never a hint of the invitation to re-visit Russia.

From the vantage points of Cambridge and Edmonton, Janek had watched developments in post-war Poland, which had like its neighbours continued as a Soviet satellite state. Gomulka remained in power, surviving the student riots in Warsaw and the Soviet invasion of Czechoslovakia in 1968 in which he supported the Soviet invaders, because by then, he needed Russian support for his deteriorating hold on power. His popularity and credibility were gone by the time of the 1970 uprising in the Baltic ports. He was replaced by Edward Gierek who was to last ten years.

In 1973 Janek returned to Poland. He made the trip after much soul-searching, which was combined with fears that he would be prevented from returning to the West. He relates his experiences in his own words:

"When I revisited Poland in 1973 I was able to see members of my family again, including Stryj. Along with other scholars of Polish descent, including my brother Staszek, a Professor of Mathematics at the University of Western Michigan in Kalamazoo since 1957, I had been invited by the Polish Academy of Sciences to a scientific congress celebrating the 500th anniversary of Copernicus. My daughter Clare had already independently arranged a trip to Europe including a visit to Poland with a friend, and joined me and her uncle, Staszek. It was thirty-three years since we had last seen our homeland. A previous invitation to me a few years earlier had been declined on the advice of the Canadian Government who felt at that time it would have been unwise for a Canadian citizen with my history to risk a detention behind the Iron Curtain.

"The 1973 Copernicus meeting took place first in Warsaw and then in Kraków. It was full of pomp, ceremony and receptions attended by the highest dignitaries of the country. Two incidents remain in my memory. A day or two after arrival in Warsaw I decided to contact some of my former colleagues from the Staszic Gymnasium, which I

Staszek and Janek returned to Poland in 1973 to be reunited with two of their brothers Franek and Wicek and their sister in Maria at the family home in Grodzisko.

attended for seven years, before I moved with Stryj and Stryjenka to Kraków in 1936. For those seven years I had shared a double desk with the same pupil, Kazik Kozniewski, who since the war had made a name for himself as a journalist and had also written several novels. I phoned him at his home, and after asking for Kazik heard the familiar voice. When I announced myself as his fellow desk mate, there was a long silence. I repeated my name, and asked if he had forgotten me. The response was astonishment, and an enquiry as to where on earth I was speaking from. Kazik had believed that I had died in 1944 during the Warsaw uprising, and had actually attended my 'funeral'.

"When I had disappeared in 1940, it was assumed that I had gone to France and joined the Air Force, which they had known was my intention. In 1944 one of the planes dropping supplies for Warsaw during the uprising had been shot down over the district in which Kazik and others from Staszic had held positions against the Germans. Among the debris, they found bodies, one of which had an airman's book in the name of Jan Leja. They all assumed that it was their old schoolmate and buried me as a former pupil of the Staszic Gymnasium. The sad part was that we arranged to meet the following

ronii p. .cę .
z funkcji z wy...er.   ... .em).
W 1957 przenosi się ao *Western
Michigan University Kalamazoo,*
tamże do tej chwili jest profesorem
matematyki, wybitnym dydakty-

gimn...jalnej, .. .vici..
talentów (przewiduje się wysokie
nagrody, 1,5 tys. dolarów dla naj-
zdolniejszych i najlepiej przygoto-
wanych).
    W ciągu tych 34 lat tylko 7 razy

The newspaper article published in Poland when Janek and Staszek returned in 1973.

day, and did so for about twenty minutes. Kazik was an avowed supporter of the communist regime—and we quickly ran out of any common ground for conversation. After finding out what had happened to the various boys from our class and scout groups and teachers, I left.

"The other incident took place in Kraków. Most of the foreign participants in that meeting had been interviewed by the Press, and so were the two Leja brothers, the only pair of brothers attending this meeting. The journalist Zbigniew Swiech spent nearly two hours with us at our hotel, and ended by taking us outside for a photographic session. Asked about our wartime experiences, both Staszek and I told him about deportation, prisons, concentration camps, slave labour and starvation, all of which was taken down in shorthand. Then briefly we told him of our subsequent life since the war, and our present University life. When the interview was published in the '*Przekrój*' Crossection No 1478, August 5 1973, P.4, our Russian experiences were described in a shorthand of its own; my account ran: '**He happened** to find himself in the USSR'. Staszek's story was similarly abbreviated: '**He spent his time** in the USSR'. The rest of the information, on events since that '**happening**' was reproduced accurately and without omissions or changes. No doubt this wording—curious to a Westerner—was instantly recognizable to Polish readers as a code which conveyed to them a truth familiar to all, in a country where nearly every family had relatives or friends who had experienced Russian 'hospitality' when '**they happened** to find themselves in the USSR".

Janek's daughter Clare noticed a change in her father after his visit to Poland. He had never told his children anything of his wartime experiences and he seemed to have cut himself off completely from his Polish past. After Janek had seen his family again he seemed reassured and more able to assimilate his past into his present life. "He became more open with us and seemed much happier within himself," said Clare.

There was fresh hope for Poles in exile when Cardinal Archbishop of Kraków, Karol Wojtyla, was elected Pope in 1978. This caused embarrassment to the authorities in Poland, and even more so when his pilgrimage to Poland in 1979 made it obvious to the whole world just how little effect the years of anti-religious propaganda had had, re-emphasized by his second visit in 1983. Between these visits Solidarity appeared in 1980, when Gierek's regime, bankrupt both of ideas and money, collapsed with the Gdańsk strike. There was a brief period of relative freedom when for the first time, uncensored news about the war was able to circulate, until the imposition of martial law in December 1981 by General Wojciech Jaruzelski.

Janek remained in Vancouver until his retirement in 1983 after publishing a standard book on flotation, "Surface Chemistry of Froth Flotation", and still works as a consultant in this specialist field. After retiring he was able to indulge his dream of building a house to his own design in a forest on the plot of land that Mary and he had chosen twenty years previously, about fifty miles from Vancouver. In 1987 a new link was forged between the Leja families in exile when Janek's second daughter Kate married Staszek's younger son Stanislaw. The link was strengthened in 1988 by the birth of a mutual granddaughter, Anya Renée. Janek has told his story so that his children and grandchildren will understand the Polish nation's fight for survival and will remember the thousands of Poles who died in the struggle against foreign domination.

Appendices

Miniature Biographies

Alexander II (1818-81), Tsar from 1855, emancipated serfs 1861, suppressed Polish Insurrection 1863, victorious war against Turkey 1887-8. Assassinated 1881.

Anders, General Wladyslaw (1892-1970), Reserve Officer Tsarist Army 1914; 1917 1st Polish Lancer Regt. After Bolshevik Revolution with Pilsudski in Battle of Warsaw, 1920. C.O. 15th Lancer Regt. Two years École Supérieur de Guerre, Paris. Opposed Pilsudski's coup in 1926. G.O.C. Cavalry Brigade until 1939. Wounded end September 1939, taken prisoner by Soviets, released from Lubianka (by Beria and Merkulov) June 1941 on appointment Commander of Polish Army in Russia. HQ Buzuluk Sep 10 1941, later at Yangi-Yul. 1942 supervised evacuation Polish Army from USSR to Persia in two waves, March and September. HQ at Quizil Ribat near Khanaqin in Iraq. Army trained 1943, Jan 1944 moved via Egypt to Italy. Naples 6/2/44 Monte Cassino, Ancona, Bologna; acting C-in-C when Bór Komorowski became POW after Warsaw Rising. See "Army in Exile" (bibliography).

Arciszewski, Tomasz (1877-1955), Participated in 1905 uprising. Cabinet Minister 1st Independant Government 1918-19. Socialist Party leader, Air Bridge escape from Warsaw July 1944. Succeeded Mikolajczyk as Prime Minister London Government Nov 1944.

Beck, Colonel Józef (1894-1944), Foreign Minister in Colonel's regime 1932 until September 1939. Interned in Romania.

Begin, Menahem (born Brześć 1913), freed from Russian camp 1941; evacuated from USSR with Anders; deserted from Polish Army, joined terrorist organisations aiming to evict British forces from Palestine. Later Prime Minister of Israel.

Beria, Lavrenti (1899-1953), Georgian Bolshevik, NKVD Chief, Predecessors Yezhov executed in 1938, and Yagoda 1936. Beria executed 1953 after death of Stalin.

Berling, Colonel Zygmunt (1896-1980), Polish Army captured by Russians Sep 39; underwent political training near Moscow, joined Anders Army 1941; remained in USSR, joined Union of Polish Patriots, became Commander of Polish Army under communist control.

Bierut, President Boleslaw (1892-1956), President of Provisional Government set up in Moscow July 1945. Replaced Gomulka 1948 as Chairman and First Secretary, ran Stalinist Poland until 1956. Died in Moscow as Krushchev denounced Stalin.

Bohusz-Szyszko, General Zygmunt (1893-1982). After Narvik battle head of Polish Military Mission to Moscow Aug 1941; Staff Officer to General Anders, remained in Yangi-Yul in charge of Liquidation Committee, then deputy Commander 2nd Polish Corps to Anders.

Bór-Komorowski, General Tadeusz (1895-1966), Cavalry officer, 1939 organized Underground in Kraków, 1943 followed Grot-Rowecki as Commander of (Home Army); Warsaw Rising 1,8.'44; P.O.W. when Rising collapsed 5.10,'44. Feb 1945 Colditz. Liberated by Americans.

Catherine II, (The Great) (1729-96), Empress of Russia 1762 when husband Peter III (1728-62) dethroned and murdered. Enlarged Empire by First Partition of Poland, Turkish wars 1774, 1792, Swedish war 1790, Second & Third Partitions of Poland.

Chamberlain, Neville (1869-1940), Prime Minister Great Britain 1937-40

Copernicus, Nicholas (1473-1543), founder of modern astronomy, born at Toruń.

Curie-Sklodowska, Madame Marie (1867-1934), physicist and radiation chemist, Nobel Prize 1911 after discovering Polonium and Radium 1910.

Cyrankiewicz, Józef (1911-1989), Premier Polish Communist Government 1947; President 1970-'72 People's Poland.

Dmowski, Roman (1864-1939), leader of National Democrats 1893, member of Tsarist Duma, President Polish National Committee Paris 1917-19, delegate Peace Conference 1919, Minister of Foreign Affairs 1923, retired from active political life 1924. Author of many books on Political affairs.

Gierek, Edward (b.1913), Communist politician; replaced Gomulka after Gdansk strikes 1970.

Goering, Hermann (1893-1946), Represented Nazi Government at Pilsudski's funeral 1935; Field-Marshal, Hitler's Air Force chief. Committed suicide after Nuremberg verdict.

Gomulka, Wladyslaw (1905-1982), Polish Communist leader Lublin Committee 1945, ousted from power in 1948; regained positions of Premier and First Secretary 1956. Ousted finally 1970 after Gdansk strikes.

Grabski, Professor Stanislaw, Speaker of the Parliament-in-Exile, Economist, attended meeting with Stalin with Mikolajczyk in August 1944.

Hess, Rudolf (1894-1987), Hitler's Deputy-Fuehrer, parachuted into Scotland during war; at Nuremberg trial defence exposed secret-protocol to Molotov-Ribbentrop pact; USSR insisted Hess remained in Spandau where he committed suicide in 1987.

Himmler, Heinrich (1900-45), Head of Gestapo, committed suicide at end of war.

Ivanov, Semen Pavlovich (b.1907), Red Army General Third Ukrainian Front Oct 1944-May 1945 who promised immunity to Polish Underground leaders in 1945 to negotiate formation of Provisional Government for Poland. They were arrested.

Jankowski, Jan Stanislaw (1882-1953), Deputy Premier London Government, Chief Delegate to Underground, among 16 arrested by USSR 1945. Died at end of 8 years sentence.

Joseph II, (1741-90), Hapsburg Emperor from 1765, acquired Galicia, Lodomeria, Zips from First Partition of Poland 1772.

Kalinin, Mikhail Ivanovich (1875-1946), President of USSR (1919-46).

Kalugin, Captain Konstanty, liaison officer from Rokossovsky to Bór-Komorowski 1944 Warsaw Rising.

Karasziewicz-Tokarzewski, General Marian (1893-1964), initiated Resistance Movement in Sep 1939 before fall of Warsaw; sent to Lwów by Sikorski, arrested by Soviets on way. Released under "amnesty" joined Anders in 1941. 1944 GOC III Corps Middle East.

Kopański, General Stanislaw (1895-1976), Commander of Carpathian Bgde 1940, 1943-46 Chief of Polish General Staff and military spokesman when Katyń corpes found.

Kościuszko, General Tadeusz (1746-1817), Polish hero of insurrections against Tsarist Russia.

Kot, Professor Stanislaw, (1988-1975), Polish Ambassador in Moscow 1941-2 from Sikorski's Government.

Krushchev, Nikita (1894-1971), Organised "elections" in Lwów in 1939 for Ukrainian Assembly; later successor and denigrator of Stalin.

Kukiel, Marian (1895-1973), Commander Polish 1st Corps in Scotland, Minister of National Defence 1942-7 when Katyń corpes found.

Marie Antoinette (1755-93), Queen of France 1774, brother of Joseph II, husband of Louise XVI (1754-93). Both guillotined.

Mikolajczyk, Stanislaw (1901-1966), Peasant Party leader after Witos went into exile in 30's. Escaped via Hungary to France Oct 1939; Deputy Premier to Sikorski whom he succeeded after his death in 1943. Resigned in 1944 after failure of Warsaw Rising and negotiations with Stalin. Agreed after Yalta to join Lublin Poles in forming Provisional Government. Failed to win fraudulently conducted election 1947; forced to flee from post-war Poland. Died in USA. Published memoirs—see bibliography.

Molotov, Vyacheslav (1890-1986), USSR Foreign Minister, signed pact with Nazi Germany August 1939, with secret protocol carving up Poland and Baltic states.

Mustafa, Kara, Grand Vizier. In command Turkish forces defeated by Jan Sobieshi at Vienna 1683.

Nowak, Jan (b.1913) Army Courier from Underground to Polish Government-in-Exile, witness to Warsaw Rising; finally returned to England before Yalta conference. See bibliography "Courier from Warsaw".

Okulicki, General Leopold (1898-1946), organizer of Underground after September campaign 1939. Soviet prisoner until 1941 "amnesty"; Anders' Chief of Staff; returned by parachute to Home Army May 1944; after Warsaw Rising, succeeded Bor-Komorowski as commander of Home Army which he disbanded Jan 1945. Arrested with other Underground leaders after accepting safe-conduct offer to negotiate Provisional Govt; tried in Moscow in June 1945. Sentenced to 10 years, died in Russian captivity.

Osóbka-Morawski (b.1909), Edward, Socialist leader accepted Communist domination of Provisional Government; first Prime Minister in 1945.

Paderewski, Ignacy Jan (1860-1941), Prime Minister 1919, famous international pianist.

Pelczyński, General Tadeusz (1892-1984), Chief of Staff Home Army (AK) 1941-44 ("Grzegorz").

Pilsudski, Marshal Józef (1867-1935), Organized clandestine resistance in Russian Partition, edited Robotnik, formed Riflemen's brigades as nucleus of future Polish Army; imprisoned at Magdeburg with aide, Sosnkowski. Released Nov 1918, and reached Warsaw with help of Germany. Won Polish Soviet War 1919-20. Head of State 1918-1922, organized coup in 1926; Prime Minister 1926-28, 1930. Inspector General of Armed Forces and Minister of War 1926-35, devised new Constitution, introduced 1935.

Poniatowski, Stanislaw Augustus (1732-98), elected King of Poland 1764, abdicated 1795. Died at St Petersburg.

Puzak, Kazimierz, Puzak (1883-1950), Speaker of Underground Parliament, Secretary General Socialist Party. Among the 16 Underground leaders arrested 1945, tried, imprisoned,. After release sent to Poland, arrested and died in Polish communist prison.

Raczkiewicz, Wladyslaw (1885-1947), President 1939-47 of Government-in-Exile.

Raczyński, Count Edward (b.1891), Polish Ambassador to Britain 1934-1945. Acting Foreign Minister 1941-43. Later Foreign Minister of Government in Exile, President 1979-1986.

Rehbinder, Professor Petr Aleksandrovich (1898-1972), Soviet Physical Chemist described how adsorption lowers mechanical strength of solids, (Rehbinder effect) 1928, Academician of the Academy of Sciences of USSR 1946, Hero of Socialist Labour 1968.

Ribbentrop, Joachim von (1893-1946), Hitler's Foreign Minister, signed pact with Molotov Aug 1939, executed after Nuremberg trial.

Rokossovsky, Marshal Konstantin (1896-1968), Russian Commander of 1st Byelo-Russian Army on Vistula when Warsaw Rising began. Imposed on Poland as Defence Minister and Commander-in-Chief Polish Armed Forces 1949. Dismissed 1956 when Bierut fell.

Romanovs Dynasty of Russian Tsars, founded by Michael 1613, hereditary until 1762.

Romer, Tadeusz (1894-1978), Ambassador to Japan 1937-1941; Foreign Minister in Mikolajczyk's London Government. Attended conference in Moscow with other Polish leaders from London during Warsaw Rising 1944.

Rowecki, General Stefan (Grot) (1895-1944), appointed commander of Home Army (AK) 1939, arrested by Gestapo 30 June 1943; executed in Sachsenhausen concentration camp on Himmler's orders during first week of Warsaw Rising August 1944.

Rudnicki, General Klemens (b.1897), lecturer Staff College in Warsaw 1934-8. Commander 9th Lancers Cavalry Regiment, German prisoner after Warsaw fell, escaped and joined Underground. Liaised with Warsaw (General Tokarzewski), Kraków (Col Bor-Komorowski), and Lwów. 25 Feb 1940 Rudnicki captured by Russians. After "amnesty" in 1941 joined Anders' Army. Deputy to Col Okulicki. Last to leave Krasnovodsk in 1942. Italian campaign (Bologna), Commander 1st Polish Armoured Division in Germany. Met Bor-Komorowski freed from POW camp in 1945.

Rzepecki, Colonel Jan, (1899-1986) succeeded Okulicki as commander of AK units who refused to be disbanded in 1945, under control of London Government in Exile, fought on against Soviet occupying forces after August 1945 amnesty by Provisional Government. Later imprisoned.

Sapieha, Archbishop Prince Adam (1867-1951), Archbishop of Kraków 1911-51. Cardinal from 1946.

Sikorski, General Wladyslaw (1881-1943), 1920 commanded 5th Army, Battle of Warsaw 1920, Chief of Staff 1921–22, Prime Minister 1922-23, Minister of War 1924-25, retired 1928. Critic of Sanacja regime, held no command in 1939 so was not interned by Romania as were Government and Army personnel escaping from Poland in September; formed Government-in-Exile 1939 in Paris, then Angers; to London after collapse of France. Killed in air crash leaving Gibraltar in 1943.

Śmigly-Rydz, Marshal Edward (1886-1941), Inspector-General of Armed forces in pre-war Poland after Pilsudski's death in 1935, Supreme C-in-C Sept '39; interned in Romania after defeat.

Sobieski, Jan, (1624-96), Elected King 1674 after defeating Turks at Choczim 1673; raised Turkish siege of Vienna 1683.

Sosabowski, General Stanislaw, (1892-1967), Commander of 1st Polish Paratroop Brigade at Arnhem.

Sosnkowski, General Kazimierz (1885-1969), Chief of Staff Legions 1914-16, Magdeburg with Pilsudski 1917–18, 1920 GOC Reserve Army. Minister of War 1920-23, Inspector of Army

1927-39. GOC Southern Front 1939, joined Sikorski in Paris Oct 1939; directed Home Army (AK). C-in-C after Sikorski's death in 1943; dismissed near end of Warsaw Rising September 1944.

Stalin, Jozef (1879-1953), Succeeded Lenin in 1924 as dictator of USSR. Eliminated rivals in purges and show trials 1936-38.

Stolypin, Pĕtr Arkad'yevich (1862-1911), Tsarist minister after whom were named Prisoner carriages; assassinated at Opera House.

Tabor — General Stanislaw Tatar (1896-1980), London director of Home Army after return from Warsaw.

Tukhachevsky, Marshal Mikhail (1892-1937), Soviet military Commander Western Front defeated by Pilsudski at Battle of Warsaw 1920. Executed by Stalin after show trial 1937.

Vyshinsky, Andrei (1883-1954), State Prosecutor in show trials 1936-38. Deputy Foreign Minister 1939-49.

Walewska, Marie (1789-1817), Polish Countess, had son (by Napoleon) Count Walewski (1810-68) French diplomat.

Wallace, Henry (1888-1965), Vice-President USA 1941-45.

Wasilewska, Wanda (1905-1964), Polish Communist, accepted Russian nationality, organized Polish Communist party after destruction by Stalin in 30's; with Berling formed Union of Polish Patriots. Colonel in Red Army; married to Soviet Commissar Kornietchuk.

Weygand, General Maxime (1867-1965), French Staff Officer with Pilsudski's forces in 1920. Later Commander of French forces that surrendered to Germany in 1940.

Witos, Wincenty (1874-1945), Leader of Peasant Party, Prime Minister 1920-21, 1923, 1926, voluntary exile 1931. Following arrest by NKVD 1945, was unfit to take office in post-war Provisional Government.

Zaleski, August (1883-1972), Pilsudski's emissary in London World War I, Foreign Minister 1926-32, disagreed with Pilsudski's foreign policy, Foreign Minister 1939-41, disagreed with rapprochement with USSR; President Government-in-Exile 1947-72.

Zhukov, Marshal Georgi (1896-1974), NKVD General allocated to deal with problems of Polish Army on Russian soil under General Anders; organized evacuation to Persia.

Chapters 1–4 Parallel Chronology

1883 Janek's father Josef Leja born.
1885 Janek's uncle Franciszek (Stryj) born.

1899 Franciszek starts teaching at 14.
1901 Franciszek joins Pilsudski's PPS.
1904 Franciszek to Lwów University.

1908 Josef Leja marries Aniela Pawlik.
1909 Franciszek teaching at Drohobycz.
1910 Maria born (Janek's only sister).
1912-13 Franciszek at Sorbonne in Paris.
1912 Stanislav (Staszek) born, Janek's elder brother.
1916 Franciszek refuses to take loyalty oath to Germany.
1918 Jan (Janek) born 27th May.

1920 Franciszek (Franek) born (Janek's second brother).

1923 Vincenty (Wicek) born (Janek's third brother).
1925 Feliks (Felek) born (Janek's youngest brother).
1927 Janek adopted by Stryj → Warsaw.
1929 To 2ry school Gimnasium Staszica.
1932 Scout camp in Bukovina.
1934-35 Scout camp at Zakopane.
1935 Feb-July Janek has Rheumatic Fever.
1936 Stryj & family (incl Janek) move to Kraków.
1937 Janek enrols Kraków University.
1938 Janek starts second year at Kraków University.
1939 Staszek marries Basia Smialek 10 April '39.
 July—Janek goes to Ostrowiec; receives half-diploma.
 Aug—Returns to Kraków.

1867 Birth of Pilsudski.

1886 Polish League formed by Milkowski.
1891 National League reorganized by Roman Dmowski.
1892 Polish Socialist Party (secret) formed—effective leader Pilsudski.
1904 Russo-Japanese War.
1905 Revolution in Russia, risings in Poland.
1908 Pilsudski takes part in mail-train robbery at Bezdany near Wilno.
1911 Pilsudski with approval of Austrian General Staff organizes Riflemen's Associations to provide nucleus of future Polish Army, (Galicians and Eastern Territory Poles).
1916 Pilsudski imprisoned at Magdeburg.
1918 Nov 11. After 123 yrs Poland regains independence. Pilsudski Head of State.
1919 Treaty of Versailles.
1919-21 Polish-Bolshevik war.
1920 Battle of Warsaw "Miracle on the Vistula" Aug 15.
1921 Poland and Bolsheviks sign Treaty of Riga (Mar 18)
1922 Pilsudski resigns as Head of State; first President Narutowicz assassinated.
1923 Hyperinflation leads to General Strike.
1925 Grabski signs Concordat with Vatican.
1926 May Coup. Pilsudski takes over effective Government.
1929 Wall St crash produces economic slump in Poland.
1934 Polish-German non-aggression pact.
1935 Death of Pilsudski.
1936 Spanish Civil war.
1937 Stalin Show Trials, Red Army chiefs purged—Tukhachevsky shot.
1938 Karol Wojtyla (later Pope John Paul II) enrols Kraków University.
1939 March. Hitler invades Czechoslovakia.
 Mar 31 Gt Britain guarantee to Poland.
 Apr 28 Germany renounces Polish-German pact.
 Aug 23 Nazi-Soviet non-aggression pact with secret protocol.
 Aug 28 Poland orders general mobilization; but cancelled at request of France and Great Britain.

World War II starts.

1939 Sep 1st   Germans bomb Kraków.   1939 Sep 1st   Germany invades Poland.

Chapters 5 and 6

1939 September

1 Germans bomb Kraków. Janek puts Stryj on train for Grodzisko.
3 Janek starts walk across Poland to join up.
6 On barge on Vistula to Szczucin; after being machine-gunned from German aircraft, travels on minor roads.
10 Crosses River San at Rozwadow continues to walk towards Kowel and Wlodzimierz Wolynski.

22 Signed on with Polish Army; given uniform.
24 Captured by Russians at Wlodzimierz Wolynski marched 55km to Luck.
27 Escape from Luck military barracks; hides below floor in local school; cattle train to Lwów.

29 Arrives Lwów; meets Staszek at his flat—discussion about future events— Staszek advises that only illiterates will survive under Russian rule.

October

Train to Tarnopol and walk to Bialozorka to rescue Basia (9th or 10th Oct) after avoiding Ukrainian vigilante groups.

mid Oct Return to Lwów with Basia.
As unregistered person Janek has to move before communist supervised "election".

late Oct Janek sets off for Warsaw, arrives 30 Oct—All Souls Day commemoration in Warsaw; sees street graves.

November

6 Stryj and Kraków University staff arrested, taken to Oranienberg Concentration camp
Janek returns to Grodzisko and family.

December

Excursions to Warsaw, Przemyśl, Jaroslav to survey escape routes—discussions with seminarian Wojtek Szklany about plans for leaving to join Polish forces abroad.

1940 January

8 Janek, Kazik Markocki and Wojtek Szklany leave to join Sikorski's army.
15 Captured by Russians at Sieniewa, taken to Przemyśl Fortress Prison.

September

1 Hitler invades Poland. Invites Stalin to join the attack; Stalin prefers to wait.
3 England & France declare war on Germany.
6 Polish army retreats to Vistula; abandons attempt to defend boundaries.
7 Polish Government leaves Warsaw.
16 German communiqué falsely announces fall of Warsaw.
17 **Fourth Partition:** USSR invades.
18 Polish Government escapes to Romania; its members interned. President Mościcki sends resignation to Paris. Replaced by Rackiewicz; Sikorski Prime Minister.
27 Defence of Warsaw ended; collapse of organized armed opposition.
28 German-Soviet convention and amendment to secret protocol signed. Line of R. Bug and R. San formed new frontier.
29 Gen Anders captured south of Lwów at Jesionka Stasiowa, taken to Stary Sambor (Soviet Army HQ) and on to Lwów.
30 Polish Government in exile formed in Paris under Sikorski. Moves to Angers in November. Tokarzewski and Okulicki organize nucleus of underground army.

October

5 Last Polish unit capitulates at Kock. Hitler holds victory parade in Warsaw.
8 Western Poland incorporated into Third Reich.
10 USSR cedes Wilno to Lithuania
12 Hitler decree on German occupied territories.
mid Oct K. Rudnicki joins Undergrd Army.
21 Plebiscite held by Soviets in Eastern Poland to "elect" assemblies.
27 Lwów: West Ukraine Nat Assem.
29 Bialystok: White Russian Assem; both join USSR, supervised Krushchev.

November

1 Moscow incorporates Western Ukraine and Byelorussia into USSR.
30 Russia attacks Finland.

December

Germany deports Polish Jews.
Polish Parliament in Exile formed with Paderewski its President.
27 106 Hostages shot at Wawer. Ghetto started in Warsaw for Jews.

1940 January

23 First meeting Polish Parliament in Exile; Mikolajczyk deputizing for Paderewski.

Chapter 7

1940 January
22 Transferred to Przemyśl fortress; incarcerated there for two months—in adjoining cell to Wojtek Szklany.
February
March
Stryj released from Oranienburg and returns to Grodzisko
19 Janek taken from Przemyśl Fortress prison by cattle train via Lwów.
24 Arrives Nikolaev near Odessa.
Interrogation—maintains pretence of being illiterate—sleep deprivation—death of Boris Gumenuk—meeting with Wlodzimierz Gorzecki—differences from Przemyśl prison—criminal element and their code of behaviour—maintenance of order—lice and bedbug infestation unaffected by rare steam disinfestation or equally rare baths—refusal of food after finding rat tail—hears constant wailing from women and children's prison—regular routine of prison life—two small meals a day.
June
Staszek and Basia void earlier deportations by not sleeping at home, staying with friends etc.

29 Staszek & Basia arrested in Lwów, and deported to Siberia on last of rail transports.
In cattle truck for 6 weeks until arrival at Serov, north of Sverdlovsk in August. Basia in last months of first pregnancy.

August
Basia's daughter born in cattle truck a week before arrival at Serov.
6 Janek "sentenced" to 25 years "*katorga*" (hard labour)
9 Taken from Nikolaev by cattle train to Kiev and on to Kharkov (23rd).
26 3 days in Moscow siding.
29 Transported in crowded Stolypin car to Archangelsk; meets Adas Skrzynski. Hears of fall of France.
September
Journey north to Arctic region.

1940 January
February
10 First of four railway convoys to deport Poles from Eastern territories to Siberia. Others 13 Apr, end June '40, June '41.
March
6/7 Tokarzewski captured by Soviet forces
12 Finland armistice with Russia. During March and April, 3 Soviet camps for Polish officers "wound up" Kozielsk, Starobielsk, & Ostashkov.
29 Anders transferred to Lubianka prison Moscow and then to Butyrki.
April
Between April & June Polish officers from Kozielsk camp murdered at Katyń.
10 Germany invades Norway.
13 2nd railway convoy of Poles deported.
May
8 Narvik Polish Mountain Brigade (Bryzada Podhalenska) takes part.
10 Germany invades Low countries and France.
June
10 Italy declares war on France and G.B.
14 Germans enter Paris. Auschwitz receives first inmates.
17 Fall of France. Petain asks for armistice. 17,000 Polish troops evacuated from Dunkirk. Carpathian Brigade leaves Syria for Palestine.
21 Polish Government moves to London; President Rackiewicz met by George VI.
29 Churchill meets Sikorski.
Third railway convoy of deported Poles.
July
14 Churchill speech "We shall fight on the beaches"—24,000 Poles reach England. Deportations of Poles from eastern territories to Arctic Circle and Kazakhstan stopped. Suspension probably due to fear of Nazi's defeat of France and expected collapse of Great Britain.
August
15 Biggest air engagement in Battle of Britain (10 July-31 October). 81 Polish air force pilots take part.
26,000 Polish troops now in Great Britain (7,000 being officers).
September
7 Sep-3 Nov Blitz on London.
Anders returned to Lubianka in Moscow. Polish mathematicians and British Secret Service break German Enigma code.

Chapters 8-9

September

At Archangelsk transit camp.
Loaded on to Coal boat transport for Nar'yan Mar; 2½ weeks on board, severe storm, one quarter of *zeks* die.

October

Barge trip on Pechora River to Ust Usa
9 Two weeks at Ust Usa transit camp.
23 Eleven day march over ice and through forest to Abez.

1940 November

3 Starts life in penal colony of 125 near Abez, in corrective "extermination" camp, constructing other camps etc for new intakes of prisoners—tree cutting—finds frozen horse.

December

Snow storm *"purga"*. Janek's colony reduced to 25 by accidents, scurvy, malnutrition.
24 Move to new camp near Abez; nearly freezes to death on journey. Shared head of fish for *Vigilia* (Christmas Eve meal).

1941 January

7 Colony now reduced to 9 survivors—Janek admitted to "dugout hospital" run by Anna Nikolaievna.

February

Recuperates in "hospital".

March

Janek transferred to "Central Hospital" for convalescence; distributing meals, removing dead bodies etc.
25 Discharged back to work—claim to be "capable draughtsman"—logging team—manipulating norm—Wasyli Nikoforowich foreman—belief of freedom from Russia within three years—horsemeat stew—telephone lines Abez-Kotlas.

September

Battle of Britain at its height.
Blitz on London begins.

October

28 Italy attacks Greece.
31 Battle of Britain ends.

1940 November

3 Daytime blitz on London ends. Night attacks begin, and on other cities.
12 Molotov visits Berlin.
14 Warsaw Ghetto gates closed.
Polish Army training in Scotland.

December

6 North African campaign. Wavell's British Army destroys Italian army. Polish "Carpathian" Brigade available but unable to take part initially because Sikorski had omitted to declare war against Italy.
9 Battle of Sidi Barani.
18 Hitler orders plan for invasion of USSR (Operation Barbarossa).

1941 January

21 Tobruk captured.

February

Polish brigade ready reinforce Greece.
12 British troops capture Benghazi.

March

Polish brigade on standby for Crete.
Polish underground reports German troop concentrations on USSR's western borders.
27 Coup in Yugoslavia. King Peter installed after Regent Paul ousted.
31 Rommel offensive starts in North Africa.

Chapters 10-11

March

25 Discharged back to work—starts as a "capable draughtsman"—joins logging team—manipulating norm—Wasyli Nikoforowich foreman—belief of freedom from Russia within three years—horsemeat stew—Telephone lines Abez-Kotlas.

May

1 May day holiday digging out snowbound convoy.

June

Snow melts, hunting bodies buried in winter snow, rerouting winter road.

22 Poles segregated from multinational work brigades when news of Nazi attack on USSR becomes known—given heaviest work—shifts of 18 hrs—many Poles die under this regime.

August

17 Janek collapses, admitted to barrack hospital, bleeding from scurvy of intestines. Unconscious 11 days—almost buried—slow recovery—learns of agreement between Sikorski & Stalin; hears *zeks* names being listed for possible release—determines to get put on list despite weakness.

Staszek and Basia near Serov, issued with papers after "amnesty" permitting travel to Yangi-Yul; the overcrowding there caused diversion to Turkestan north of Tashkent, where Staszek was employed on *kolkhoz* digging irrigation canals.

September

1 Janek gets his name put on list of Poles to be "amnestied".

2 Released from camp. Collapses outside—Barge trip to Kozhva camp—looked after by Kazil Markocki—released from prison status.

17 Struggles on foot to reach railhead in Vorkuta district to catch train to Kotlas.

March

27 Coup in Yugoslavia.

31 Rommel offensive in North Africa.

April

1 Sikorski & Mikolajczyk to USA & Canada.

6 Germany invades Yugoslavia & Greece. British Expeditionary force to Greece.

18 Yugoslavia capitulates.

23 Greece capitulates.

May

3 Mikolajczyk addresses 230,000 Chicago. Stalin warned about imminent attack by Germany. Stalin disbelieves warning.

end German parachutists capture Crete.

June

Last rail convoy of deportees to USSR from Eastern territories of Poland.

22 Germany invades USSR (Operation Barbarossa).

July

30 Diplomatic relations resumed between USSR and Poland; "amnesty" granted to all Polish internees (for uncommitted crimes) so that Polish Army could be formed on Russian soil. Polish-Soviet Treaty signed in London, by Sikorski and Maisky under Eden's chairmanship.

August

4 General Anders released from Lubianka.

12 USSR & Poland sign military convention.

Soviet officials treat Polish citizens of Ukrainian, Byelorussian, Lithuanian, Jewish nationality as Soviet subjects. No satisfactory explanation for missing 15,000 Polish officers.

14 Atlantic Charter signed.

22 Soviets agree to enrolment commission going to POW camps.

25 Britain & Russia invade Persia. General Anders flies to Griasovietsh camp near Vologda; learns that Col Berling had volunteered for Red Army before Germany attacked Russia.

September

5 Anders meets Polish Ambassador to USSR (Kot) with orders from Sikorski.

10 Anders flies to Buzuluk reception area.

12 Anders requests creation of further divisions for Polish Army.

14 Anders inspects 17,000 Poles (mostly barefoot) at Totskie.

16 Shah of Persia ousted, son succeeds.

1941 September

17   Train to Kotlas from railhead in Vorkuta district. Few days there, wine barge— Sverdlovsk, buys books instead of bread, meets Wojtek Szklany again.

October-November

Continues journey to Kungrad. Visits village between Kartaly & Orsk with Edek Rynkiewicz. Sees Bukhara with Wojtek Szklany; begins to learn English and Cyrillic alphabet.

December

Arrives Chardzhou early December. Transfer to barges on Amu Darya river.

23   Arrive Kungrad on Aral Sea. Brief stay on first *kolkhoz* (collective farm) after failing to pick enough cotton. To avoid bad example, transferred to another *kolkhoz* near Nukus, maintaining irrigation canals and ditches.

Staszek and Basia and family arrive at Turkestan—digging irrigation canals etc.

1942 January

Mud fish—stray dog stew shared with Polish army liaison officer—told about entitlement to rations. Demand for rations due under Polish-Soviet agreement results in yet another transfer to *kolkhoz* near Turtkul—decision to acquire food to help local Polish deportees—pig killing, sheep stealing, honey collecting etc; hearing Chekhov, Tolstoy, Dostoevsky and learning English.

March

8   News of impending departure from *kolkhoz*.

9   Final robbery of storehouse to provide food for local Polish population.

10   Embark on barges for Chardzhou and then cattle truck train. Staszek and Basia at *kolkhoz* near Turkestan; Staszek goes to Chopkar north of Alma Ata to enlist in Ander's army.

1941 September

Polish Carpathian brigade by sea relieves Australian at Tobruk.

27   Kot (Polish ambassador) sees Vyshinsky.

October

6   Kot sees Vyshinsky again. One Polish division now in UK. Moscow Government and Embassies (including Polish) move to Kuybyshev.

November

14   Kot asks Stalin about 15,000 Polish officers from Starobielsk, Kozielsk & Ostashkov. No satisfactory reply.

December

3   Stalin conversation with Sikorski and Anders, who presented a specific list of 4,000 officers who had not been released. Stalin replied "they've fled". Sikorski asked where could they flee and was told "Manchuria, for instance", or "they've been released but haven't arrived yet".

5   Declaration of Friendship and Mutual Assistance signed by Stalin and Sikorski. Red Army launches counter-attack to lift threat to Moscow.

7   Japanese attack Pearl Harbour. USA at war with Axis Powers. "Union of Polish Patriots" formed under Wanda Wasilewska formed at Saratov.

1942 January

New Headquarters for Polish Army at Yangi-Yul near Tashkent.

February

14   Home Army under Grot-Rowecki formed in Poland (300,000 by Mar 1943). Zhukov asks Anders for 15th Division from his army in Yangi Yul near Tashkent, to be ready for action on Soviet front. Anders refused; his army was to fight in full complement or not at all. Stalin halved Polish food rations.

March

Soviets tell Poles that rations to be cut to 26,000 on 20th March—70,000 men enrolled by then.

18   Anders flies to meet Stalin & Molotov. Agreement that 40,000 soldiers for whom there were no rations to be evacuated immediately to Persia. Anders convinced that whole Polish Army would have to leave USSR; not agreed until July; completed in September.

Chapter 16

1942 March

16 Arrive Kermine (Navoi). Marched to plateau within view of Pamir mountains where Polish Army was being formed. Cook tortoise to survive.

19 Janek fails medical examination by mixed Soviet-Polish commission. Separated from companions; spends three days outside camp.

22 Retakes medical, passes eye test.

26 Given Polish Army uniform.

29 Train to Krasnovodsk on Caspian Sea.

April

2 Arrive Caspian Sea; 3 days on Russian boat to Bandar-e-Pahlavi (Bandar Anzali) in Persia. Easter (5 April) in Pahlavi—first eggs—first birdsong.

14 Leave Pahlavi by truck across Elzburg mountains to camp at Qazvin. Then on to Baghdad via Hamadan & Kermanshali. Truck across desert from Habbanyah to Palestine.

29 Arrive Hadera between Tel Aviv and Haifa.
Move to Ashdod on Mediterranean south of Tel Aviv.
Remains there for 5 months.

August

15 Staszek and family leave USSR with Anders' army. Arrive Pahlavi. Basia and two children to Teheran, Staszek with army to Khanaquin.

September

20 Janek to Suez by truck to join Carpathian Brigade from Libyan campaign. Meets Jan Figiel, fellow student from Kraków. Embarks on boat through Red Sea.

1942 March

18 Anders makes agreement with Stalin that 40,000 Poles for whom there were no rations should be evacuated immediately to Persia.

April

Anders travels to Cairo, London, Scotland, to inspect troops.

May

German offensive; threatens Stalingrad by August.

June

21 Tobruk captured by Rommel.

July

8 10,000 Poles leave Kolyma; only 171 reach Anders army by September.

26 USSR informs Anders that remainder of Polish Army is to be evacuated from its territory.

August

Arrest of Polish delegates responsible to Polish Embassy in USSR.

9 1st rail transport of final evacuation leaves Krasnovodsk.

19 Anders leaves Russia with Polish 2nd Corps. Gen. Bohusz-Szyszko remains as head of liquidation Cttee until Oct.

20 Col. Berling (depot commander at Krasnovodsk) deserts to "Union of Polish Patriots".

31 Last transport from Krasnovodsk. 115,000 Poles escape from USSR.

September

Remaining Polish soldiers and civilians with General Anders leave USSR. The thousands left behind were cut off from contact with the London Government. Many were recruited into the Communist controlled Polish Army under General Berling not to emerge until March 1944.

Chapter 17 $\qquad$ Sep 1942-Mar 1943

September
20 Janek to Suez by truck to join Carpathian Brigade from Libyan campaign. Meets Jan Figiel, fellow student from Kraków. Embarks on boat through Red Sea.

October
Lands at Basra.
17 Arrives Khanaquin, near camp for units of Polish Army just evacuated from USSR.
25 With Wojtek Szklany visits camp; meets Staszek for first time since Lwów 1939.

November
23 After reorganization of Army units, Janek leaves for Quayarak (via Kirkuk, Mosul).

1943 January
2 Wojtek Szklany leaves for seminary in Beirut to complete studies for priesthood. Janek as dispatch rider until he wrecks his motor cycle.

Winter
Staszek and Basia's two children die in Teheran, during typhus epidemic.
Basia goes to Palestine as truck driver—later returns to teaching.

March
Janek volunteers for Polish Air Force; rejected due to poor vision. Accepted for Parachute Brigade.

September
Remaining Polish soldiers and civilians with General Anders leave USSR. The thousands left behind were cut off from contact with the London Government. Many were recruited into the Communist controlled Polish Army under General Berling not to emerge until March 1944.

October
Russians inform Polish Foreign Minister (Raczyński) no further enlistment of Poles to be permitted to Anders' army.
23 British victory at Alamein.

November
8 Allied landing in North Africa.

December
Sikorski visits Washington for last time; discussions with Roosevelt.

1943 January
9 Himmler visits Warsaw Ghetto.
14-25 Casablanca Conference. Sikorski flies to London.
16 Molotov to Polish Embassy in Kuybyshev "all persons on Polish territories occupied by Soviet forces 1-2 Nov 1939 must consider themselves Soviet citizens." Sikorsky returns to London.
31 Stalingrad victory by USSR. Von Paulus surrenders.

February
19 Russians claim Eastern Poland in article by playwright Korneytchuk (3rd husband of Wanda Wasilewska).
25 Polish Govt in London protests about accusation of wanting to move frontier to Dnieper & Black Sea.

March
2 Russia replies accusing Poles of wanting to dismember Ukraine & White Ruthenia. Curzon Line proposed.
4 Poles reject Curzon Line as not a frontier but a proposed Armistice Line of 1920. Home Army now 300,000 strong.

Chapters 18 and 20

March
Janek joins Polish Parachute Brigade.

April
3 Truck to Baghdad, Damascus, and on to Suez.
10 Transit camp.

May
1 Embark on Île de France (troop ship).
16 Durban—Rio de Janeiro—English conversation practice on board, becomes "interpreter".

June
11 Freetown (Sierra de Leone). On to New York, Iceland.
20 Arrive Greenock in Scotland.
July
3 Arrive Elie (Fife) for start of parachute training. Meets Estonian student who had joined Poles escaping from Russia, and Estonian authorities extricate him from Polish Army.

September
2 At Largo, continues parachute training.
28 At Leslie, continues parachute training.
Oct 1943: Parachute training at Ringway (Manchester) 4/10-15/10
23/10 To London for studies at Royal School of Mines to complete course started Kraków 1937.
Dec First visit to Birmingham—meets Mountford family, including Mary.
Jan 1944 Registers as student with University of London. Student until 1947.

March 1943
Spring: Mysterious weapons developed at Peenemunde; Underground tells London.
Home Army now 300,000 strong.
April
13 Germans announce discovery of graves at Katyń.
16 Polish Government asks Red Cross to investigate.
19 Warsaw Ghetto Rising.
26 USSR breaks with Polish Government.
May
5 Polish Ambassador leaves USSR.
8 Russia forms Kościuszko Division with General Berling as commander.
12 German forces capitulate in N. Africa.
16 Warsaw Ghetto overwhelmed by Germans.
June
30 Grot-Rowecki (Commander of Home Army) arrested by Gestapo.
July
4 Sikorski dies in plane crash Gibraltar.
8 Sosnkowski succeeds as C-in-C.
10 Sicily invaded by Allied forces.
14 Mikolajczyk succeeds as Prime Minister.
17 Bór-Komorowski replaces Grot-Rowecki as Commander of Home Army.
25 Mussolini arrested.
August
2 Kopański appointed Polish Chief of Staff.
15 RAF raid on Peenemunde, V2 Rocket site, after information from Underground.
17 Sicily liberated by Allies.
19 Quebec conference between Churchill & Roosevelt opens.
23 Quebec conference closes.
September
Himmler sends SS Major-General Kutschera to Poland to suppress resistance movement.
3 Italy invaded by Allied Forces (Calabria).
8 Italy surrenders. Germany takes over resistance to Allied forces.

October
5 Mikolajczyk asks Eden to help re-establish relations with USSR; refuses permission to negotiate away pre-war boundaries.

Chapter 21

Chronology of Polish and related events

1943 November

12 2½ Polish divisions in Persia delegated for Italy.

22 Eden meets Mikolajczyk prior to Teheran. Asks for meeting with Churchill; refused because "such might cause Stalin to back out".

28 Teheran conference. Polish post-war boundaries decided; Polish Government not represented nor told of decisions.

December

Operation Tempest (*Burza*) policy: Bór-Komorowski to co-operate with Red Army in liberation of Polish territory.

1 Teheran Conference ends—Churchill ill.

6 Communiqué vague and brief.

15 3rd Carpathian Rifle Division to Italy.

1944 January

1 Bierut in Warsaw from Moscow: "new Polish Government to be formed. Polish Committee of National Liberation appears in Moscow (Communist controlled).

3 Red Army crosses eastern border of Poland.

20 Churchill tells Mikolajczyk "post-war Poland will be free from Curzon Line to the Oder". Mikolajczyk: "he must consult his Government and Underground."

February

6 Anders flies to Italy to command Polish 2nd Corps.

15 Mikolajczyk to Churchill: "Government cannot agree to surrender of half of Poland, agrees to temporary demarcation line; but Stalin refuses.
Allies bomb Monte Cassino.

22 Churchill in House of Commons: Teheran agreement would move Poland westward.

24 Romer (Polish Foreign Minister) protests to Foreign Office.
Underground "Parliament" (Council of National Unity) rejects proposals for Curzon line in East.

March

Stalin demands Curzon line, dismissal of Kukiel, Sosnkowski, Kot, and Raczkiewicz.

April

Operation Tempest (*Burza*) starts in eastern Poland; Kowel and Wlodzimierz Wolynski in Polish Volhynia; Home Army officers arrested, others conscripted to Berling units or to USSR. Tempest (*Burza*) synonym for betrayal.

6 Operation Jula: Home Army paralyses German rail traffic for 48 hrs. Bridge over Wislok at Przeworsk-Rozwadow blown up. Example of possible co-operative action with Red Army.

May

11 Polish assault on Monte Cassino.

17 Monte Cassino captured.

20 V2 rocket captured River Bug Underground hides it from Nazis.

21 Okulicki parachuted into Poland to join Home Army.

June

3 Mikolajczyk asks Polish underground in France to rise with Maquis.

4 Rome liberated.

6 D Day Invasion of Europe from England by Allies.

7 Mikolajczyk meets Roosevelt who claimed to have got on better with Stalin than Churchill did. Roosevelt's request to Stalin to receive Mikolajczyk turned down.

1944 July

Churchill urges Stalin to receive Mikolajczyk; invited Aug.

17 Ancona taken by Polish 2nd Corps.

20 Attempt on Hitler's life.

21 Bór-Komorowski and Okulicki decide on Warsaw rising.

23 Lublin committee masquerading as Provisional Government comes to Lublin.

25 Operation Bridge: Dakota from Brindisi (with Jan Nowak to brief Bór-Komorowski), from occupied Poland brings captured V2 rocket to London.

27 Mikolajczyk, Romer, Grabski leave for Moscow, arrive 30 July.

28 Moscow communiqué: Rokossovsky's troops approaching Warsaw.

29 8.15pm Kościuszko Station (Moscow) urges Poles in Warsaw to rise.

31 Order for Warsaw Rising given by Bór-Komorowski.

Chapter 22

Warsaw Rising

August

1 1st Polish armoured division to France, Falaise sector of front.

1 Warsaw Rising begins 5pm. Mikolajczyk in Cairo and Teheran en route for Moscow learns Lublin Poles had agreed administration to be in hands of Red Army, Home Army members to be surrendered & deported to Russia, Curzon line accepted. Mikolajczyk tempted to turn back; Churchill & Roosevelt wire Stalin to change attitude to London Government. Bleak reception, Molotov ignores messages from London and Washington: "Mikolajczyk must meet Lublin Poles before seeing Stalin."

3 Mikolajczyk meets Stalin, accuses Home Army of not wanting to fight Germans.

6 Lublin Poles to Mikolajczyk: "Bierut had reported no fighting in Warsaw"; Wanda Wasilewska "Curzon line was most just for Poland".

7 Bierut offers Mikolajczyk Premiership in new Government, himself to be President.

9 Stalin meets Mikolajczyk; trump card of rising ignored. Mikolajczyk becomes supplicant for Home Army.

10 Leaves Moscow. Osóbka Morawski alleges: "Bór-Komorowski not really in Warsaw."

12 Churchill appeals to Stalin for help for Warsaw fighters. Stalin to Mikolajczyk "Warsaw action is a thoughtless adventure; cannot take any responsibility for it."

14 Joint appeal from Churchill & Roosevelt to Stalin.

16 Curt refusal from Stalin.

20 Further request from Western allies.

24 Roosevelt replies to London Poles re help for Warsaw; urges agreement with Lublin Group. Paris liberated by Allies after citizens had risen. Bór-Komorowski notes good fortune of Paris to have co-operative forces nearby.

30 Mikolajczyk's Government & Underground submits new plan, future Polish administration, 4 main parties + Lublin representatives. Britain and America accept. No reply from Russia who passed it to the Lublin group.

September

8 First V2 bombs on London. Authorities forewarned by Polish sending V2 to London.

11 Bór-Komorowski appeals to Rokossovsky for supplies and co-ordination with Home Army. Churchill & Roosevelt joint message to Stalin urging help for Warsaw garrison.

12 Stalin gives permission for Flying Fortresses to use Russian airfields after supply drop.

17 Arnhem operation starts, Polish Parachutist Brigade takes part.

18 First drop of supplies by American Flying Fortresses after bad weather.

21 Polish Parachutists under Sosabowski in action at Arnhem.

22 Berling's unit with Red Army make sortie towards Warsaw garrison, without artillery cover. Berling sent to Russia for "further training".

25 Arnhem forces retreat north of Rhine.

30 Sosnkowski dismissed as Commander-in-Chief by Polish President Rackiewicz.

October

2 Warsaw rising collapses; Bór-Komorowski surrenders. Okulicki new Commander of Home Army. Goes underground. Bór-Komorowski appointed Commander-in-Chief—becomes POW.

Lublin Poles change policy to Home Army, after Warsaw Rising.

13 Mikolajczyk, Romer, Grabski, "Tabor", Churchill, Eden, Harriman, & Stalin and Molotov in Moscow: Plan of Aug 30 fails with refusal to accept Curzon Line. Churchill & Mikolajczyk argue; latter would consider Curzon Line if Lwów, potash and oil deposits retained. Rejected by Stalin.

17 Unofficial meeting between Milolajczyk and Bierut.

27 Churchill in Parliament hopes Mikolajczyk will lead new Polish Government.

November

Until Spring of 1945, arrests of Home Army members stepped up.

24 Mikolajczyk resigns as Premier. Succeeded by Tomasz Arciszewski.

December

Stalin: "Mikolajczyk not to return to Poland while Red Army was there".

26 3 British Officers parachute into Poland, Military Mission to Home Army.

31 Lublin Committee becomes "Provisional Government of Liberated Democratic Poland".

1945 January

Communists begin to equate Home Army with the Gestapo.

3 British Military Mission reach Okulicki; Polish Underground state in ruins. Germans raze Warsaw as they retreat before Red Army.

5 Russia recognizes Lublin Government.

12 Last great Soviet offensive launched with Berling's units participating.

17 Russians enter ruins of Warsaw.

19 Germans abandon Kraków (undamaged).

19 Okulicki disbands Home Army, to help members avoid NKVD roundups.

23 Red Army units reach River Oder.

31 Beneš on behalf of Czechoslovakia recognizes Lublin Government.

February

Home Army describe as "armed agency of the landowners" by the Communists.

4 Yalta: Stalin, Roosevelt & Churchill; Major tragedy for Poland. USSR gets Baltic states & free hand in eastern Europe. Stalin rejects Mikolajczyk as unacceptable to Lublin Poles. Decisions cause bitter reaction from Polish 2nd Corps in Italy (from eastern Poland). Anders considers withdrawing 2nd Corps from front, but loyalty to Allies precludes this.

9 Polish Govt confirms disbandment of Home Army; ignored by many units.

20 Anders flies to London.

21 Anders meets Churchill who defends Yalta decisions. Council of National Unity in Underground Poland reluctantly accepts Yalta decisions and puts hope in promised free elections; Jankowski in the Underground follows Mikolajczyk's line, splits with London.

24 Anders pleads with Mikolajczyk not to go to Poland and join Lublin Poles.

26 Anders appointed acting C-in-C while Bor-Komorowski is P.O.W.

27 Molotov repeats that Mikolajczyk is unacceptable to Lublin Poles.

March

5 44 Countries at San Francisco form United Nations; Poland excluded.

6 Russians invite Okulicki, Jankowski and other Underground leaders to meeting; personal safety guaranteed. Okulicki told by Anders & Kopanski (Chief of Staff) to stay hidden.

25 Underground National Council of Ministers and Council of National Unity agree Okulicki should emerge to meet General Ivanov, Russian commander who insists on his presence.

27 Okulicki, Jankowski, Puzak emerge from hiding to meet Ivanov.

28 Further 13 Underground leaders come out of hiding to join meeting. All 16 disappear, arrested, taken to Lubianka Prison in Moscow. No announcement made.

31 Wincenty Witos, veteran Peasant leader arrested by NKVD and taken to Brest-Litovsk; later released in poor health.

April

6 Anders flies back to Italy to lead last battle of 2nd Corps. Poland on brink of civil war with disappearance of the 16 Underground leaders. Soviet units attack Polish Underground units under guise of "pacification".

7 Stalin to "use his influence" with Lublin to accept Mikolajczyk if he accepts Yalta decisions.

9 Spring offensive opens on Italian front with British 8th army.

12 Roosevelt dies. Succeeded by Truman.

21 Mikolajczyk accepts Yalta decisions.

21 Poles liberate Bologna. London Government makes final attempt to discuss frontiers with Stalin.

28 Germans surrender in Italy. Polish Corps in Italy now 112,000, + 10,000 civilians.

30 Hitler dies in Berlin bunker.

May

3 Molotov tells Eden in San Francisco missing 16 Polish Underground leaders arrested and awaiting trial. Eden refuses further negotiation on Polish Provisional Government.

7 VE day. Peace in Europe but fighting continues in Poland between guerilla forces (ex-Home Army) and Berling's units.

Post-war deterioration in Poland   Jun 1945-Oct 1947

June
17 Mikolajczyk, Lublin Poles, Bierut, & Osóbka-Morawski in Moscow. Mikolajczyk's proposals and similar from Kiernik arriving from Poland rejected.
21 Show Trial opens in Moscow after 11 weeks of interrogation of 16 Underground leaders. Okulicki, despite ill-health & sleep deprivation castigates trial as political. Sentenced to 10 years. Jankowski to 8; both die in captivity.
27 Mikolajczyk humiliated leaves Moscow with Lublin colleagues for Warsaw. Underground Political organization formally disbanded; announced July 1st.
end Mikolajczyk visits ailing veteran leader of Peasant Party Witos.

July
6 Poles in Russia given until Nov 1st to file application for repatriation. Britain recognizes Warsaw Provisional Government and withdraws recognition from London Poles.
Polish Underground organization formally disbanded.
Bierut, Wincenty Ryznowski (Foreign Minister) & Mikolajczyk represent Poles at Potsdam (17 July-2 Aug); USSR to settle Polish repatriation claims from its share.

August
2 Democratic forces in Govt gain amnesty for Home Army members, but not its leaders.
mid Poles summoned to Moscow to discuss frontiers & reparations. Stalin retracts concession by Molotov and forces Bierut & Osóbka-Morawski to renew original agreement.
20 Bevin urges Poles to return to assume responsibility in rebuilding the new Poland.
Mikolajczyk's Peasant party, larger than all pro-Communist bloc parties, refuses to merge with "Communist Peasant Party". Wladyslaw Kojder (Executive Cttee) murdered.

October
mid Mikolajczyk in Quebec to negotiate UN-RRA aid; Gomulka describes Mikolajczyk as "Trojan Horse" servant of capitalists.

31 Wincenty Witos (veteran Peasant Leader) dies.

December
5 Boleslaw Scibiorek, secretary of Congress Peasant Party, murdered by Security Police.

1946 February to September
Increased polarization, proposal for "electoral bloc" defeated 22/2/46.
Violence against Peasant party members increased from February.

June
30 Referendum—to delay election, but disastrous for communists, though rigged. Official result not published until 10 days later. Kielce Jews murdered by Army.

August
Note from Britain criticized conduct of referendum.
28 Communists & Socialists to Moscow; Stalin gives instructions for conduct of election; the real results to be sent to him "I want to see how influential you really are".

October
7 Peasant Party decides to fight election independently of Government Bloc.
10 Mikolajczyk Memorandum to Stalin re reign of terror, recalls Yalta, Potsdam, and Moscow pledges for free elections; no answer, so sends it also to US and GB in Dec.

1947 January
19 Poland has Communist rigged elections. Official result 80% for Government Bloc. Stalin informed true result 74% supported Mikolajczyk's Peasant Party.

February
5 Bierut elected President.
6 Józef Cyrankiewicz Premier of "new" Government; retained power until 1972.

October
20 Mikolajczyk flees with help of US and Britain; Churchill "surprised to see him alive".

Chapter 24

1947 April 10 Janek marries Annabel Mary Mountford in Birmingham.

30/3/48 Daughter (Magdalena Aniela) born in Birmingham.

May 1949 Moves to Abenab in South-West Africa, now Namibia.

18/10/49 2nd daughter (Catherine Anne) born in South-West Africa

31/7/51 Son (Marek Franciszek) born in South-West Africa

1952 Returns to UK, Cambridge. Research work in flotation.

7/2/54 3rd daughter (Clare Georgina) born in Cambridge.

1956 Moves to Edmonton, Alberta in Canada. Continues research in flotation.

1957 Aunt (Stryjenka) dies in Poland.

10/2/59 4th daughter (Gabrielle Mary) born in Canada.

10/8/60 2nd son (John Josef) born in Canada.

1962 Mother dies in Poland.

1963 Father dies in Poland.

1965 Moves to Vancouver as Professor of Mineral Processing Engineering at University of British Columbia.

1973 Revisits Poland with Staszek, Professor of Mathematics at University of Western Michigan in Kalamazoo to attend congress for 500th anniversary of Copernicus.

1976 Revisits Poland with Mary and youngest two children, Gabrielle and Josef to meet Stryj now 91, and his surviving family.

1979 Uncle (Stryj) dies in Poland.

1982 Publishes "Surface Chemistry of Froth Flotation".

1983 Retires to Mission and builds retirement home in forest.

1985 Sister (Maria) dies in Poland.

1987 New family link with Staszek when daughter Kate marries Staszek's son Stanislaw.

1988 Link strengthened with birth of mutual grandchild Anya.

1947 Communist Government installed Feb. Mikolajczyk flees to West in Oct.

1948 Gomulka ousted from leadership. Stalinist period begins—Berlin airlift.

1949 Church property confiscated.

1951 Gomulka arrested.

1953 Death of Stalin. Cardinal Stefan Wyszyński arrested.

1954 Swiatlow (UB chief) defects. Gomulka released from gaol.

1956 Feb. Krushchev denounces Stalin. Bierut dies in Moscow.

Jun Riots in Poznań.

Oct Krushchev flies unannounced to Warsaw. Gomulka back in power.

Nov Hungarian uprising suppressed by Soviet tanks.

1968 Russia invades Czechoslovakia. Mar Student riots in Warsaw

1970 Riots and strikes in Baltic ports. Gomulka replaced by Gierek.

1972 Gierek launches modernization plan.

1976 Riots in Radom, Ursus (Warsaw).

1978 Cardinal Karol Wojtyla of Kraków elected Pope John Paul II.

1979 First Papal pilgrimage to Poland.

1980 August, Strikes in Baltic ports lead to agreement of Gdańsk, with rise of Solidarity—Gierek replaced by Kania.

1981 Feb. Gen. Jaruzelski: Prime Minister.

Mar "Bydgoszcz Incident" Security Police beat up Solidarity members.

May Rome: Pope wounded by Turkish fanatic.

Dec Jaruzelski declares Martial Law—suspends Solidarity.

1983 Second Papal visit. Martial Law ends—general amnesty.

1984 Murder of Fr Popieluszko.

1986 Second amnesty for political prisoners.

1988 Solidarity leader Lech Walesa invited to talks with Government.

Bibliography

Prisoners' and Deportees' Experiences

Buca, E.—*Vorkuta*—Constable, 1976, translated from Polish. (Pole who organized strike in Vorkuta camp and lived to be released.)

Bukowinski, Wladyslaw—*Wspomnienia z Kazakhstanu* (Reminiscences from Kazakhstan)—Spotkania 1979. (Posthumous account of a priest's life in Kazakhstan in Polish.)

Ciszek, Walter J. (S.J.)—*With God in Russia*—McGraw-Hill, 1964. (Account of a Jesuit priest's life in USSR prisons and lagers; released after 23 years in 1963.)

Dolgun, Alexander & Watson, Patrick—*Alexander Dolgun's Story*—Alfred A. Knopf, New York 1975. (American's life in USSR prisons and lagers.)

Herling, Gustaw—*A World Apart*—Heinemann, London 1951—Reissued Oxford University Press 1987. (Experiences of a Polish deportee in Soviet labour camps.) A literary account by a professional writer.

Kuczynski, Józef—*"Między Parafią i Lagrem"*(Between parish and a lager)—Spotkania 1985. (Priest's life among prisoners and free settlers in Asia).

Rawicz, Slavomir—*The Long Walk*—Constable, London 1956. (Polish cavalry officer escaped with six from Yakutsk via Baikal, Mongolia, Tibet to India.)

Solzhenitsyn, Alexander—*The Gulag Archipelago 3 vols*—Collins & Harvill, London 1974-1978.

Teczarowska, Danuta—*Deportation into the Unknown*—Merlin Books Ltd, Devon 1985. (Experiences of a Polish doctor deported to Siberia.)

Memoirs by participating Characters

Anders, General Wladyslaw—*An Army in Exile: the Story of the Second Polish Corps*—Macmillan 1949.

Bór Komorowski, Tadeusz—*The Secret Army*—Victor Gollancz, London 1950

Calvocoressi, Peter—*Top Secret Ultra*—Cassell, 1980. (The Enigma story.)

Churchill, Winston—*The Second World War*—6 Vols—Cassell and Co London 1948-54.

Jones, R.V.—*Most Secret War*—Hamish Hamilton 1978. (Account of Enigma, V1 and V2 rockets.)

Maisky, Ivan—*Memoirs of a Soviet Ambassador—The War 1939-43*—London 1967.

Mikolajczyk, Stanislaw—*The Pattern of Soviet Domination*—Sampson Low, Marston & Co., Ltd, London 1948.

Mikolajczyk, Stanislaw—*The Rape of Poland, Pattern of Soviet Aggression*—Greenwood Press, Westport, Connecticut 1948. American edition of previous.

Nowak, Jan—*Courier from Warsaw*—Collins 1982. Poland under Nazi occupation.

Pilsudski, Józef—*Memoirs of a Polish Revolutionary & Soldier*—Translated and edited by D.R. Gillie—Faber & Faber 1931.

Rudnicki, General Klemens S.—*The Last of the War-Horses*—Bachman & Turner, 1974.

General works

Ascherson, Neal—*The Struggles For Poland*—Michael Joseph 1987. (History of Poland's fluctuating fortunes, to accompany TV series, illustrated.)
Ascherson, Neal—Television Series—*The Struggles For Poland*—Channel 4, 1987. (Nine programmes, available on video.)
Davies, Norman—*God's Playground: A History of Poland (2 vols.)*—Oxford University Press, Oxford 1981.
Davies, Norman—*Heart of Europe: A Short History of Poland*—Oxford University Press, Oxford 1986. (Concise version of above, updated.)
Freemantle, Brian—*KGB*—Holt, Rinehart and Winston, New York, 1982.
Heine, Marc E.—*Poland*—B.T. Batsford Ltd, London 1980.
Krok-Paszowski, Jan—Photographs Bruno Barbey—*Portrait of Poland*—Thames and Hudson 1982.
Roos, Hans—*A History of Modern Poland,* (translated from the German by J.R. Foster)—Eyre & Spottiswoode 1966. (Geschichte der Polnischen Nation) 1961.
Werth, Alexander—*Russia, Hopes and Fears*—Simon and Schuster 1969.
Wilmot, Chester—*The Struggle for Europe*—Collins 1952.
Zamoyski, Adam—*The Polish Way*—John Murray, 1987. (Comprehensive history of Poland to present time, illustrated, and with many maps.)

Poland between the wars 1918-39

Machray, R.—*The Poland of Pilsudski*—George Allen & Unwin, London 1936.
Polonsky, Antony—*Politics in Independent Poland 1921-39*—O.U.P. 1972.

World War II 1939-47

Ciechanowski, Jan—*The Warsaw Rising of 1944*—Cambridge University Press 1974. (Politics of the Resistance.)
Coutouvidis, John & Reynolds, Jaime—*Poland 1939-1947*—Leicester University Press 1986.
Garliński, Józef—*Intercept*—J.M. Dent & Sons, 1979. (Secrets of the Enigma War.)
Garliński, Józef—*Poland in the Second World War*—Macmillan 1985. (General history of 2nd war.)
Garliński, Józef—*Poland, SOE and the Allies*—George Allen & Unwin 1969. (Describes relations between Polish London Government and Allies with Underground.)
Irving, David—*Accident—The Death of General Sikorski*—William Kimber, London 1967.
Litynski, Zygmunt—*Warsaw—a Warning*—MaxLove, 25/8/44. Booklet published in London during Warsaw Rising (6d) five weeks before it collapsed.

Poland after 2nd World War

Ascherson, Neal—*The Polish August*—Allen Lane 1981. (Solidarity's development.)
Lapedz, Leopold—*The Use & Abuse of Sovietology*—A Special Anthology—Survey, Institute For European Defence & Strategic Studies, Vol 30, March 1988.
Szczypiorski, Andrzej—*The Polish Ordeal, (The view from within)*—Croom Helm, London & Canberra 1982. (Interned by the military rulers of Poland at end of 1981.)
Siedlecki, Julian—*Losy Polaków w ZSSR w latach 1939-1986* (Fate of Poles in the USSR in 1939-86)—Gryf Publications Ltd, London 1987.
Stankiewicz, W.J.—*The Tradition of Polish Ideals*—*Essays in History and Literature*—Orbis Books (London) Ltd 1981.
Steven, Stewart—*The Poles*—Collins/Harvill, 1982. (View of an English journalist married to a Pole.)
Syrop, Konrad—*Poland in Perspective*—Robert Hale, London 1982.
Tucholski, J.—*Cichociemni* (Silent and Blind)—Pax, Warsaw 1985. (The fate of parachutists sent to Poland as emissaries of London Government to Home Army; published under auspices of present regime in Poland.)

Glossary

arba(s)	cart(s) (with 2 wooden wheels 6-8 ft diameter, used in Asia)
bania	bath
blatnoys	Russian criminal element
bolnoy	sick
boumazhka	piece of paper (applied to rail ticket + release document)
burza (Polish)	tempest
chai-khana	tea house
diesiatnik	supervisor/evaluator/overseer of 10 people—in theory
jigoura	grain producing plant, native to Central Asia
katorga	hard labour
khalats	long robes
khorosho	good
kipiatok	hot water (substitute for tea)
kolkhoz	collective farm (from *kollektivnoe khozyaĭstvo*)
komiak	nomad, native of Republic of Komi where Vorkuta is situated.
kulak	rich peasant farmer (especially in the Ukraine)
lager (lagier)	concentration camp
parasha	toilet bucket
politruks	NKVD officials responsible for inculcating *zehs* with communist theory
purga	snowstorm
stakhanovite	a (Russian) worker who increases his output to an exceptional extent, from Alexei Stakhanov (miner). His letter in *Tribune* (23/7/48) is reproduced in an appendix to Gustav Herling's "A World Apart" as well as Herling's reply (*Tribune* 6/8/48).
stolypin	Russian railway carriage with barred windows for carrying prisoners, named after Tsarist minister who introduced them
taiga	forested waste land in subarctic region, swampy
tundra	Arctic waste land, with scattered trees and bushes
Urząd Bezpieczeństwa	UB, Polish equivalent to the NKVD (Security Service)
valinki	felt boots
vozchik	driver
vrach	medical orderly
wadi (Arabic)	stream or dry river bed
zek	prisoner in Russian hands (from zaklyuchenny)

216

Index